First published by Carl Scully, 2017

First reprint 2017

© Carl Scully 2017

This publication is copyright. Apart from any use as permitted under the Copyright Act 1968, no part may be reproduced without written permission from the publisher. Requests and inquiries regarding reproduction and rights should be addressed to the publisher.

National Library of Australia Cataloguing-in-Publication entry

Creator: Scully, Carl, author.

Title: Setting the Record Straight : A Political Memoir / Carl Scully.

ISBN: 9780646970011 (paperback)

ISBN: 9780646973333 (hardcover)

ISBN: 9780646971995 (ebook)

Subjects: Scully, Carl.
New South Wales. Parliament--Officials and employees--Biography.
Politicians--New South Wales--Biography.
Cabinet officers--New South Wales--Biography.

Book cover design and layout by eMatti
Printed by IngramSpark in Australia
Keywords:
    Politics
    Pre-selection
    Campaigning
    Government
    Minister
    Leadership
    Infrastructure
    Major Projects
    Motorways
    Railways
    Transport
    Privatisation
    Olympics

Setting the Record Straight

A Political Memoir

by

Carl Scully

In memory of

Patrick Charles Scully

My Grandfather

State MP for Namoi 1920 to 1923

and

William James Scully

My Great Uncle

State MP for Namoi 1923 to 1932

Federal MP for Gwydir 1937 to 1949

Minister for Commerce and Agriculture 1941 to 1949

To my wife
Ann
and my children
James and Sarah
who were there for most of the journey

and

to my pre-selection comrade
Anwar Khoshaba
who made the journey possible

No Enemies

YOU have no enemies you say?

Alas! My friend, the boast is poor;

He who has mingled in the fray

Of duty, that the brave endure,

Must have made foes! If you have none,

Small is the work that you have done.

You've hit no traitor on the hip,

You've dashed no cup from perjured lip,

You've never turned the wrong to right,

You've been a coward in the fight.

Charles Mackay, 1915

Acknowledgements

I would like to thank a number of people who have assisted me in writing this memoir.

My wife Ann often encouraged me to record my account, gave valuable feedback and has been a constant source of advice on how best to present my story.

My good friend Charlie Monti provided legal advice and my former senior staffers; Brent Thomas, Gary Sargent and Simon Miller provided feedback on sections of the book as did Stephen Loosley, former NSW ALP General Secretary. Arthur Smith former Deputy CEO of the State Rail Authority provided wonderful practical examples of what went wrong when economic rationalists took over the railways and Chris Ford, former RTA Director, had some great stories to tell on delivering transport for the Olympics.

Colette Vella gave some very useful advice on an early draft. My good friend Robert Ishak also provided valuable practical advice and has promoted my story wherever he can.

I want to also thank the many hundreds and hundreds of people who over a long period of my public life shared the journey with me and who contributed in so many different ways to all the stories which underpin this book. I thank them all.

And finally, I want to thank the people of my electorate of Smithfield who through five elections, had the confidence in me to be their MP for nearly 17 years. It was an honour to serve and represent them.

CONTENTS

PREFACE		1
CHAPTER 1	The early years – what drove my passion to serve?	5
CHAPTER 2	Joining the ALP – the dream begins	15
CHAPTER 3	The campaign for pre-selection – climbing the political Mt Everest	23
CHAPTER 4	The backbencher – reaching for executive power	45
CHAPTER 5	The illusion of freedom of speech – over-reaching on 'sacred' ground	61
CHAPTER 6	Law & order – the cases of Vo and Lewthwaite	71
CHAPTER 7	Winning government – exercising executive power	87
	A day in the life of a minister – what is it really like?	111
CHAPTER 8	The Sydney Motorways – what it took to build them	117
	The Eastern Distributor	120
	Difficult media management – Competent vs Incompetent	127
	The Cross City Tunnel	129
	The M5 East	137
	Power and consent	138
	The M7 Motorway	141
	How the M7 funded the Abbotsbury Parklands	146
	The M7 Cycleway	149
	Final approval of the M7	150
	Costa kills off the M4 East Motorway	152
	Battling the Commonwealth Government	154
	The Sydney Harbour Bridge Toll	154

CHAPTER 9	**Road safety – saving lives**	**157**
	Death and complacency on our roads	158
	Double demerit points	162
	Digital speed cameras	163
	Graduated licensing for young drivers	163
	The Sea Cliff Bridge	164
	Seat belts and the Premier	167
CHAPTER 10	**Connecting communities – anecdotes along the way**	**169**
	The Shires Conference	171
	The demise of Ray Chappell	174
	The road with no cars	176
	Tony McGrane	177
	The Copmanhurst Approach	183
	The Moree to Mungindi Road	185
	Calling the bluff	187
	Stymying Clover Moore	188
	The Tugun Bypass	189
	Michael Caton gives it to the RTA	192
	Gate crashing a press conference	193
	Profanities over a cup of tea	195
	Luxury cars and the Hunter Valley	196
	The 'Carl' Expressway	197
	Shining shoes	197
	Cyclists leak too	198
	Traffic lights at Edensor Park	200
	Vegetarian in the Louvre	200
	UTS Railway Station	201
	Tunnelling under Lane Cove River	203
	The weighted average cost of capital	205
	Thwarting FOIs on crime statistics	206
	Reviving Country Rail services	207
	Not his son's father	209
	Why Malcolm Turnbull joined the Liberal Party	211
	Banning jet skis on Sydney Harbour	213
	Protecting Sydney Harbour Bridge after 9/11	215

	Wran waits for Klugman too	216
	Fairfield City	217
	The demise of the king and queen maker	219
PHOTO ALBUM		**222**
CHAPTER 11	Running the railways – managing unbridled economic rationalism	257
CHAPTER 12	Delivering transport for a successful Sydney Olympics	297
CHAPTER 13	The premiership denied – what really happened?	321
	Bowen almost swaps with Tripodi	322
	The Chiefs of Staff	323
	Waterfall	324
	The Government attacks itself	330
	The attacks come to an end	338
	The nuclear codes	343
	The contenders	344
	Developing a programme for Government	345
	Obeid and Iemma plan for the succession	358
CHAPTER 14	The dream ends – Iemma strikes again	385
CHAPTER 15	Privatising electricity – The destruction of a Labor Government	433
	Plan A: 'Back to the future'	446
	Plan B: 'Communication breakdown'	447
	Plan C: 'A parallel universe'	448
CHAPTER 16	The aftermath – transition, renewal and new beginnings	457
EPILOGUE		**469**
A brief history of Carl Scully's political and business career		475

PREFACE

"**I want your resignation**", mumbled Premier Morris Iemma in his Parliament House office, without making any eye contact.

That brought to an abrupt end the dream and desire of my whole adult life to serve and make a difference. What began as a 17-year-old with a dream awakened by the re-election of the Whitlam government in May 1974, ended on the 25th of October 2006 as a 49-year-old in the cold, harsh reality of political life.

It had been a very long journey and a much tougher one than I had ever envisaged it would be in my teens and early 20s.

Friends and family had often asked that I record my story since my earlier than expected retirement from politics in March 2007. I have thought on more than a few occasions of putting pen to paper, but decided instead to let time pass, let some scars heal and the dust settle somewhat on what had been a high profile public career before doing so. It now seems opportune to record some thoughts and recollections from a personal, political and professional perspective.

I am mindful of what the late Neville Wran, former New South Wales Labor Premier, and in my view, a titan of New South Wales politics, once said to me when I asked him why he had not written an account of his rich political life: "Too many of the bastards are still alive". I thought this was classic Wran to the last. Brilliant, witty and to the point. It also emphasised the main risk

Preface

in writing a political account from a personal rather than an independent perspective.

It is usually a lot easier to leave it all well alone than run the risk of former colleagues, journalists and many interested parties strongly disputing how events are described or recalled many years later. This was a factor in my not wanting to put pen to paper. But, after several years out of politics and with most of the 'bastards' still alive, I decided it was time to record the events as I remember them.

I had dreamed since the age of 17 of one day leading the great Australian Labor Party and whilst I did not quite achieve that political mountain, I did go a lot closer to it than many. And on that long path to just below the pinnacle of power, I had a rare privilege of service and achievement which few can look back upon over their working lives.

This is the story of my own personal journey in serving the great cause of Labor and of the community, including the joys and challenges of delivering to Sydney and New South Wales, new motorways, freeways, rail lines and housing estates, delivering transport for the Sydney 2000 Olympics, running for the premiership and being hurled from Office on a whim by the man who beat me to that position. It is a journey, rich in battles won and battles lost – a journey of achieving great things and being denied in the end the opportunity to do much more.

It is also an opportunity to correct the record, or at least to add to the record on both the wider circumstances of my unsuccessful bid for the premiership, and the suggestion by many journalists and media outlets that I had misled the Parliament about the existence of the Cronulla Riot report and as a result was forced to resign.

Misleading the house is a vague notion, ill-defined and lacking any process for assessing guilt or innocence. On most occasions, including my own, when the allegation is made, it is usually the media acting as 'Prosecutor' before what they believe is the 'Court of Public Opinion', which they have in turn whipped into a frenzy. An experienced Premier like Bob Carr was well aware of the pack-like mentality of many political journalists and often stared them down until a 'crisis' of their making had passed. But, Iemma was never going to be a Bob Carr. By removing me from the ministry at the height of the media frenzy over unfair and unsustainable allegations of 'misleading the house', he left me appearing in my view, as if I had to resign for some kind of dishonesty. This hurt deeply, was blatantly unfair and untrue. I had always valued my reputation in both words and deeds for being an ethical, honest and moral person in all my personal, professional and political dealings. My late parents would have expected no less.

That a dubious interpretation could possibly be made to how I had conducted myself both publicly and privately was deeply wounding to me and took a long time to heal. The assurances to the contrary in more recent years, from MPs from both sides of politics and even some senior journalists, have been greatly appreciated.

I have also welcomed the opportunity to draw some closure on what had been a pretty tough time in my life. I am aware that MPs are expected to be made of 'sterner stuff' and take whatever life dishes up to them, but we are no less human than the citizens we represent.

Thank you for allowing me the privilege of sharing my memoir with you.

Preface

CHAPTER 1

The early years – what drove my passion to serve?

When I look back over a long public life and the process of getting, and then remaining there to make a difference, I do wonder sometimes what drives a person to do it. It was tough, often hard, yet it had a strange, compelling mix of exhilarating victories and shattering defeats. It certainly felt like a roller coaster of emotions when the highs and lows were coming all at once, often on a daily basis.

All the battles I had to go through, all the factional and Party warfare to survive and endure, all the undermining from colleagues and leaders and the endless challenges dealing with hostile press and stakeholders, more often than not, left me feeling like I was in a war zone minus the bullets. It leaves me wondering if all that was the norm for a long life at the top of the political game.

This is not a game for anyone to fall into! So, why do it?

What is it that makes a young man or woman seek a public life of community service? What causes the drive and passion to serve which overcomes any usual human inclination to have a calm, quiet, professional life, the pursuit of maximum financial gain and the wish and need to enjoy a good family life?

Yes, there are many MPs who are not so driven and have either chosen a public life as just an alternative career path, or have fallen into it more by accident than design. But, these MPs tend to be less successful and are more likely to fill the backbench than senior ministerial ranks. If they get to the senior ranks, they usually do not last long nor make much of a difference. In my view, the successful long-term politician without exception is the soldier of determination, self-confidence, daring and chance.

I once heard a young Paul Keating asked at a New South Wales ALP right faction forum, "… how does a person know if he or she is suited for a life of politics?" His reply is one I have never forgotten and one I have regularly passed onto young party members who have asked me similar questions from time to time: "If your drive to serve in public life is so strong that the thought of not doing so burns a hole in your heart so large and the thought of doing something else sounds abhorrent to you, then you are suited to a life in politics. Otherwise, the job will be just too hard".

I was 23 when I heard this and I thought immediately – yes, that sounds like me. I can't possibly imagine a life without public service.

But, I have often wondered where the drive came from. When I hear servants of religion speaking of their chosen life as an unstoppable calling, I think this is pretty similar to what I actually felt as a young man about serving as a parliamentarian and no less so during my years in Ministerial Office.

If it is possible to explain the drive as being caused by DNA or family genetic makeup, then I have my fair share. My grandfather,

Patrick Charles Scully, was elected in 1920 as the ALP member for the State Electorate of Namoi in the New South Wales Parliament. In those early days, Lower House seats had three members for each electorate, so in a strong Country Party seat like rural Namoi, the ALP could still expect to get one of the three elected. He died before I was able to meet him, but I recall in 1972, as a 15-year-old meeting his younger brother, Ern Scully then aged 96. Uncle Ern told me how he had often helped his brother Patrick out on the hustings and how Patrick would address local voters from the back of a truck. "The finest public speaking voice I ever heard" I still remember him saying. I always like to think I was not too bad a public speaker and wondered how much of that may have been inherited.

For reasons, I have never been able to discern, he served until only 1923 when he resigned. As his brother, William Scully had been next on the ALP ballot paper at the previous election, he filled the casual vacancy and then held the seat until 1932, which he then lost in the big Lang Labor defeat that year.

My great uncle then served as the ALP MP for the Federal Electorate of Gwydir from 1937 to 1949 and served as a Minister in both the Curtin and Chifley Governments. He was Federal Minister for Commerce and Agriculture from 1941 to 1949. The football grounds in Tamworth known as 'Scully Park' are named after him. I never met either of them, but I am enormously proud of their service. I did, however, get a lot of pleasure at Australian Transport Minister's meetings, in regularly reminding the National Party Deputy Prime Minister and member for Gwydir, John Anderson, that the last Labor Member for Gwydir was my great uncle and a Scully to boot! Currabubula Primary School near Tamworth as a then single teacher school, produced two Federal

Ministers (including Fred Daly) and a State MP. Not bad for State education in the bush. And two of the three were Scullys!

Neither of my parents were Party members and rarely spoke of how they voted. I recall my Mum saying she voted for Whitlam in '72 but not in '74. I grew up seeing my Dad as a soft Labor supporter and my Mum as fairly strong Liberal supporter. Whilst our home was free of Party dogma, there were constant conversations between my parents on the current affairs of the day. My earliest recollection of such a conversation over our small breakfast table, was of them discussing an issue concerning Arthur Calwell and Gough Whitlam. I had no idea who they were and what my Mum and Dad were talking about. I must have been about eight years of age at the time.

I do think the constant discussion on issues which mattered between two people who were very important in my life must have slowly instilled in me a lifelong interest in current affairs. But why the Labor cause?

None of my three sisters, Kathy, Marie and Maryanne nor my brother Martin, have more than a passing interest in politics and none of them have ever desired to serve in elected roles or commit to the Labor cause. I suspect our very modest circumstances and my early schooling had a big impact on my views of the world generally and on religion in particular.

Our upbringing was very happy, loving and Catholic. For the first three years of my schooling, I attended Our Lady of Dolours School at Chatswood on Sydney's Lower North Shore – they were a pretty miserable three years. My memories of this time in the early 60s are not pleasant. The nuns who taught us seemed to relish meting out regular punishment: ruler on the back of the hand, feather duster on the back of the legs, soap in the mouth and regular isolation. And all in an infants' school and all from a group of God's messengers.

A few years ago, I drove past the school and noticed that the hall where I shared year 2 with 69 other kids had been knocked down. Even then, all those years later, I felt relieved. I can still see the nuns and picture the mistreatment. It must have coloured my views on people of religion doing these things. Like most people, I remember little of my very early schooling, but these experiences are etched in my memory bank as if they had happened yesterday. My experiences were mild compared to what many others had to endure elsewhere.

With my own experience of Catholicism, it is perhaps little wonder then that at age 13, having gone through the Catholic sacraments of baptism, communion and confirmation, when my mother told me that I was old enough to decide if I wished to go to church or not, I chose the latter. It was one of the most liberating things my parents could have done for me. There and then, I decided I would never again be a Catholic and never again due to my own faith would I attend a church service of any kind. And so it has been for over 45 years.

I don't know why, but even at an early age, I wanted to be noticed in the crowd. The one sure way of doing this at school was to be the worst behaved in the room. I picked that up pretty quickly.

The New South Wales Labor right had always been the bastion of the Irish Catholics, but has changed somewhat in more recent years. I was always treated by the faction as being part of that club and just momentarily 'un-financial' as some would like to put it. But, the scar of my very early Catholic experiences lingered well into adulthood. In fact, it was only after I decided as

Chapter 1: The early years

Transport Minister to allow Mary Mackillop's Order of Nuns to name a new ferry after her that I finally felt I had made my peace with a lifetime of angst towards the Catholic Church and could put it behind me. I felt confident enough after that to ask anyone who owned up to having gone through Catholic Schools in the 1960s: "Were you beaten?" It seems to always get a positive response and we have a good laugh. I guess that this would be called 'gallows humour'.

I grew up in a wider family environment with a sense that Catholics were Labor through and through especially Catholics with Irish heritage. This must have had an impact on where my political sentiments would fall.

After entering politics in the New South Wales Legislative Assembly, as the Member for the South West Sydney Electorate of Smithfield, the Liberals just loved reminding me that I had grown up in Chatswood on Sydney's well to do Lower North Shore and had gone to the very middle-class Chatswood High School. They neither had any knowledge of my family circumstances nor any appreciation of how proud I am of completing most of my schooling in the public education system.

We lived at 112 Beaconsfield Road in West Chatswood for all of my childhood and a large part of my young adulthood. Whilst on a large block, our home was an old two-bedroom house built in the late 1940s. It had been purchased by my maternal grandmother and my parents purchased it from her estate after their marriage in the early 1950s with a long term low interest war service loan. My Dad had served in the Air Force as a radio operator in Northern Australia for the last 18 months of WWII. It would have been a tight fit for a family of three or maybe four at a stretch, but for a family of seven it was really tough.

The house was not heated except for a cosy in the lounge room, which we lit up each winter night from a stack of coke in the backyard. The floors were bare of carpet long before the polished version became fashionable. My brother and I shared for many years a tiny room with a double bunk which had been squeezed into a converted veranda. The louvered windows kept little of the cold out. Perhaps one of the few things my wife and I disagree about is the temperature of our home. Just about every winter my refrain is: "I grew up in a cold house and that is how I like it".

The leafy lined streets of today's West Chatswood do not hint at all about how tough a struggle it must have been to rear five kids on one modest public servant's income. We were poor but did not know it. We were all loved unconditionally and all of us were provided with the opportunities for a good education – the two essential ingredients, in my view, for a happy and successful life. It was only after we grew up that we realised that relative to our peers and neighbours, we had had few holidays and few luxuries. But our parents did their best with careful planning and husbandry of their modest income to shield us from that reality. Even now, in my early 60's, I just love grocery shopping and delight in how I can now freely put anything I want in the shopping trolley. Every time I do the shopping I remember how Mum would pass by all the goodies in the aisles and tell us that we could not afford them.

In later years, my parents would describe the early years with a young family as lean and tough and requiring constant meticulous budgeting to get through. My mum would not let us go without, but I would learn from my sisters that Mum would often deprive herself to do so such as buying a new dress. But, I do think that growing up in the environment I did, must have been a catalyst to cause me to comfortably and naturally commit to the Labor cause at a young age.

I also think my Mum must have encouraged in me a great level of self-confidence and drive which I have taken through life. My Mum would often tell me from an early age that I was going to university and that I would be successful. There was never a 'might be' attached to it. Just statements of fact from a very confident mother. When I was 13 she said to me "I have saved up some money for you to have some golf lessons" and when I asked why she simply replied: "You are going to be successful and all successful men need to be able to play golf." I dutifully went down the road for my first of five lessons and loved it from the first moment. I even dreamed of being a pro one day, but soon realised I would never be good enough.

It was at about this time of my life that I decided to become a lawyer. I do wonder with today's kids who often don't have a clue about what they wish to do with their lives, how I could be so certain at such a young age that this would be my professional calling.

The turning point for me and thousands of young people across the nation was the emergence of Gough Whitlam as a political force. I was 15 when the Labor Government was elected in 1972 and the excitement and energy of those early days of the new Government awakened something in me. By the 1974 election, I was a committed Labor man, had a photo of Gough on my bedroom wall and decided that one day I would lead the Labor Party.

My Mum took me to a 1974 candidates forum at Lane Cove Town Hall. A very young John Howard was the Liberal candidate at his first election and Dick Hall was the ALP candidate. I remember listening and watching their performances and thinking to myself, I could do that! Many years later, I told John Howard I had been there that night and he replied, "so was Kerry Chikarovski" who for a short period was the leader of the New South Wales Liberal Party.

I told my Dad at the time that I intended to be a Labor MP and that I was going to do a law degree which would help me to be a Parliamentarian. He was sceptical: "You will need to live in a different area for that and you will need to get preselected by the Party first" I recall him saying. At 17, I was aware of these two necessities but not how tough it would be to achieve that goal.

Two awful events occurred in 1975. One personal and the other political. Despite a reasonably good Higher School Certificate (HSC) score, I missed out on getting into the Macquarie University Law School by a whisker. Just like a lift door when it shuts and you are not in, I felt as if I had been shut out from my dream of being a lawyer. I was devastated.

The second awful event that year was the demise of the Whitlam Government. For me it felt like a death in the family. I just couldn't grapple with the nation not sharing my unbridled awe of this man and the Government he led. It was my first introduction from a distance of the trials and tribulations of political life and the rise and fall of the Party's fortunes. I was angry at the way Fraser and Kerr had abducted our elected Labor Government, took the Constitution hostage and then stole Government itself by manipulating the timing of an election. I did 'maintain the rage' as Gough had asked for some years afterwards.

Chapter 1: The early years

CHAPTER 2

Joining the ALP – the dream begins

For me, joining the Labor Party was a solemn decision as was signing the Party's pledge on joining 'to vote and assist the election of endorsed Labor candidates.' I regarded it then and still regard it now, as a noble cause to join and commit to and an even nobler one to seek the privilege of the Party's support as a candidate for Public Office. Maybe I am old fashioned, but as an 18-year-old, I took the view that once committed then always committed. I still have that view all these years later.

Then as now, I see stark differences between the two great political forces which dominate our political processes and landscape. For Labor with a deep-seated commitment to social justice, the improvement and protection of wages and conditions of every day workers, the recognition of a legitimate place for trade unions, the protection of the environment, the universal availability and quality of public schools and hospitals, and a fairer society where anyone ought to have the opportunity to achieve their true potential, was always going to be the more comfortable place for me. The Liberal Party never seemed to me to be the place where these things would be really valued and cherished.

In early 1976, I decided to join the ALP and in March of that year at age 18, I turned up to the Lane Cove branch, applied to join

Chapter 2: Joining the ALP – the dream begins

and commenced a lifetime commitment to the Party and the people it seeks to serve.

Even at that young age, I wanted to spend my professional life as a full-time elected MP. In joining my local branch of the Labor Party, I believed I had made an essential first step on what I knew would be a long journey.

In May 1976 at age 19 and a brand-new member of the ALP, I was asked by our candidate in the imminent New South Wales State election to hand out Party material at The Lane Cove Shopping Centre on the Thursday nights leading up to the election. It was main street Lane Cove and even if the Liberal Party fielded the devil himself as a candidate, the locals would still reject the ALP. Less than 10 minutes in to my first assignment as a Party stalwart, an irate middle-aged and very overweight local Liberal positioned himself almost nose-to-nose with me, took one of our pamphlets, ripped it into several pieces, scrunched it into a ball and with a hard throw of it to the pavement, looked at me triumphantly and said: "That's what I think of Labor" and then stormed off. I thought to myself, "Gee, this path I have chosen is going to be a lot tougher than I had imagined."

Whilst I missed out on Law School, I had been accepted into a Bachelor of Arts at Macquarie University concentrating on accounting and economics with a few indulgent arts subjects for good measure. I decided I would study harder than anyone else in my first year and do so well that my transfer into law school at the end of the year would be a 'fait accompli'. It was not easy, but it showed me that really hard work trumps luck most of the time.

The State Election campaign in 1976 came to Campus and one lunchtime, Neville Wran addressed students on the front lawn about the 'bread and butter' issues of the campaign. I found him inspiring and wondered quietly to myself if one day I might return to do a similar thing.

John Faulkner, a future Asst. Secretary of the NSW ALP and Federal ALP senator, was also a student at Macquarie University at that time and my first introduction to him was in a small nondescript university lecture hall when he gave hell to senior State Liberal MP, Peter Coleman. This was a puny audience fronted by a small political man who would never cut the mustard against a colossus like Neville Wran, but I did think he ought to be allowed to state his case. One of our WWII air aces, John Waddy, and Liberal MP for Kirribilli had just lost pre-selection to Bruce McDonald and Faulkner used what I think is one of the most ear-piercing and penetrating voices I have ever heard in politics to constantly rattle the back walls of the room with: "What about John Waddy. Why did you rat on him?" I thought at the time it was more than a little uncivil, but it did introduce me to a tough uncompromising political player who I would later come across in Young Labor. And Bruce McDonald would go on to lose his seat to an independent in the 1981 'Wranslide' and disappear into the footnotes of New South Wales parliamentary history.

As we know, Neville Wran won the 1976 election by a one seat majority and presided over a first-class government of social, legislative and constitutional reform. He made me feel proud to be a Labor member and he thoroughly beat the Liberals, election after election.

I felt very happy at the 1977 Lane Cove Branch Annual General meeting, when I was asked by the leaders of the branch to nominate for election as a delegate for one of the vacant electorate Council positions. But, I was crestfallen when later told by one of them, that I had been elected on the Left ticket who brazenly commented: "We didn't tell you at the time because we didn't

Chapter 2: Joining the ALP – the dream begins

think you would be happy about it." Too right I wasn't! This was my first introduction to factions which up to that point, I knew little about and became my very first experience of left trickery.

I then explored in detail the role and differences of the Party factions and it seemed to me that they were far more about organising a large body of people effectively and establishing personal control and influence, than about anything of great policy substance. Both sides were committed to doing good things for the community and to the cause of Labor to improve the quality of life of our citizens. But, it also seemed to me that the left was reckless and inclined to throw fortune to the wind to achieve a pure position on an issue. The right was clearly the dominant and more pragmatic of the two and certainly the one I needed to join if one day I was to lead the Labor Party. I wanted to be head of government in an ALP administration and I was certain that that would never happen to a left winger. How times have changed since then. A left wing Prime Minister in Julia Gillard, a left-wing Premier in Nathan Rees and now a left-wing Leader of the New South Wales Opposition in Luke Foley. In the late 1970s this was unimaginable. I am sure if the 1970s giant of the New South Wales ALP and union movement and the then absolute ruler of the New South Wales ALP right, John Ducker, was alive today he would be horrified. I can almost see 'Bruvver Ducker' turning in his grave.

In February 1978 over a Chinese meal with Michael and Shane Easson in Dixon Street, Sydney I joined the New South Wales right of the ALP. Shortly thereafter, I was ushered into an audience with the factional leader and General Secretary of the New South Wales branch, Graham Richardson. At 20, I had applied and been accepted into the most dominant and politically successful faction in the country. Another small but significant step forward in my goal of high elected Office.

I now needed factional battle experience. I had attended my first quarterly Young Labor conference in early 1978 at Bondi Beach and I used the opportunity to demonstrate to my new faction that I was their man if they wanted the left attacked on the conference floor and bested in argument and debate. The left was always providing positions and views extreme enough to make good copy for robust ridicule and rebuttal. I got noticed and the next month, I was on the right Young Labor Council ticket for the Young Labor Executive and was elected.

Things were looking upwards and onwards. I was also enjoying my 2nd year of Law studies.

I had a ball on the Executive of the Young Labor Council (YLC). We basically reversed the roles the grown-up factions played in the main Party, with us causing havoc and the left trying to act responsibly. I eventually had four years on the YLC including an unsuccessful stint in 1982 at becoming President. The left kept winning, but I learnt a lot about public speaking in turbulent situations, campaigning within the Party, factional loyalty, affiliation with the major political players and where and how each faction dominated branches and regions across Sydney. This was invaluable, critically important knowledge on how the Party really worked. My involvement with the right faction at this early age and my contribution to date, meant that when I did make a move to a target area, I would be well known by the faction's leaders as a loyal and capable trooper and hopefully be granted consent and approval as the faction's favoured operative in that area.

My Party experience by the end of 1982 had been pretty tough and in-your-face factional encounters. When I eventually was elected to the New South Wales Parliament, it constantly amused me no end that old hands and the media would always refer to the

Chapter 2: Joining the ALP – the dream begins

Legislative Assembly as the 'bear pit'. In my 17 years as an MP, the so-called bear pit at its roughest, never seemed close to the roughhouse environment of Young Labor conferences and on occasions the annual conference of the main Party as well.

By contrast, the Libs who got elected to Parliament often seemed a little overwhelmed when put under the spotlight of robust and aggressive debate. Young Labor was in my mind an excellent training ground for a frontline role in Parliamentary engagement.

Perhaps the greatest gift Young Labor gave me was the opportunity to meet my future wife and life partner, Ann Leaf. Whilst the executive and quarterly conferences of Young Labor were the training and battleground of both the left and right, the local suburban Young Labor associations were a much tamer affair. I had been almost fully engaged in constant warfare with the left, and I had never met a woman in the Party who I was the least bit interested in. But that all changed one November evening in 1979.

Ann Leaf was in her final year of a modern languages / teacher's degree at Macquarie University. The local Young Labor Association covered the boundaries of the Federal Electorate we both lived in and we met once a month at the Gladesville Bowling Club. I was immediately overwhelmed. Beautiful, smart, articulate, political and Labor. What more could a young bloke want! I met her again a few weeks later on the Sunday of the Australian Young Labor Conference held over the January Australia Day weekend. It was at Sydney University and we had both decided separately to attend to listen to the guest speaker and rising star Paul Keating who was then a Shadow Minister in Bill Hayden's Federal Opposition. However, this was one occasion when we both found each other a lot more interesting than we did our future Prime Minister.

We have remained committed to each other ever since and as Gough once said of his wife Margaret: "My finest appointment." And now, just on 37 years later, I am still just as smitten as I was when we first met. I was then just 22 and Ann was 21.

I felt I had found my soul mate and a couple of months later, I shared with Ann my ambition to move to a strong Labor area, campaign for pre-selection and commence a life in politics and maybe one day becoming Attorney General in a Labor Government. She immediately supported the idea, but I will never forget her response: "But why stop at Attorney General. Why not aim to be leader?" I had tried to be modest and I think she saw through that almost immediately.

My six years of full-time study at Macquarie University came to an end in 1981. I had graduated with a Bachelor of Arts and a Bachelor of Laws with Honours. On the 14th of February 1982, Ann and I moved in together to a small two-bedroom apartment in Eastwood. After six more months of full-time study undertaking the practical legal training course at St Leonards, I decided I needed a break. I was washed up and needed a 'gap' year. From July 82 to March 83, I worked seven days a week as a laundry truck driver, service station attendant and barman. It was a great nine months that gave me a much-needed intellectual break. Ann and I then went on a five-week driving holiday around Malaysia and Singapore which was my first overseas trip.

By the beginning of 1983, it was time to start thinking seriously about getting a job as a solicitor and moving in to an area where I could commence my campaign to win a seat in Parliament.

Chapter 2: Joining the ALP – the dream begins

CHAPTER 3

The campaign for pre-selection – climbing the political Mt Everest

Perhaps the toughest seven years of my life would have to be the period from early 1983 to late 1989 when I was finally pre-selected as the ALP candidate for the by-election for the safe Labor State seat of Smithfield in the New South Wales Parliament.

It was a journey I would not recommend for the faint-hearted, self-doubters or those lacking a huge dose of self-determination.

The first step I had to undertake was a dual one: find a strong ALP area to move to and hopefully a job close by.

Four years of active service in Young Labor had given me invaluable knowledge of the ALP factional makeup of the Sydney region. I had long before decided, that I was not going to throw myself to chance in winning a marginal seat, only to see it taken from me a term or two later when the electoral wrecking ball came over to our side of the house.

I was determined to serve in a safe Labor seat for 20 years which would give me a period in executive government and hopefully keep me in the game long enough to have a serious tilt at the leadership. I had seen many a talented person on both sides

Chapter 3: The campaign for pre-selection

of politics come in flashes of light and then go with great thunder. I did not intend to be part of that sort of political sideshow.

But there was no point in moving into an area controlled by the left faction of the Party. I was well aware that once the left got wind of my arrival let alone the slightest whiff of local activity on my part, then I could expect a prompt and aggressive response. At least in a marginal seat I would get a chance, but in a strong left controlled area, I would be politically dead before arrival. The left in Young Labor had shown themselves to be very deft at resistance, recruitment and retribution. Over time, I had come to respect their sheer blood and guts determination and combativeness in protecting or enhancing their interests. Young Labor battles with the left had blooded and trained me in ALP factional combat, but I did not see a great future in engaging in the trenches with them on ground they controlled and would fiercely defend as their own property. I certainly respected them and decided that giving them a wide berth at this next phase of my political path was the much wiser choice.

I got hold of a huge map of Sydney and superimposed on it all the State and Federal electoral boundaries. I separated out in different colour codes ALP seats and Liberal seats then held by each Party and then designated which of the ALP seats were regarded as marginal ones and would swing to or away depending on the whims of the electorate. I then marked left held ALP seats and all marginal seats as a large no go zone. This left a good number of right held State and Federal seats to choose from, but I needed to be far more strategic than just picking one of those from the hat.

My time in Young Labor had not only taught me well as to which seats were controlled by the right and the left, but had also taught me which right wing ones were tightly controlled by

Tammany Hall style local warlords and which ones were just a loose confederation of like-minded conservative Party members. There was no point in moving to the former as I would also be 'dead on arrival'.

I needed an area which was regarded as safe Labor, with the local branches controlled by a loose and dispersed group of right faction loyalists, where no one and no group was all powerful, and where the left was weak and disinterested. Such an area would allow me to move-in unhindered and hopefully unnoticed, to establish myself, take charge and then eventually win a pre-selection. Being unnoticed was an ambitious aim, but critical to being unhindered as I commenced my work in the new area.

However, picking an area which was soft right with a weak left was not enough. I needed an area with an aging local MP who still had a couple of terms to go before voluntary retirement. Taking on a sitting MP is usually just too difficult and if one does succeed, the MP is usually left in a cloud of local animosity. I did not wish to go down that path. At the time, the only Federal seat which satisfied all my criteria was Prospect, broadly-based around the Fairfield area of South West Sydney.

Dick Klugman had been the Federal Member for Prospect since 1969. He was tired and had made no secret of his interest in only doing a few more years. The electorate did share a boundary with the Federal Electorate of Reid covering the Guildford area, which was an absolute monarchy run by the Jack Ferguson machine and his sons Martin, Laurie and Andrew. The risk that the Ferguson machine could at any time launch a factional recruitment attack on Prospect was something which worried me deeply for years.

Chapter 3: The campaign for pre-selection

Having identified my target area for a long pre-selection campaign, I then managed to secure my first job as a solicitor in March 1983 in the Fairfield town centre right in the heart of Prospect. This also provided huge cover for me whenever branch members inquired as to why I had moved all the way from Eastwood to Fairfield.

In July 1983, Ann and I moved into our first rented home – a three-bedroom fibro tile house at 22 Thorny Road Fairfield West on a large block of land backing on to Orphan School Creek. Having just moved from a small apartment, three floors up with no lift, near a rail line and surrounded by apartments full of noisy university students, we were very happy. We were just inside the boundary of both the Federal Electorate of Prospect and of Fairfield West branch of the ALP. The real journey was about to begin.

I was more than a little anxious fronting up to my first meeting of Fairfield West branch of the ALP. I envied the activists in the Party who had grown up in strong Labor seats and who by the time they were ready to pursue Party pre-selection would be at a decided advantage. I had moved to a place in Sydney where I had no family, no relatives, no friends, no links and no contacts. Apart from Ann being at my side as much as she could, I did feel pretty alone at the start.

I had been right to a degree on the area being loosely right wing, without a dominant factional machine and no warlords. However, the recently elected State MP for Fairfield, Janice Crosio, was a powerful, inspiring and frightening personality. She was a larger than life trail blazer for women in politics, but just as importantly, also a trail blazer for both Fairfield and Western Sydney. I loved her in-your-face confidence and optimism that is more lacking in Public Office than many would think to be the case. Paul Keating had once said to aspiring politicians: "When you walk in to a room, always assume that you are in charge". That was certainly Janice Crosio.

Janice was so well regarded, so passionate about the Labor cause and in everything she said and did, and so highly respected by the local branches in her electorate that had she chosen to do so, she could have quickly stopped me in my tracks from the very beginning. To my eternal debt, not only did she not do that, but she actually welcomed and supported all my activities and interest in local Party affairs and forums. Her husband, Ivo, was equally supportive and in a sense the unsung hero of Janice's very successful political career.

When I attended my first meeting of the ALP Prospect Federal Electorate Council in October 1983 and my name was announced as the newly appointed alternate delegate from Fairfield West branch, one of the rusted on left wing delegates from Fairfield South branch asked: "Who is Carl Scully?" My fiancée was with me that night and chuckled quietly in my ear: "They won't be saying that for too long."

By February 1984, I managed to secure my appointment as Education Officer of Prospect FEC which I had correctly assumed would be a very effective vehicle for raising my profile across all the branches in the Federal Electorate. I put on BBQs, film nights, social events and ran a newsletter called 'Prospects' as well as speaking at as many branch meetings as possible. In less than six months, everyone in the local ALP had now heard of me.

There were a lot of branches covering the Prospect Electorate: The right controlled Fairfield, Fairfield West, Smithfield, Canley Heights and Cabramatta. The left controlled Carramar, Greystanes, Fairfield South and Guildford West. The left branches

Chapter 3: The campaign for pre-selection

were not large ones and I naively thought I could reach out to at least some of their members. My favourite memory would have to be of Carramar branch, where I would leave feeling like I had been an unwelcome visitor to a western Sydney outpost of the Soviet Embassy. They were old school left who hated the ALP right more than they did the Liberal Party.

The real gem in the pack in addition to my own branch was Smithfield branch. This was Janice Crosio's branch and the one with the largest membership and the largest number of delegates in the two state and federal Electorate Councils. I was welcomed by the branch with open arms and by contrast with elsewhere in the Electorate, it seemed like the red carpet had been rolled out. I figured that if I was able to win over the Smithfield branch and the other right branches, then I would be on my way to a public career.

Canley Heights and Cabramatta branches were right wing, but were under the sway of Alderman John Newman who had spent years preparing for his own career in State politics. He was an aggressive and physically intimidating individual with a short fuse. He did not welcome anyone on his patch who he deemed might be a threat to him succeeding Eric Bedford when he retired as the then current MP for the State Electorate of Cabramatta.

In time, John and I would both become MPs for adjoining electorates and throughout that period in that capacity, we would develop a good rapport. But well before that happened, it was an in-your-face 'get out of my patch' sort of intimidation. John turned out to be a great MP for Cabramatta and a stalwart for his area. His career and life were cut short in 1994 when on the orders of fellow local Party member, Phuong Ngo, he was gunned down on the driveway of his Cabramatta home.

Despite the tough landscape, I had taken it all in my stride and believed that my non-stop performance as Education Officer would show all the members, irrespective of faction, that in due course, I should be supported as their MP. I would soon be given a very big wake-up call.

Smithfield branch did have the massive Crosio presence, a large membership and a welcoming mat, but it also had Anwar Khoshaba. Anwar was to prove the most rusted on, loyal, effective and persistent supporter I would ever have in my entire professional life. Success in life often depends on having a sponsor and Anwar was to become mine in spades. He and his immediate family had migrated from Iraq in the early 1970s and like many Assyrians before and after him, chose to settle in the Fairfield area in South West Sydney. Over the years, I would learn of his fascinating story in Iraqi underground politics, his service in the military, how he learnt to speak five languages and above all, how he was able to play a dominant role in local Assyrian affairs. The story is worthy of a book on its own.

Anwar seemed to take a liking to me; he supported my Education Officer activities and was always keen for good conversation. He struck me as very smart and I have no doubt that had he been born in Australia and had the language and education which would have fallen naturally to him, it would have been he and not me, who would have made it as MP. As it was, he would later spend many years as a Councillor on Fairfield City Council, including the position of Mayor.

Rather amazingly one Sunday afternoon in 1984, Anwar came around to my house to see me with a friend of his from the Assyrian community. He said he wanted to talk to me about something very important: "Carl, you are a highly-educated man. You are a solicitor and you are the sort of person this area needs as

Chapter 3: The campaign for pre-selection

a Member of Parliament. If you are agreeable, we want to support you and help make that happen." I almost fell over with excitement, but had to feign pleasant surprise and pretend that the idea was a little new to me and assured him I would be more than prepared to do it. We both agreed it would be a few years away with both Dick Klugman and Janice Crosio keen to continue as MPs for some time.

Apart from Ann, I had not spoken a word to anyone. I could not believe that my hard work and effort had resulted in such an outcome in less than 18 months. But then came the Annual General Meeting of Prospect FEC.

By March 1985, the left knew what I was up to and were very unhappy about it. Instead of being thanked for a year of hard work, I was defeated as Education Officer by a complete unknown who was then a young factional combat soldier by the name of Mike Smith. Mike was from the left and worked for the Miscellaneous Workers Union. I lost 21 to 17 to a guy who had just turned up on the night unannounced.

I could not believe what had just happened. One of the old-time lefties was even smug enough to say: "We couldn't leave you in that position. You were doing too good a job." Ann had been with me at the meeting and shared my great sense of defeat. It would not be the last time we would share such a raw emotional moment which most people spend their whole lives never experiencing. That night, I also learnt the hard way that one should never ever take anything for granted in politics. I became more determined than ever to succeed.

I did not feel dejected for very long! I decided that I would find a way to keep in-the-faces of branch members and keep up at least some level of activity. I again went back to the Party rule book and in particular the rules in relation to electorate Councils for positions to be filled at annual general meetings. I was delighted to find that State Electorate Councils could, if they so wished, appoint an organiser of the electorate Council. The role was not really defined and it seemed to be an effective way for me to continue to do my education officer activities, at least for the branch members within the Smithfield electorate. The boundaries of Janice's electorate had been reduced for the 1984 election to accommodate the huge growth in the new suburbs, which had sprung up in the western part of Fairfield. The new seat was called Smithfield, and left-wing Jeff Irwin became the new Member for Fairfield.

I discussed with Janice and Ivo the possibility of taking up the organiser role and both were very supportive. The Smithfield Electorate Council held its AGM a couple of weeks after the one for Prospect FEC, and I was duly appointed Organiser.

I was back in business. Mike Smith must have wondered whether he had actually been elected Education Officer, as I continued at an even greater pace, except now within the boundaries of the State Electorate. I was down, but was far from being out!

Many years later, when I had been a State Minister for some time, I met up with Mike for a cup of tea and a chat outside my Electorate Office in Fairfield. I thanked him and the left for the role he and they had played in the clear and blunt message in those earlier years: If I wanted a career in politics, I would have to recruit new members into the Party in large enough numbers so as to render irrelevant the views or actions of existing members. It was a pleasant discussion and he was even generous and cheery about the feedback. Old warriors can yarn about old battles won and lost,

Chapter 3: The campaign for pre-selection

but when they are actually happening, it is a whole lot less pleasant.

Anwar and I held a Council of war and agreed that the only course of action was to start recruiting from the Assyrian community. I did not have any local community relationships, so I was totally reliant on him. The area of focus would primarily be within the boundary of the Smithfield branch, as that was where most of Anwar's recruitment targets lived.

What we then embarked upon was a huge endeavour - We created a factional machine literally from scratch, which in time would dominate the branches and the pre-selection of MPs. I look back today, some 30 years later and I wonder just how the two of us did it. When I see the number of MPs parachuted into safe Labor seats today, with barely a few weeks' local effort, I do lament a little at just how much sheer hard work, blood and guts it took for me to win my own place in Parliament.

The start Anwar and I tentatively made in 1984 was followed by five solid hard years of effort. But we saw progress. Gradually, slowly, inexorably, our influence and control emerged in time to be a strong political force to be reckoned with.

I felt I now had a good plan to overcome what had been a surprise blitzkrieg from the left: Work hard as SEC Organiser and work harder still with Anwar in recruiting as many new members as we possibly could.

The critical period for Anwar and I was from the beginning of 1985 through to the end of 1987. To be eligible to vote in an ALP pre-selection, a member of the ALP needed to have had at least two years' membership and have attended at least three of their local branch meetings in the preceding 12 months. It was also essential that a member had correctly applied to join both the Party and the local branch and the latter to have been correctly recorded in the Minutes of the relevant meeting. And it was critical that the member not only be financial each year, but that the membership dues had been paid each of the previous two years by the date designated in the rules of the Party. If that was not enough, it was necessary also to be a financial member of the appropriate union covering their employment.

I cannot describe how onerous it was to ensure full and complete compliance by all new recruits and existing members with these requirements. Prior to any pre-selection, the returning officer was required prior to the day of the ballot, to hold a credentialing day when all the branch secretaries would present for inspection and scrutineering the branch Minute Book and the Attendance Book. It was usually aggressive stuff, and both factions would pull every trick in the book to convince the returning officer to either add or detract individuals from the voting list. I knew it was do or die stuff and it would take any serious contender years of effort to recruit supporters and then literally hundreds of hours to ensure compliance. The final list was then subject to appeal to the internal Party Review Tribunal.

Anwar's job was to find the recruits which I would assist in selling the Party message to, but it was my job to make sure when the day of credentialing eventually arrived that ALL of our recruits would withstand scrutiny and make it to the official pre-selection voting list. Anwar and I would spend as many evenings as possible painstakingly visiting Assyrian families and signing up in their lounge rooms all the family members over the age of 15. On other occasions, Anwar would visit me in my office in Fairfield with a batch of application forms duly signed which would give me a euphoric lift every time.

Chapter 3: The campaign for pre-selection

I had to be organised, so I prepared a large sheet of Cardboard about the size of a piece of butcher's paper. I listed down the left side of the page every single member in each branch that I had recruited which was mostly Smithfield branch and a little in Fairfield West branch. Unless I was certain a member not recruited by either Anwar or I was a 100% supporter, I did not include them on the list. If they wanted to vote, then the left could make sure they would be eligible. After the debacle of the 1989 Liverpool pre-selection where Mark Latham lost votes because he unknowingly challenged some of his own supporters, I decided that I would not be using that device to disenfranchise party members. If I was going to win, then I would do it by having an overwhelming majority by the time the vote was held.

Along the top of the paper I listed eighteen columns to cover eighteen months of attendance signatures ticked off and evidenced by the attendance book. There were columns to provide for the dates that the person applied to join the Party and the branch, the date of the branch meeting they were accepted, the category of membership, the dates membership dues were paid for the previous three years, union membership and whether or not this was financially up to date.

This document was a work of art in itself and would prove of incalculable value as a ready reckoner on a rolling time line to ensure compliance at any one time. I usually ensured that my recruits had about five or six signatures in the attendance book, to ensure that no matter when the previous twelve months was calculated from, that they would still be eligible. The biggest labour was entering the data, keeping it up to date and making sure the branch books corresponded with what was on the list.

Since moving in to the Smithfield branch in early 1986 after buying our home in Bossley Park, I was elected Branch Secretary at its Annual General Meeting soon after. Holding this position was almost as important as the recruitment itself. I was the custodian of the books and no one else could get access to them except on a credentialing day.

On a typical weekend prior to the monthly meeting of Smithfield branch, I would make 50 to 60 phone calls asking members to turn up and sign the attendance book at the meeting. The book was kept on a desk at the front of the meeting hall and there would often be a queue going for metres outside the door as folks waited to sign the book. It was a sight I just loved to see. The longer the queue the better. During any particular week, I would usually visit one or two families on my way home from work to keep up the interaction. As a local solicitor, I was often called upon by Anwar to do pro bono work for members in need. My professional, personal and political life seemed to be all directed at one thing: the pre-selection. It was never far from my thoughts and I was very focussed on it day and night.

At one branch meeting in 1987, Dick Klugman approached me and used one of the oldest pre-selection tricks in the book by asking me to nominate him for pre-selection. It was a technique to either out a competitor or if not, it would put a person in an invidious position if whilst seeking pre-selection they had earlier nominated someone else for the position. Dick also apologised at the time: "Sorry Carl, but I have decided to run again at this year's election and I'd like you to nominate me". "Of course", I quickly responded. But I was thinking quietly to myself: "Dick, are you kidding. I'm not ready, my recruits are not yet eligible to vote and I need you to run for another term". It was just as I had planned.

The year of 1988 was a bit of a watershed for the Labor Party and the local branches. The New South Wales State Government was defeated in the May elections and Janice Crosio was

Chapter 3: The campaign for pre-selection

consequently no longer a Minister of the Crown. It was well known by then that Dick Klugman would not be seeking a further term at the following Federal election expected sometime in 1990. And the vultures were swooping!

Frank Walker, the high profile left wing Attorney General, had just lost his seat at the State election and it was rumoured that he was looking at Prospect as a possible gateway to a Federal parliamentary career. I had also heard that Bob McMullan, then an ALP senator from the ACT, had expressed an interest in the 'vacant' seat as well. After all the hard work that I had put in, I was mortified that the Party or either faction of the Party would allow or actually orchestrate the parachuting in of a complete stranger to succeed in the seat.

I arranged for an audience with the then General Secretary, Stephen Loosley and sought an assurance that as far as the right faction and the Party were concerned, the seat would be mine. "Keep working at it" was the only assurance he was prepared to offer despite my concerns of a 'foreign invasion'. I had naively expected someone in his position to roll out the red carpet for my elevation to Federal Parliament. Stephen Loosley and I are now good friends and often chat about military and political history, but back then in the late 1980s, I was crestfallen that my claim on a Federal seat was not readily endorsed by him. However, I still regard him as easily the smartest General Secretary the New South Wales ALP has had in the last 50 years and always respected that he had a wider responsibility to the Party than just looking after one ambitious factional colleague.

More recently, Loosley informed me that Prospect had been considered by then New South Wales Premier Neville Wran as a vehicle for a federal career. It was certainly rumoured during the Wran political hegemony that he might or even would transfer to

Canberra with a plan of becoming Prime Minister. Wran had even privately suggested that he appoint Dr Dick Klugman, then MP for Prospect, as the Director-General of New South Wales Health and then take his seat in Federal Parliament. Wran apparently came to the view that the Murdoch press would have been unforgiving in attacking such a tawdry transaction, so he pulled the plug on it. Probably just as well.

Many years later when Wran had been long retired and I was a State Minister, I asked him why he had never gone to Canberra: "Hawkey jumped the queue" was all he had to say, alluding to the 1980 entry of Bob Hawke into Federal Parliament and then his election as Prime Minister in 1983. But no mention of any dubiously defendable shuffle with Dr Klugman.

Nick Greiner, when Premier of New South Wales, was not so cautious as he clumsily attempted to move Terry Metherill MP from the New South Wales Parliament to a senior job with the Environment Protection Agency and lost his job over it.

Until my meeting with Loosley, I had strongly believed that I was seen by my faction as part of generational renewal, that I had rightfully staked my claim to the Federal seat of Prospect and that when the time came, the machine would roll in and back me 100%. How naïve I had been.

The reality was unfortunately nothing like this. I went home that afternoon from this meeting with our faction leader feeling forlorn and worried that when the time did come, a well-known 'star' candidate might be conscripted to take the seat. I decided that I needed to take a course of action which would effectively take the faction leaders and Party office out of play and leave me guaranteed a parliamentary career.

Chapter 3: The campaign for pre-selection

Factional loyalty and dependence was one thing, and risk management of my future was entirely another. Assuming that loyalty and fealty to the tribe would mean much when an individual sought and expected support in return, has stymied many a career in politics before it began. I resolved that I would not be in that category. But, I would have to give up something very valuable to me to achieve this. I had to trade away my dream of becoming a federal MP. It was a big price to pay!

Janice Crosio was an extremely popular, high profile and much-loved individual. Having lost her ministerial position following Labor's defeat at the 1988 state election she was still the local MP for Smithfield but I suspected she was feeling more than a little unfulfilled if not unappreciated. This combined with the fact that all of the new members which Anwar and I had brought in to the Party were within the boundary of the Smithfield State Electorate made for a compelling discussion.

However, to guarantee a parliamentary career I had to give up my plan to be a major player in National politics. I was just not sure enough that I could get the votes in the face of WW111 from the local left so I opted for caution and threw my dream to the wind. One evening in late 1988, at Janice Crosio's home in Bossley Park, we did the deal. She would take the vacant federal seat in the 1990 federal election and I would then follow in a by-election as her replacement in the state seat of Smithfield.

Despite wrenching away my federal ambition I was still so excited about the prospect of a Parliamentary career that I had to pinch myself to make sure it was actually happening. Once Janice announced her intentions to the Party office, the branches and the wider community, it was all over. In March 1989, she was duly pre-selected in a one-sided contest with the left and became the new federal member for Prospect at the 1990 election.

I have often wondered over the years what might have been. I had always sought a federal political career and sometime after this pre-selection some old lefties in the area believed I would have won it had I persevered. Would I have? And if so, what national political role might I have achieved? Wondering is nice now and then but it doesn't really achieve much except regrets. I had made a conscious risk management decision to guarantee a political career rather than run in a battle where such a career might be just a maybe or even a probable but never guaranteed. I made the decision based on an assessment of the landscape as it appeared before me and in the same circumstances I would make the same decision again.

On the 2nd of December 1989, the pre-selection ballot for the Smithfield Electorate took place. It was held on a sunny Saturday at the St James' Anglican Church Hall on the Horsley Drive, Smithfield. The returning officer was a very young 16-year-old Chris Bowen, who had already been a Party member for nearly two years and had shown promise, talent and interest. I had taken him under my wing and he was loyal. It was a big call to entrust something as important as this to a 16-year-old, but I was more than confident he would excel at it. At the Annual General Meeting of the SEC held in April of that year, I had secured his appointment. He did not let me down. But we still have a chuckle even now, at how we both put a kid in charge of something so important.

There were three candidates: myself, Patrick Mulhall and Genene Euridge. Patrick Mulhall was a fellow branch member and a person I thought was a friend and supporter until he unexpectedly nominated. Genene Euridge was the left candidate. At the close of polling we all piled in to the hall as the ballot box was emptied by the returning officer in front of scrutineers and a

Chapter 3: The campaign for pre-selection

large audience which had filled the hall. A separate pile was set aside for each first preference vote given to each candidate. With each ballot paper unfurled, examined and allocated, my pile was getting bigger and bigger. Ann squeezed my hand and without saying a word we both knew a magic moment of enormous consequence to our lives was upon us. I cannot describe the electrifying feeling of seeing this unfold in front of me.

The Returning Officer announced the result of the ballot:

Carl Scully: 110 votes
Patrick Mulhall: 15 votes
Genene Euridge: 10 votes

I was declared elected.

I have often wondered what it must feel like for a mountaineer the moment he or she reaches the top of Mt Everest. Well this was my Everest and I had climbed it! I think this must also be close to the enormous feeling of relief, excitement and sheer joy for an athlete at the moment an IOC official places a gold medal on them. If ever there was a gold medal moment in Party politics, then this had to be it.

During a long career in Public Office littered by numerous minor to major successes and disappointments I would on only three occasions feel the dizzying high of substantial victory: My pre-selection on the 2nd of December 1989, my election as a new MP on the 23rd of June 1990 and my commissioning as a new minister on the 4th of April 1995. I would also on only three occasions feel the despair and abyss of significant defeat: In February 1985 when I was defeated as the Education Officer of Prospect FEC, on the 29th of July 2005 when I realised I was unable to win the leadership of the New South Wales Parliamentary Labor

Party and on the 25th of October 2006 when I was sacked by the person who beat me to that job – Morris Iemma.

There would be in a career spanning seventeen years including nearly twelve years in the Cabinet, countless minor to mid-level wins and setbacks but they pale when compared to these major life changing wins and losses. And on the 2nd of December 1989, the day of my pre-selection, of all my three big highs this was 'the sweetest of them all.'

The evening of my pre-selection win and the following few days were a very emotional time for me. On the Tuesday of the following week, the local Fairfield Advance Newspaper ran a front-page photograph of Janice Crosio and me, with a story announcing that I would be the next State MP. I was ecstatic and the photo showed it. Ann with that wonderful cheeky sense of humour I have grown to love over the years, picked up the paper, had a good look at it, gave me one of her looks and lamented: "Huh! You look happier here than you were on our wedding day." That was one I was not expecting and I am not sure how I got out of it.

A short while later I was endorsed by the New South Wales ALP Administrative Committee. It was also pointed out to me that I had been pre-selected on the anniversary of the election of the Whitlam Government in 1972 and on the same day that the Goss Labor Government was elected in Queensland. I thought how fitting to be amongst such august Labor milestones. One great tradition which my local returning officer, Chris Bowen, has steadfastly maintained on every 2nd of December from then on right up even to this day, is to call or send a note congratulating me on the anniversary of my original pre-selection win. He and I well know that no pre-selection means no Parliamentary career.

Chapter 3: The campaign for pre-selection

My 14-year campaign including six and a half years in full Party factional combat mode was over. My time had come. It had been a long hard slog. When I reflect back upon those long campaign years of pursuit and endeavour I do wonder how I had the unrelenting drive and energy to do it.

I was eighteen when I took those first nervous, tentative steps in joining the Lane Cove branch of the ALP and then at 32 I was standing on the victory dais. I had started as a teenage kid and was now a grown-up veteran of internal Party combat. It was now time to look beyond the Party and to the electorate.

Anwar and I had created a broad, far reaching and effective political machine out of nothing. It not only delivered my pre-selection but substantially underpinned the Federal Prospect pre-selection of Janice Crosio in 1989 and delivered the pre-selection and a Parliamentary career for her successor, Chris Bowen in 2004. It also contributed to Fairfield State Electorate pre-selections, had a big say on who would serve as Councillors on Fairfield City Council and finally, provided substantial factional and Party stability in an important area of south west Sydney. This continued for over 25 years.

When Janice Crosio made it clear that she would retire at the 2004 Federal election, Anwar and I determined that Chris Bowen would succeed her. Anwar and I ran the ALP factional machine in the area, they were our numbers and would have done as we asked. Anwar always conducted himself as if he was the head of my local ALP Praetorian Guard. He first and foremost sought to protect my political position and to implement my political will within the local ALP branches. Our choice of Chris Bowen as the next MP for Prospect was no different. Without our backing, he would not have had a political career at either local or federal level.

I always acknowledged whenever I could, the role Anwar had played in launching my political career. In time, I would arrange for right faction war lord, Graham Richardson, to visit Anwar in his Bossley Park home and thank him for his contribution to the faction and to the Party. But that was later. Anwar was my Campaign Director and Chris Bowen was my Assistant Campaign Director. There was work to do.

Chapter 3: The campaign for pre-selection

CHAPTER 4

The backbencher – reaching for executive power

"Are you from the ALP" bellowed the response from the back of a Smithfield home as I announced my candidacy from an open front door which soon followed with a very solid: "Then get the fuck off my property". This is perhaps my most treasured memory of my first campaign.

I started campaigning for the by-election almost immediately. Railway stations, posters, pamphlets, newspaper stories and doorknocking. Lots of doorknocking. In fact, almost the whole electorate by foot!

Bob Carr would say at the time that folks appreciated the personal effort and would remember it years later. He was right. When I announced my retirement from politics in early 2007 I received a very nice note from a woman who lived in Merrylands reminding me that I had met her family whilst doorknocking in January 1990 and that it was still the only visit they had ever had from a politician. The local shoe mender got a lot of work from me at that time.

The Premier, Nick Greiner, announced that the Liberal Party would not be fielding a candidate for the by-election. And he was in no rush to announce the date either. I had a field day lambasting the government for this twin contempt of the people of Smithfield.

Greiner eventually set Saturday June the 23rd 1990 as the date for the by-election. A few independents nominated but as expected no one representing the government. I had arranged for a small room near to our campaign office to receive the count from our scrutineers. Ann was with me as was Anwar, and Chris Bowen had the job of recording the numbers as they came in.

The first one was from Horsley Park which was a small booth in a rural area of the electorate, and the only one which had just about always voted a majority to the Liberal Party in all previous state and federal elections. But I assumed with no Liberal candidate and my comprehensive coverage of the area with personally addressed letters, with brochures and with doorknocking, that I would be a shoe in. When Bowen showed me the count I had to check it twice before realising that I had not received a majority of the votes and even on a distribution of preferences I may not win the booth. I was devastated. I was so upset I withdrew to the stairwell with Ann and in tears said: "I may not win. This is all I want to do with my life. I don't want to do anything else!"

Ann calmed me down as always and then Bowen came in and assured me that this was a very small booth in 'enemy territory' and the later bigger booths would tell a wholly different story. He was right and I was elected by a thumping majority. But my emotional reaction at the beginning of the night showed me just how much it meant to me to serve and would, I am sure, have satisfied the Keating test on a suitability for a life in politics. The victory Party that night with 200 Party members and supporters, family and friends is probably the one I cherish most.

Shortly after being elected, I was invited with Ann, to do a tour of Parliament House, to settle in to my new office and to meet the various administrative officials who kept the place running. I managed to meet up with ALP legend, Johnno Johnson, who despite the loss of the 1988 election, was still the President of the Legislative Council. Johnno was very much part of the right faction Catholic mafia and a stalwart in Bob Carr's branches. He suggested that for my 'swearing in' as a new MP I should buy a new Bible for the occasion but when I responded with: "I am an atheist Johnno, I will be doing an affirmation and not a swearing in", I thought he was going to collapse. The sheer look of horror on his face, that one of his factional own could have just said such a thing, left me wondering for a moment whether we needed to call for medical assistance.

Parliament did not resume for the spring session for a few weeks which gave me time to move in to my electorate office, select staff and run constant stories in the local paper, blaming every local evil on the state government and to prepare my maiden speech.

My grandfather Patrick Charles Scully was elected in 1920 as the MP for Namoi for the multi member rural electorate in the New South Wales Parliament. He served until 1923 when his brother William Scully, my great Uncle, would take over the seat from 1923 until his defeat at the Lang debacle election of 1932. William Scully would then serve as the federal member for Gwydir in the National Parliament from 1937 until 1949 and a Minister in the Curtin and Chifley governments.

My grandfather was keen to ensure decent salaries for our teachers and he had spoken on this very thing in the very place I would now be speaking. I decided to not only quote from him in my maiden speech but to adopt his words of the 23rd of November

Chapter 4: The backbencher

1920: "For many years, I, in company with my fellow teachers strongly advocated the payment of salaries which would to some extent remunerate the teachers for the many sacrifices they were called upon to make, and which they are still called upon to make".

I recently went back and re-read my grandfather's speech in the house on that day and was even more thrilled to see, that he had been very active in setting up a Teacher's Association which was an early form of a union for teachers. No wonder I joined the Labor Party.

I felt much moved by not only referring to his speech but being able to do so in front of my father who was in the gallery listening, as was my Mum and my four siblings.

About 18 months before delivering my first parliamentary speech my mother had been diagnosed with kidney cancer at the age of just 58.

By the time of my maiden speech in September 1990, my Mum was gravely ill but just well enough to attend. She could barely walk up the stairs to the front entrance of Parliament House, even with assistance and was hardly able to eat a thing at the pre-speech dinner in the dining room I had laid on for my family, friends and a few branch members. John Dowd, the Greiner government Attorney-General and Leader of the House, did my Mum and I a big favour by allowing my speech to be given straight after the dinner break. It was the first and only time my mother would visit Parliament house.

I will be forever grateful for what did John Dowd did. Some would say it was just a small thing and when I repeated this story to one of the Leaders of the House in the Wran/Unsworth Labor era he replied: "I wouldn't have done that". Well I would have.

When I eventually became Leader of the House from April 2003 to October 2006 I tried as much as possible to be accommodating to requests from the opposition as to when and on what they wanted to speak. My ALP colleagues sometimes used to gently challenge me with: "Why do you give those bastards a break" and I would usually respond with: "We can't win the day in the electorate by denying the opposition the opportunity to speak and put their case. The day we are worried about the quality of their argument against ours is the day we start to lose it in the community." I have always believed that the weight of numbers in an argument is only convincing on its own for a while and if you can't convincingly argue your case on the floor of a Young Labor Conference, on the floor of the New South Wales Conference of the ALP or even on the floor of the New South Wales Parliament, then sooner or later you will have those numbers taken off you. But an element of my approach whenever asked when Leader of the House was to think of how I was treated many years before by one of their own.

I had not long been an MP when I asked a few of my right-wing colleagues one evening, "When do we get stuck into them?" When asked: "What do you mean?" and I responded with: "You know, the left, when do we start getting stuck into the bastards?" I was somewhat perplexed at first with the response: "Carl, we don't do things that way in here. I know you have come from battling the left in your branches but in here the factions work together. We are all focussed in taking the fight up to the Liberals". I said, "Shit that's novel", did a 180-degree change of direction and from then on focussed on giving the Government as hard a time as I possibly could in both the Parliament and in my local community.

Chapter 4: The backbencher

My only up-close experience with the Liberals had been handing out 'how to' vote cards at election time. But after years and years of devoted combat duty to ensure the left never ventured anywhere near controlling the Party, I did need a sober reminder of who our real political opponents were and what my Party responsibilities were in that regard in Parliament.

I wanted to be noticed by my colleagues; I wanted to stand out amongst them, so that after the next election which was due the following year, my performance and capability would elevate me to the front bench. I wanted to make a difference and the only real way to do that was to be in the Cabinet. But, I was rather naïve back then thinking that performance alone would do the job! I spoke on as many bills as I possibly could.

If I wasn't in the House speaking or getting ready to speak, I was in my office preparing for one. I thought I was doing well.

The first six months of 1991 were some of the most eventful six months both personally and politically in my entire 17 years in politics. My daughter Sarah was born in April, I was re-elected in May and in June, my mother passed away.

Incredibly, Nick Greiner almost threw away government in one quick term after his devastating win in 1988. Greiner is a very smart guy and not surprisingly, corporate Australia has sought his skills and talent in his life after politics. But, at politics he was not that effective. He approached government as if it was a company balance sheet to be presented to the once four yearly meeting of voting shareholders. The books had to be balanced, staff sacked, taxes increased, levies raised and every charge he could get his hands on increased.

It was as if the New South Wales Government had become the economic rationalist capital of the world. But government is so much more complicated than a board room or a share register. It is supposed to compassionately regulate our affairs, arbitrate between competing interests and to the best of its ability, deliver the services, infrastructure and quality of life its citizens expect. Greiner did not seem to me to have a fundamental grasp of these essentials. His early approach to 'corporatising' government was to cost him dearly.

The huge increases in taxes and charges by the government gave Bob Carr a mantra which took him to within three seats of victory at the 1991 election. An amazing result from where the Labor Party had been just three years earlier.

From June 1988, when the first set of large increases were imposed by Greiner right up to the May 1991 election, Bob Carr talked about the issue of taxes and charges so incessantly that we began to quietly complain. Carr's response was classic: "When you are so sick of hearing the same message over and over again to the point where you almost want to vomit if you hear it again, then always remember, that this is when folks are finally hearing the message for the first time." He was right. It is often hard to break through the 'message clutter' of the modern world and deliver a political message to a mostly uninterested polity.

As the count was going on straight after the 1991 election, I had high hopes of just maybe becoming a minister, if not an Opposition front bencher. I rang one of the right faction leaders, Paul Whelan, who said tartly: "I'm not even thinking of that now." I interpreted that comment as: "I have thought about this a lot indeed and you my lad, do not even get a mention." I assumed that the old guard had already divided up the spoils of office win or lose and I was not even in the discussion, let alone the play. I was not going to let that happen next time.

I ran into Brian Langton, who had been a very capable Shadow Minister for Transport, one day and mentioned to him my wish to be considered for promotion. He was at least frank and honest about it: "There is no doubt about your ability, it's just that it's not yet your turn." And with that, I was left on the backbench for four more years.

So, in six short months of 1991, my mother had died, our daughter was born, I had been re-elected as the MP for Smithfield and then refused entry by the old guard onto the front bench. Every one of those events would have a lasting impression on me. It was a tumultuous year.

Morris Iemma and Eddie Obeid were natural allies for me in Parliament in the early 1990s. We had all either grown up with or experienced the Party with Graham Richardson as the undisputed right faction war lord. And both Iemma and Obeid were front and centre creations of Graham Richardson. Iemma had worked on Richo's staff when the latter was a Minister in the national Parliament. Obeid had developed a personal friendship with Richo who in turn would sponsor Obeid into the Upper House vacancy caused by the retirement of Jack Hallam.

The three of us in particular were unimpressed that the parliamentary right and therefore in turn the parliamentary party, were controlled by an old guard remaining from the remnants of the 1988 defeat who were either unwilling or unable to share power with a new generation of MPs. The Opposition whip at the time was the Member for Broken Hill, Bill Beckroge. He was old guard and a signed-up member of the Trog sub faction in the right of the parliamentary party. His approach to newcomers and sharing the decision making was best summed up one day when I asked him what the tactics were going to be for Question Time: "You're a rower Scully. We'll tell you when you need to know." Paul Crittenden, the new MP for Wyong, received similar treatment from Beckroge and was so seething with anger about it, he became devoted to the disempowerment of the Trogs.

The analogy was starkly clear: New MPs were no more than the equivalent of slaves rowing a Spanish galley in ancient times. We would often joke about it over the years particularly with our own new MPs, but at the time, we saw it as a complete failure to recognise that we ought to be included in the decision-making process. A few of us began to discuss how to deal with the situation. Iemma was blunt with me: "I see you are doing a lot of speeches in the House. If you think that is going to get you in to the Ministry you are mistaken. You get ahead in here from having friends not giving speeches and you need to make more friends." I didn't need any convincing that the Trog grip on the decision-making in the faction was ever likely to elevate me to the Ministry or front bench anytime soon. We were young and ambitious and wanted a say in how the faction and the Party was run. It was not going to be handed to us. We would have to seize it.

We talked to a number of fellow right wingers and soon there was a consensus among a number of us that we needed to create a new sub faction to take over the right and to control the parliamentary party. We intended to determine who would and who would not be on the front bench of the parliamentary party and in what order MPs would be promoted. Our message was pretty simple but very effective: "Under the current arrangements you are never going to get ahead. Join with us and know that when it's your turn, the weight of the group will propel you in to the position you seek".

Chapter 4: The backbencher

People often ask how Eddie Obeid became so influential in the parliamentary party. The answer is simple: No one was as consummate as he was at convincing MPs that without the Terrigals their careers were doomed, but joining the new tribe would in time guarantee it.

And what he was good at and in fact better at it than anyone I have seen, was that he was able to soothe egos, gently massage ambitious tendencies downwards to a more realistic timetable, give individuals a sense that he really cared about them and their futures and corral a disparate 'herd of cats' into one solid voting force which would in time dominate the New South Wales political scene for many years.

Obeid from the start presented as a successful businessman who wanted to put something back into the community. He was a consummate professional in projecting an older godfatherly concern and empathy with all the actual and potential Terrigal flock. It was impressive and effective.

Obeid had a holiday house on the beach at Terrigal and as our first meeting was held there, our sub faction became known as "The Terrigals". There would be a number of gatherings at his holiday house, but most of the effort occurred in Parliament House in Obeid's 12th floor office which became a drop-in centre for the new group. All the disaffected, disappointed or disenfranchised would regularly drop in for long chats about what a bunch of bastards the Trogs were and how something had to be done about them. We grew stronger and stronger as each month went by in the new four-year term.

Obeid was one of the most successful influencers I have ever seen in politics. From a standing start of almost zero in 1991, within a year or two he was a major player in factional, party and parliamentary politics. Looking back, it was as impressive as it gets.

He was older, seemed less interested in the spoils of office than in making sure everyone achieved their potential. Obeid was exceptionally good at making every MP within his orbit feel like he worried about them, their prospects and their place in the sun. No one was anywhere near as good at this as he was. Politics is a lonely life and even lonelier still for the ambitious. Obeid was able to convincingly act out the role of being each and every Terrigal MPs career protagonist. Even I got duped with lines such as: "I'm only staying in politics to see you become Premier" or even one of his favourites with me: "You are like a son to me". By devoting himself to the cause of each and every Terrigals' eventual advancement and political wellbeing, he became influential and in due course, very powerful.

But he did not arrive entirely without connections and influence. He never hid his close relationship with Graham Richardson. In fact, it was his badge of honour which we all respected very much. 'Richo' as he has always been affectionately known, was still an ALP factional and party heavyweight, even though he had left the Sussex Street machine for the Hawke Cabinet. We had all grown up in the faction and the Party, with Richo as the undisputed king of every decision that mattered.

Obeid was known for being a close friend of Richo and that it was Richo who had steered him to the vacant position in the Upper House. Many of us saw Obeid as Richo's eyes and ears in the caucus and far from this troubling anyone, it actually enhanced Obeid's position from the start. I certainly assumed that we were organising a more effective faction to enable closer cooperation with the Sussex Street ALP headquarters and the leader than the Trogs were ever going to provide.

Chapter 4: The backbencher

Obeid made it clear that he was often talking to Richo, which in our new and young eyes, just added to Obeid's weight and influence. At the time, it all made sense: take control, support head office, support the leader and get our talent onto the front bench. In time, the influence of Richo waned and in due course Obeid was able to work his 'magic' on MPs a little more freely. This was even more so as Joe Tripodi emerged as a Terrigal spear carrier and Obeid Mr Fix it.

Michael Knight became a prize acquisition for both the Terrigals, the right faction as a whole and in due course, the Labor Government. Prior to entering Parliament, I had only known Michael Knight as a fire-eating, right-hating, left winger from Campbelltown who was the enemy incarnate. However, when I was elected, I was given a spot on the backbench sitting right next to the man himself.

What astonished me was that he seemed human, seemed genuinely concerned about our people and seemed to take an interest in me as a new MP. In fact, he was the only guy who took any interest in me at all when I first arrived. It really is a dog eat dog life in Parliament and there is no manual or buddy system to smooth a new comer into the ways and culture of a very unusual kind of workplace.

Knight was always keen to help and even warn me as I slowly learnt the ropes as an MP. I couldn't see how it would help him other than doing a colleague from another faction a good turn. We became friends and remained so during our ministerial careers and beyond. I am firmly of the view that this solid friendship had a lot more to do with a successful delivery of the Olympic Games in Sydney than perhaps either he or the general public realised.

I did feel for him in the early 1990s. He had been an MP since 1981 and had been constantly prevented by the left from attaining even the remotest chance of a front bench position. It seemed that for whatever reason, he attracted negative emotions from within both factions. The right hated him and the left didn't trust him. But from the moment I started dealing with him, I could see talent and friendship rather than bastardry and disloyalty.

His reputation followed him. One evening, when Janice Crosio visited the New South Wales Parliament, she saw me sitting next to Knight during Question Time. She later said to me: "Why are you sitting next to Michael Knight. He just can't help himself. You will regret ever having anything to do with him". I ignored her comment and spent many years working closely and productively with him.

Graham Richardson had let it be known that he wanted Knight in the faction particularly as he believed that the left was too dumb and stubborn to ever let him in on the front bench. Obeid and the Terrigals went to work and despite Trog Opposition, secured his admission to the right Caucus. He immediately became an important part of the Terrigal group and was a regular visitor and contributor to Obeid's 12th floor office. Faye Lo Po and then Knight himself would secure front bench vacancies well before the 1995 State Election.

With Knight and Lo Po already secured on the front bench in Opposition, Obeid secured within the Terrigals, a consensus that I would be the next cab off the rank and worked on Carr and others in the right to sell that message. But my colleagues made it clear that I also had to work for the position so that when the time came, my elevation would not be a fight but would be recognised as appropriate by both factions. And I still had a lot of work to do to reach that sort of position. I didn't yet stand out enough to justify my promotion on performance alone and I now intended to do something about that at every available opportunity.

Knight did me a favour on one occasion, when he was unable to do the launch of a petition in Castle Hill that called for the removal of the local MP, Tony Packard, for breaching the Listening Devices Act 1984 whilst running a car yard in what would be part of his future electorate. Knight said: "Sorry mate, but I will be away so I need you to launch this out in Castle Hill for the bastard's local newspaper. We will issue a media alert that you are holding a press conference, but I don't expect much interest."

He had to be kidding! I had never before done a full-on news conference. When I turned up expecting a journalist from the local paper and a photographer, what I got was five TV journalists – yes, even SBS turned up, plus radio journalists and representatives from both the Sydney Morning Herald and the Telegraph. I took it in my stride and rather liked the encounter. I moved onto the main street and had lined up my father in law, Alf Leaf, to be the first passer-by to wander up and sign the petition. He did so with relish and added a flourish which was all his own: "He's got to go". The cameras loved it and so did the journos. My mother in law, Rose Leaf, was tickled pink by Alf's performance.

The story took off and only fuelled the problem for the local MP who would soon resign from Parliament and disappear into obscurity. I am not sure Knight meant to give me that much of a leg up, but he seemed happy that I had performed under pressure and told me the leader was impressed. That to me at the time was manna from heaven.

Life as a backbench MP was certainly very different to the life I had had as a solicitor. I was loving it, but knew I needed to work harder to get the balance right between family and my parliamentary and electorate responsibilities. Ann and I do have one particular fond memory of this time when my job was new and our family was young. It was 1994 and James, our son, was five and Sarah, our daughter, just three. We had had lunch in the parliamentary dining room and Ann and the two kids went up to the upstairs gallery to watch Question Time. Kevin Rozzoli, the Speaker, was having a hard time keeping the House orderly and kept bellowing "order, order". Sarah asked her Mum: "Why does that man keep saying 'order order'"? and Ann responded: "Because they are being naughty and too noisy". The House just at that moment, actually went quiet long enough for Sarah to give a very audible "order, order" of her own. Carr was quick to add: "your daughter I presume?"

One thing no one knew about in the House, was that Kevin Rizzoli and I were related on my father's side. As a keen student of American civil war history, I was always proud of that fact that I was a direct descendant of a union soldier by that surname who is buried in Arlington cemetery. At least I was until I learnt that he had the same name and was related to a doyen of the Tories, an enemy of the ALP and no less than a Speaker of the House to boot! My civil war veteran was the father of my father's grandmother. I am not sure who was more embarrassed about being related 'across the aisle.' I didn't tell anyone and I don't think Mr Speaker did either. It has remained largely secret until now.

Chapter 4: The backbencher

CHAPTER 5

The illusion of freedom of speech – over-reaching on 'sacred' ground

I had always been impressed from a distance that some Labor federal backbenchers had produced from time to time, thought provoking policy papers on issues of the day. When I became a New South Wales State MP, I thought it was a shame that only Shadow Ministers provided this sort of contribution to policy debate and backbench MPs were just mostly asleep. I decided in addition to participating in debates on legislation, finding more friends in the Labor caucus and rigorously defending the interests of my electorate, I would also produce some policy papers of my own. A good idea intellectually, but a very unwise idea politically.

Much against what others would call my better judgement, I decided to venture onto the hallowed grounds of immunisation policy and practice. And what a learning experience of intellectual intolerance it would turn out to be.

I researched not what unqualified people had said on the issue, but what medical practitioners themselves had said in published medical journals. I was astonished to find a wealth of material in the medical literature which more than indicated that in some cases, the side effects could be reasonably serious and for some vaccine recipients, the alleged immunity did not occur. I found that unlike the public-approved narrative, there was a range of different side effects and vaccine effectiveness for each different vaccine.

It seemed pretty clear to me that parents were being given a mantra more than a reasoned set of facts from which they could make an informed judgement about their children.

The lawyer in me found this information rather insulting; it would hardly stand up if scrutinised in a proper process of adversarial assessment. It seemed to me that on this area of public health, there was no real debate, no weighing-up of information by parents to come to an informed view, and no tolerance of any possibility that the public mantra might be just a little overconfident. 'The science is settled' is still 20 years later, a favourite refrain when on any other area of study and learning 'science is a hypothesis' until later disproved or at least until challenging evidence emerges from scientific research and enquiry. But such was not the case on immunisation.

I then embarked on a course of action which I knew would be ill-advised politically, but one I thought I needed to take. I decided to record what my research had found and in 1992, I produced a book on the side effects of vaccines detailing what doctors themselves had reported in respected medical literature. I was pretty sure that very few parents, journalists or even health ministers would have been aware of this before giving or following the almost universally accepted and unchallenged pro-vaccine creed.

I also wanted to know if the claim of vaccinations being the 'wonder drug' in eradicating disease from our midst stood the test of close scrutiny. I researched the level of disease in our community for the previous 150 years and surprisingly, I found that in the 100 years **prior** to the introduction of all modern vaccines, that the most precipitous decline in incidence of disease, followed improvements in community health and hygiene and not, contrary to the medical mantra, when the vaccines were introduced.

The evidence showed unquestionably that following the introduction of vaccines, the incidence of disease continued to decline but at a much slower rate. I found it very misleading that the published graphs of the effectiveness of vaccines only showed the period of decline following the introduction of the vaccine and not the whole story of huge decline that was already on the way for decades beforehand. One senior MP told me that the graph I was using was too convincing and I should not have used it, as it would lead people to question the role vaccines had obviously played in improving public health.

I had now touched on a real raw nerve. In a democratic society like Australia, we take for granted the right to free speech, the right to express a view on public policy and to put an argument. On just about every area of life, government, religion, industry and politics there are a thousand discussions across the continent every day from individuals to journalists to shock jocks all the way to the Cabinet rooms of this great nation about all manner of things, as one side puts its case to the other.

I simply put the case that parents should find out first as much information as possible and then make an informed decision before having their tender newborn injected with pharmaceuticals at such a young age. But that was enough to be labelled all sorts of things for daring to challenge the norm.

What for me as a lawyer was an obvious balanced way to approach an issue, was to health authorities simply heresy. It just

Chapter 5: The illusion of freedom of speech

did not seem to matter how reasonable I tried to sound or how worrying the research on the side effects may have been: 'The benefits always outweighed the risks' and what was more important, someone in my position in the community, should not be saying these things.

And life soon got a lot tougher for me on this issue.

Eddie Obeid made it absolutely clear to me that a Party heavy weight had made some strong commentary to him that if I wanted to get ahead then I needed to stop talking about immunisation. I heeded the warning. I had sought a career in politics to make a long-term difference, not to campaign on one issue and then wilt on the backbench. I assumed Carr must have also had some similar conversations, as around this time, he expressed the view that I had probably said enough on the issue.

I wanted to get ahead in politics and the issue was not that important to me that I was prepared to stake my future on it. So, I went quiet on the issue and never again spoke unprompted on it. This does illustrate all along what I had been saying. You are simply not permitted a questioning or inquiring view or approach on immunisation. It is, conform or else. It would have to be the least scientific of all the sciences I can think of.

This whole experience for me was not a pleasant one, but I still look back with some degree of pride on the nerve and dare I showed in the face of some risk and not inconsiderable opposition.

But the sacrosanct aura around this issue continues unabated today if not more so. The media and health authorities continue to present the science not as science, but as irrefutable, unarguable fact that is above debate. We even now have policy debates at a national political level about the degree to which government should take the discretion to vaccinate away from parents and effectively into the hands of public health authorities. Family and tax benefits are now being restricted for non-complying parents, as well as restrictions on access to child care facilities, and greater intrusion into parental care and management of the health and wellbeing of their children is more likely to happen than less likely.

In January 2015, a concerted effort got underway to deny an entry visa to anti-vaccine American campaigner, Sherri Tenpenny. And this was followed up by a Sydney Morning Herald (SMH) journalist: "You have a right to peddle nonsense, but you don't have a right to peddle nonsense as truth." Wow! And this newspaper proudly boasts on its front page of every daily edition: 'Independent. Always.' Consistency of approach from the SMH would compel opposition to a visit to Australia by US President Donald Trump and his retinue of 'fake news' specialists.

Being an MP and trying to have an intelligent discussion with sensible educated people in this country on the issue of immunisation, is going to be about as successful as a US congressman calling for a discussion on the existence of God, or maybe even the benefits of sensible gun control. It would seem that neither discussion would be tolerated in two great countries professing democratic, free and intellectually curious values. I am not sure when science stopped being curious, as it seems to have done, on this aspect of health and on the causes of climate change.

The issue of immunisation would 'hover' around me for the rest of my time in public life. A full 11 years later and just after the 2003 State Election, a right faction ALP opponent would show with glee his copy of my paper to at least two newly elected MPs boldly stating: "I am going to make sure that this never disappears from the light of day". The one rewarding thing I have of this particular MP, is that he never produced any policy papers of his own, never contributed as a minister and has now retired to political oblivion. But, he did contribute in a somewhat tawdry way.

When Bob Carr retired from politics in 2005, a copy of my paper was sent to every member of caucus with the sole purpose of damaging my credibility and certainly not because of some unexpected interest in an intellectual discussion on an issue of importance. Joe Tripodi was the MP for Fairfield, which was the adjoining electorate to my electorate of Smithfield. Despite having been a friend and close colleague for over 20 years, Tripodi relished the opportunity of using the document I had written 13 years before, as a weapon of political attack. I was reliably told by an MP, that Tripodi in his telephone canvassing for Iemma, would regale against me in the following way: "He is not fit for leadership. He does not even believe in immunisation." I remain unenlightened as to what Tripod's actual expertise is on either leadership or immunisation.

The claim he made was, of course, ludicrous. But the claim was made only to damage, not to entertain some kind of intelligent discussion. Whenever I had been asked during my then 10 years of ministerial life on what my views on immunisation were, my stock response was always: "Government policy on that is set by the Department of Health" and I would have done the same as Premier. Prime Minister Tony Abbott was often on the receiving end of somewhat more difficult questioning around his trenchant personal opposition to abortion and while Minister for Health, the availability of the 'morning after pill'. His stock reply was always: "On these things, I rely on the advice of the Department of Health."

More than 20 years on from when I wrote my contribution, the debate on immunisation is no longer a debate. By 2017 'the science is settled' and ineligible for debate, whereas in my time in the early

1990s, the Department of Health, medical practitioners, journalists and Government would have at least talked about the 'benefits outweighing the risks', in at least some acknowledgement that there was a discussion to be had. Even that mantra is no longer relied upon, in what is now a much nastier and more intrusive approach to the issue. The positions taken by these stakeholders is now a whole lot more aggressive than anything I experienced.

In April 2015, even the ALP Federal ALP Opposition, complained that parents needed to be labelled for what they are: 'vaccine-refusers' and that such parents ought not to be allowed to masquerade as 'conscientious objectors'. I often found that trying to get ahead of the tabloid press or shock jocks on morning radio was bound to take you down some ill-tempered burrows. So, the position of the Party I have belonged to for over 40 years, is that any parent who chooses not to vaccinate has not one element of thoughtful or considered parenting in them and are given, as one monolithic group, a broad tabloid-disparaging brush; not its finest hour, but certainly good populist politics. Best not to argue with the Daily Telegraph on these sorts of 'group think' issues. Now in 2017 just two years on from 'vaccine-refusers', the label 'flat-earthers' is now applied. The irony is enormous, in that there was a time about half a millennium ago, when the 'science was settled' and anyone claiming that the earth was round, was subject to ridicule and condemnation.

So, no further debate, discussion or argument is needed on what is best for our children – just an attack on anyone who wants to be part of it. This is a big change from the time I dared to put my toe in the water and call for parents to make informed decisions. Maybe I would not have dared if this is how it would have played out. Politics despite occasionally welcoming the bold, mostly requires populist conformity to avoid denigration and loss of support.

My concern these days, however, is much less with the issue itself and far more about the erosion of freedom of expression and respect for an alternative view in an otherwise robust democratic country. Perhaps this is the state of the world we now live in.

I still wince whenever I hear: 'The science is settled' as if certain knowledge and enquiry is locked in a bottle and inviolable from challenge and counter argument. We all fondly remember Kevin Rudd once proudly boasting that "climate change is the great moral challenge of our generation". In office, the issue soon became one where 'the science is settled' and doubters like Tony Abbott, were denigrated as 'climate change deniers'. As on immunisation, the issue became far more about abusing those who dared to challenge prevailing orthodoxy than in calmly and confidently continuing to argue the case and presenting the evidence. It was not Labor's finest hour!

Despite the continuing tabloid environment of denigrating parents who choose not to immunise their children, an April 2017 study of the Royal Australian College of General Practitioners found that over 50% of parents who immunised their children were uneasy in doing so. This creates an interesting fork in the road for the tabloids and health professionals: either present the evidence and prosecute the case convincingly in an environment of intelligent discussion with concerned parents, or simply denigrate them as complying versions of 'flat earthers'. I will watch with interest which course is taken.

In my own case, in the early 90s on a political level, I had certainly overreached on the subject of immunisation, but there were, thankfully, other issues upon which I could and did draw much credit both in the caucus and in the wider community.

Chapter 5: The illusion of freedom of speech

CHAPTER 6

Law & order – the cases of Vo and Lewthwaite

> *"Mate, keep it to yourself that this conversation never occurred. By any chance, did you drag someone out of a car and give him a clip under the ear hole? ... I was having a boring day until that happened ... Is this the Gook? ... They've got photographs of a gook being pulled up ... something went on there ... We've got to get a good story ... back to the cone of silence."*
> (Intercepted police phone conversations re Vo)

It is often said that hard work often produces its own luck, but I have never been sure about that. In any case, whether you call it luck or just circumstances, I happened to be the MP on the backbench in Opposition when two giant issues presented themselves in my electorate. These would propel me into the debate on the decision to support establishing the Police Royal Commission into corruption on the one hand, and on the other hand, participating front and centre, to position the ALP as the Party of Law and Order. Both issues would make my case for a seat at the Cabinet table.

The first issue concerned police brutality and the second concerned the release of a murderer from jail. Both concerned

Chapter 6: Law & order

constituents of mine and both required all my energy and effort in defending their interests.

In the first case, a local resident of Vietnamese extraction came in to see me sometime in early 1991 – his name was Vo. He was a young man with limited English who clearly understood his point of complaint: Whilst driving along one of the local streets in my electorate near Prairiewood Shopping Centre, he had been pulled over by two local police who were irritated that he had got in the way of a three-point turn manoeuvre that they were in the middle of executing. The police put on their sirens and allegedly became even more irritated when Mr Vo did not immediately pull over.

What allegedly happened then was most alarming. Mr Vo claimed that after being removed from the car, both he and his passenger were frisk searched and Mr Vo was then taken to the rear of the vehicle. One of the officers then grabbed his head and banged it twice against the boot of the car. He claimed that at the end of the incident, he said to the police: "You are the police and you can do anything you like" and the police officer allegedly replied, "That's right. We are the boss and you are the shit".

He gave me the name of a local resident who he claimed was a witness to this event. I initially didn't know what to make of the claim, but wondered if he did indeed have a genuinely independent witness, then the cops may possibly have committed this assault.

I contacted the alleged witness who willingly came to my electorate office for an interview. I did feel a little like I was back in my former role of a local solicitor and if I was able to use my legal skills in this way to help a constituent, then all the better. What astonished me was that the witness was the real deal. He was a member of the local Italian ethnic community and had never met

Mr Vo before this incident. I found him convincing, independent of both the police and Mr Vo and with no reason to fabricate a story as bizarre and troubling as this one was. I believed him. He said that he had been sitting on his front veranda having a beer when the police pulled Mr Vo over, took him to the back of the car where one of them bashed Mr Vo's head against the boot at least two maybe three times. He also claimed that the police were very annoyed when he asked them why they had treated Mr Vo as they had.

I was now more than satisfied that an assault had actually taken place and that the police had committed a criminal offence against my constituent. I was incensed that this appeared to have actually happened in broad daylight on one of my local streets flagrantly in front of a witness. I decided to do something about it.

Unfortunately, in the early 1990s in pre-Police Royal Commission days, the police did most of the investigating of police, with a very light touch oversight by the Ombudsman.

On the 11th of January 1991, I wrote to the Police Internal Affairs Unit requesting that the matter be investigated "and to take appropriate disciplinary action against the police officer concerned." The likelihood of disciplinary action occurring in those days of the police investigating police was very remote indeed. But, I was keen to see just how the cops were going to look after their own in the face of an independent witness. I should have known better.

When I received the results of the initial police investigation, I was very disappointed but unsurprised that the complaint was "not sustained". I was convinced then, but had no proof that the investigating officer had looked after his mates and had just gone through the motions of an investigation. I poured over the report

Chapter 6: Law & order

and found very troubling details indeed. I expected to find significant differences in the evidence, but instead I found little difference and with almost identical evidence of the police officers, more than a smell of collusion on their part.

The statements of the police officers, the witness and the alleged victim were all consistent: Mr Vo had been pulled over, he ended up at the rear of his vehicle and eventually with his head on the bonnet. But how did his head arrive on the bonnet? The police closed ranks and stymied the Ombudsman's office to the point where it could not be taken further.

I then pretty much put the Vo matter out of my thoughts when out of the blue, in March 1993, some 14 months after the Ombudsman had closed the case, I received an ominous letter from the Assistant Ombudsman who referred to an earlier letter of January 1992 and wrote:

> *"In this letter, I advised you that from the material available to me at the time, I was unable to determine the truth of the complaint...I decided against a re-investigation and accordingly the complaint was deemed to be not sustained."*

And then the bombshell!

> *"However, since this decision was made, some further information has come to light which suggests collusion between police officers involved in the complaint. I have now decided to conduct a re-investigation into both the complaint and the subsequent police internal investigations into it".*

I was intrigued by this letter to say the least, but had to wait until the end of October 1993 for a letter from the Ombudsman himself. This proved to be more than a bombshell. It was nuclear!

The Ombudsman advised that his investigation had been completed, attached a copy of the very long report and then said:

> "You will note from the recommendations that the possibility of criminal and/or departmental action against police remains...
>
> ...This matter exposes and highlights significant problems with internal police investigations, particularly those undertaken at the local patrol level. It is impossible to estimate how widespread the sorts of practices exposed by this report may be. From the attitude of the police before the inquiry, it would be safe to assume that this is not an isolated instance.
>
> I intend making this case a special report to Parliament when I have fully considered the possible impact of public exposure on any proceedings which may flow from this report".

It is not often you get either a 'holy shit' or a 'wow' moment in life and this was both all at once. I then poured over the report and it made for very sobering and alarming reading.

For reasons never explained, the Police Internal Security Unit had been tapping phones in an unrelated operation and had chanced upon some very interesting phone conversations between the two affected police officers and the original investigating police officer. When I read through what had been accidently picked up, I could readily see, not only evidence of a crime having been committed on Mr Vo but collusion, cover-up and some serious racist and cultural problems which had much wider implications for the entire police service.

The intercepted phone calls made for alarming reading.

The subsequent report from the Ombudsman did not disappoint and was a damning indictment on many serious fronts. He recommended disciplinary action against a number of police officers including the investigating officer. He recommended that Police address improved investigation training and that "senior police in the Cabramatta Patrol issue clear instructions regarding the use of racist terms of abuse by police" and that Police report within 28 days on the implementation of all his recommendations.

It took me some hours to wade through all this material, but I could see it was just pure political gold.

I took the whole Vo file and the Ombudsman Report to the Leader's office and assumed that they would keep it for the boss to get him up on a good story. We sometimes referred to Bob Carr as 'Pacman' after the console game character which ate everything on the game board. I took the view that it was our job as MPs to find great stories and give them up to the Leader to have first right of refusal on running with them. He had the profile and he was the one the public needed to hear from on major issues.

I left the story with Carr's staff expecting to get the call: "Thanks Carl, a great yarn which Bob will run with tomorrow. Keep up the good work". But this time that did not happen.

For reasons unknown to me, I was allowed to run with this political and media dynamite and I was ecstatic. I held a news conference with our Shadow Minister for Police, Peter Anderson. The allegations of police brutality and the subsequent police cover-up got a huge run in all media outlets. It was my first serious story and doing a live interview with Quentin Dempster on the 7.30 Report, only added to the impact in the caucus and in the press gallery on the 6th floor of Parliament House. A senior member of Carr's staff said that the gallery thought I was a rising star. I could not have been more delighted.

The result for Mr Vo's family was that the findings were effectively overturned, the police officers were charged with assault and Bob Carr would use this case as one of three to justify his view that the Opposition ought to support the independent MPs call for the establishment of a Royal Commission into police corruption. I like to think I played a small, but not insignificant role in this initiative.

The second big case I was involved in concerned convicted child killer John David Lewthwaite.

After nearly two years in the job as an MP, I had done countless interviews with constituents seeking my help on just about every aspect where Government had either impinged on their lives or could make their current predicament more tolerable. One day in 1992, I had what would turn out to be the most profound and most moving constituency interview I would ever undertake in my 17 years as an MP.

One of my constituents, Gwen Hanns, was a resident of Greystanes, a salt of the earth battler who was seeking my help to keep the murderer of her daughter in jail. The Greiner Government had run hard on law and order in the lead up to its win at the 1988 State Election. For as long as anyone could remember, when a murderer had been sentenced to a term of life imprisonment, very few actually died in jail and many could expect to be released in 15 years or so from the date of sentence.

Michael Yabsley, one of the more aggressive new Greiner ministers, introduced his new truth in sentencing legislation in 1989, which effectively mandated that 'life means life'. It was strong tough stuff and directly led in time to a noticeable increase in the prison population, as the sentences which courts were prescribing were the actual period of imprisonment which convicted criminals had to serve in jail. The Government had a compelling case to the electorate that it was the Party they should look to if they wanted the bad guys put away for as long as they deserved. We could only look on in awe and give grudging support for this initiative.

With this tough stand on sentencing, the Government could have been expected to get an unassailable position of strength on the issue of law and order. The Libs, since as far back as the Askin Government of the 60s and 70s and right up to the Greiner years, had always been seen by the electorate as tougher on crime and criminals than the ALP. It was always our weak spot. It certainly did not help that the Wran Government Minister for Corrective Services, Rex Jackson, was still in prison himself for selling early departure 'tickets' for criminals who then got out of jail somewhat earlier than they should have.

However, and somewhat ironically, it was the very 'get tough on criminals' sentencing legislation of 1989 which led to an opening for the ALP against the Libs and would substantially contribute to a complete reversal of the public's attitude on this issue by the March 1995 State Election. Labor would only just win that election and the views of the voters in this regard were critical in my view on that win. And it was John David Lewthwaite and the campaign Gwen and I led to keep him in jail that played a very significant part in that amazing turnaround.

Yabsley and Greiner should have given a lot more thought on how best to deal with existing prisoners, but instead focussed on how future criminals would be compelled by legislation to serve out the terms of imprisonment meted out by a sentencing judge. Good stuff for the future, but way too little care and attention to the sentences of existing prisoners. Legislation of any kind often has transitional provisions and this one was no different. It provided that anyone who had served a specified period of a life sentence could apply to the Supreme Court and have that sentence re-determined possibly to one for a fixed period of years.

If Greiner and Yabsley had bothered to insist that the legislation provide that existing prisoners be required to actually serve the full period of their original sentence, then they would have encountered fierce opposition from the Parliamentary Counsel's Office and even fiercer opposition from the Attorney General's Department, both for altogether different reasons. The former were always trenchant opponents of retrospective legislation and the latter were always hammering on about prisoner rights. But such an initiative would have received support from the ALP and the wider community. Had they done this, I think it might have saved the Fahey Government from the narrowest of defeats at the March 1995 election. We will never know.

Lewthwaite had been rotting in jail for 18 long years, but because of the new legislation, he had been able to go back to court and seek a review of his original life sentence. The facts around the case and the impact on the Hanns family are very disturbing. But these facts had to be retold again and again to ensure that Lewthwaite was never released from Jail. In running this campaign, I tried as much as possible to keep my lawyer and politician hat on, but I found that was mostly impossible given the sheer horror of the original crime and that this man could now be eventually released, solely because of new get tough on criminal legislation. I see the irony now, but Gwen and I did not see it then. We just wanted him kept in jail until he died.

In December 1972, Lewthwaite had been sentenced in Penrith District Court to a term of six years' imprisonment with a non-parole period of 15 months for setting fires to seven schools. He was released on parole in March 1974 and shortly after, had seen through a bathroom window Gwen's nine-year-old son. Just three months after his release and whilst still on parole, Lewthwaite decided to return to the Hanns house and abduct the boy to live out a sick sexual fantasy. When unable to do so, he instead killed six-year-old Nicole.

The judgement of Justice Slattery in considering the application for re-determination of the original sentence makes for very sobering reading:

> "He arrived at the home of the deceased at about 11.00 pm…he went to a side window, he broke the glass and removed its broken pieces and fly screen…climbed through a window into what was the deceased's bedroom. After turning on the light and seeing the deceased asleep he walked through the house and into the boy's bedroom where he turned on a light. After switching off the light he went to the kitchen where he got a knife for the purpose of threatening the boy if his parents woke and attempted to stop him leaving."

> "The applicant then visited the children's bedrooms and finally the parents' bedroom where he observed them asleep. On deciding to abduct the boy, he returned to the deceased's bedroom and adjusted the

> *curtains and blinds of the window to enable him to more easily take the boy from the house. At this stage the deceased awoke, the applicant walked to her, he put his hand around her mouth and told her to keep quiet. The applicant became angry because he was not able to get the boy out of the house and he stabbed the deceased. The deceased's cries alerted her parents and the applicant fled the scene. It was then about 12.45 am. The deceased was dead on arrival at 1.10 am at Parramatta District Hospital...At post mortem Dr N.G. Malouf found 13 stab wounds on her back, four of which passed through her body to the front of the chest and abdomen. There were also four stab wounds on the right arm and one nick on the palm of the left hand. The following morning the applicant surrendered himself to police."*

It was over 20 years ago when I first read this and reading it again all these years later, still distresses me now as much as it did when Gwenn Hanns first came seeking my help.

Justice Slattery had been the original sentencing judge in 1974 and was now the one considering the application for re-determination. Despite concerns expressed by the family, by psychiatrists and even the judge himself, he changed the original life sentence to 20 years, but also ordered that if released, Lewthwaite would have to be on parole for the rest of his life. The Hanns family was devastated. Nothing they did would ever bring Nicole back, but they were determined to make sure that no other family would ever have to go through what they had endured because of Lewthwaite. I agreed to join her on this important crusade for them and for the wider community.

Chapter 6: Law & order

I poured over as much material as I could on the case, but the best summation was in the two judgements of Justice Slattery. And the more I read the more astonished I was that this man may one day be released from prison.

Even at his trial in 1974, Lewthwaite had said this to the Jury:

> *"I was supposed to get treatment when I was in jail for burning down schools, but I did not get any. I have been getting these urges about young boys for some time and I don't know what happens to me. I cannot seem to control myself when this happens."*

The medical evidence of Lewthwaite's 'condition' at the original trial was just as harrowing. It was cause enough to want to keep him in jail. But with his sentence now set at 20 years, he would become eligible for parole in 1994. I undertook to Gwen and her family to do all I could to make sure that that did not happen.

And almost as we expected, Gwen came and saw me in the early part of 1994 with a letter from the Serious Offender's Review Council stating that as Lewthwaite had completed his minimum term of 20 years, the Council was now required to start to prepare him for parole and would commence that process by letting him out periodically on day leave. We were both speechless at the letter, but we quickly went into action.

Gwen and I then started one of the most effective constituent/MP joint ventures I think the New South Wales Parliament has ever seen. Gwen had a story which was so sad, so dreadful and so outrageous that it was unavoidably compelling for the media to report every time she spoke.

I did not realise at the time that we were about to embark on a campaign together which would last years, not months and would in the words of a later ALP Attorney-General: "Keep Lewthwaite in jail six years longer than would have been otherwise been the case." But at the beginning I just wanted to target the Government really hard with a tsunami and shame them into cancelling the day release plan.

I ran the story past the Leader's office to be told that this one was all mine. They cleared the decks of any other news stories and Gwen and I hit the airwaves. John Fahey and the whole Government did not know what had hit them. It was run comprehensively by TV, radio and newspapers for days on end forcing the Government to request cancellation of the plans to put him on a day release programme. Gwen and I were ecstatic.

I had done my job for my constituent and kept behind bars a person both she and I found repugnant and extremely dangerous.

But that was just the beginning of the long campaign to keep Lewthwaite in jail. The Serious Offenders Review Council just a few months later was at it again. They wrote to Gwen advising that the Offenders Review Board had sought from them, as required by legislation, their views in relation to whether or not Lewthwaite ought to be given parole.

Lewthwaite had simply got around the issue of being denied entry onto the day release programme by asking the Offenders Review Board itself, to decide on his suitability for more permanent release. As his minimum-term had expired, the Board advised Gwen that it had no choice but to consider his application and weigh up the decision after taking in to account the views of the Serious Offenders Review Council.

I wrote to the Council requesting a right of appearance with Gwen to put our views that Lewthwaite was and always would be a danger to society. They agreed to us appearing. I did some research as did Gwen and her supporters in the Homicide Support Community, like Howard Brown. We even had Paul Wilson a well-known criminologist, to write that one in three of these sorts of criminals will randomly and indiscriminately kill again if released on parole.

The Council met at Long Bay Jail which made for great media copy as Gwen and I went in to the prison and then did a stand-up press conference at the prison gates on our way out.

The Review Council recommended against parole. We treated the application for parole to the Offenders Review Board as very serious and putting my lawyer's hat on, I prepared and submitted a detailed written argument against his release. He was denied parole.

I am sure that the Fahey Government must have hated the Lewthwaite issue, as every time the issue came up, Gwen and I would go into overdrive to oppose whatever was then being considered. The State Government came across as powerless and indifferent and as a result, looked soft on crime and soft and useless on law and order generally. I know the Leader and his office, as well as others in the Parliamentary Party were delighted with this as we were now being seen as the tougher party on law and order. In the lead up to the State Election, the public seeing us as stronger on this issue was critical for our campaign and I think Lewthwaite played a big part in that.

At the last New South Wales ALP Annual Conference in the Town Hall, prior to the March 1995 election, I spoke on the law and order debate and had the whole conference silent as I went through what Lewthwaite had done to six-year-old Nicole, what he had done to the Hanns family and what he would do again if released. I declared: "If I were Minister for Corrective Services, I would mark his papers" and then paused, formed a fist and as I bellowed into the microphone: "never to be released", brought it thumping down onto the lectern in front of me. I felt very emotional about the matter and I still think it was my finest conference performance of all. With 800 delegates on the floor and over 200 observers in the gallery, the Annual Conference of the ALP was certainly the appropriate forum for such a speech. I had been noticed.

The photo in one of the newspapers the next day showing me in a huddle at the front of the stage with Bob Carr and our Shadow Minister for Police, Paul Whelan, just polished it off. The 'coup de grace' was Gwen inviting the three of us to her home to launch our law and order policy just before the election.

As if that wasn't enough for the hapless Premier John Fahey. Carr and Whelan had been campaigning to keep another awful individual behind bars by the name of Fred Many, but the Government had been unable to do so. In a cruel set of circumstances, he was released from prison at midnight just as Election Day began. The Telegraph ran a front page of him leaving prison with a good old fashion 'put the boot in to the Government' story which only the Telegraph specialises in. I think this might have been the clincher which just got us in to Government by a finger nail.

I had by early 1995 done all I could to position myself for a ministerial position. I had helped establish a new power structure in the right faction, I had worked on getting more friends, I had contributed to discussion on as many issues of the day as possible, and I had played a significant part on the issues of police brutality, as well as corruption and the wider issue of law and order in general. I was confident that if we won the 1995 election, my case for being promoted was justified and would not cause much opposition from within the Caucus.

Bob Carr would later say to me that the Lewthwaite case was my 'Alger Hiss'. I am not sure I wanted to be compared to Richard Nixon who was propelled into the American national spotlight when as a young congressman he outed the US Government high ranking public servant as a soviet spy. Despite the unfortunate comparison, I knew that Carr was both a great student of American political history and not one to give complements lightly. So, I was pleased that he, in a roundabout way, gave me praise and recognition for the cause I had rightly pursued.

In late 2016, I ran into Howard Brown outside the Supreme Court, when about to attend the admission of my daughter Sarah as a new solicitor. Howard has for decades been a stalwart campaigner for the rights of victims and was always on hand to support the Hanns family. Sadly, he informed me that Gwen Hanns and her husband Peter had passed away. We reminisced on a fight well fought and a great tragedy which had befallen this family.

CHAPTER 7

Winning government – exercising executive power

The election campaign for the March 1995 election was by now in full swing. Again, Anwar was Campaign Director and Chris Bowen was Assistant Campaign Director. The two of them made sure all the nuts and bolts were put in place: posters erected, pre-poll staffed, polling day volunteers found and rostered while I was out doorknocking, pressing the flesh, issuing letters and pamphlets to the electorate, and running on as many issues as possible in the local newspapers. Ivo Crosio was always a reliable work horse in erecting posters all over the electorate in both federal and state elections.

One of those local issues at this time, was the determination of the Greiner Government to open up a new 1,500 lot housing estate in Abbotsbury North on land that had been set aside in the 1960s as part of a much larger buffer of green space in Western Sydney. But nothing had been locked in and it turned out the zoning and use of this large tract of land, including the space needed for the new subdivision, were subject solely to the whims of the government of the day.

The western part of my electorate was very angry about it and believed that the area had been set aside in perpetuity as public

Chapter 7: Winning government

open space. Many decided to protest openly and loudly about it. This was my first really big public issue in my electorate and whilst I was relaxed about a new estate arriving or not arriving, I did not want to get on the wrong side of a strong community angst. I campaigned hard on the issue, but it fell on deaf ears when it came to the Greiner Government.

I realised that the only way to protect this valuable open space from housing development was to position Bob Carr to commit a new Labor government to it. And the only way I was able to achieve that, was by calling on my old Young Labor friend and now candidate for the adjoining marginal electorate of Badgerys Creek, Di Beamer, and convincing Carr that her victory depended on it. Carr took the bait and did a great thing for a safe ALP seat and the community.

The ALP also had a senior source within the Fahey government public service who gave us all the details of a huge number of new National Parks to be announced by Premier Fahey on Australia Day 1995. Instead, what Fahey copped was an announcement by Carr a week before, of all that Fahey had intended to announce plus my own massive Western Sydney Regional Park. I was elated and Fahey was beside himself.

I had made sure that the proposed boundaries released to the media included the proposed Abbotsbury North residential area. When we were elected and the new Premier came out to announce the new National Park on the ridge overlooking Cowpasture Road on the edge of my electorate, I invited all the locals who had so vigorously campaigned on the issue. It was an uplifting moment, as we all knew that something special had been achieved. Di Beamer was there and to her credit she always kept her counsel on the issue.

Even though we had had to 'manage' the Leader to get this result, protecting this land for future generations of local residents is one of the accomplishments I am most proud of when I look back on my years of service as the local MP for Smithfield.

The March 1995 State Election was a much tighter run operation than I had ever imagined would be the case. Many of us were confident of victory. The Fahey Government had been a poor shadow of what a government should be about. It had seemed to wallow in indecisiveness caught between a reliance on three fickle independents and trying to balance deep challenges between the National Party and the Liberal Party in coalition.

Despite this and thinking we had them on the ropes on law and order, we only won 48.5% of the two-party preferred vote and came within a finger nail of losing. On election night, the result was too close to call and counts and recounts dragged on for over 10 days before we had a clear result.

The Blue Mountains electorate quickly fell to us and so did Gladesville after a few days counting. But it was a very drawn-out process in Badgerys Creek, where the count dragged on and on. I joined a number of MPs who descended upon the local tally room as scrutineers, and I observed a number of things which showed just what amateurs the Libs were at scrutineering. Even more astonishing, was that the Libs and its new opposition leader passed up the opportunity to challenge a number of irregularities in our 107-vote win in this crucial and final seat. One Liberal MP even confidently asserted to me that 'my job is to challenge when you challenge'. So, when a few ballot papers had a number 1 outside the box but lined up slightly closer to the ALP candidate and no challenge was made, I remained quiet. When a number of ballot papers had unclear numbers, which could be a 1 or a 7 or sometimes something else but in favour of the ALP, there was no challenge. And when a number of postal votes for the ALP had been postmarked after the necessary due date, there was still no challenge from these Liberal Party scrutineering geniuses. Instead of assuming that their backbench MPs were professional at scrutineering, the Liberal Party should have had experienced Court of Disputed Returns lawyers acting as their scrutineers. This election should have been won and lost in the court room, not the tally room.

My favourite irregularity was The Scalabrini Retirement Village which had delivered 90 votes to the ALP out of a total voting pool of 90. To accommodate the old folks living there, the New South Wales Electoral Commission had designated the village a polling place, which meant that the residents could effectively vote from home. It defied belief that in a fair and transparent process, every single resident would vote for one candidate over all others. During the count, I asked one of my MP colleagues how this had occurred and he gave me a cryptic reply: "Don't ask, you don't want to know."

I feared that if an appeal was launched to challenge the result, the Liberal Party lawyers would have a field day questioning the old and infirm residents one by one, on how or by whose hand they had all come to vote ALP.

But a challenge never came. The best the Liberal Party could say on the issue was five years later when Peter Collins, the former Leader of the Opposition, claimed in his autobiography: "In another key seat, Badgery's Creek, an entire Italian retirement village voted Labor in an unbelievable demonstration of unanimity." That was it! No challenge! No Court of Disputed Returns. Just a weak side-slap many years after the event. The whole election could have turned on this if a by-election had been ordered.

If a mere 54 people in that electorate had voted the other way, then the Carr Labor Government would not have been elected. A mere 54 people out of a total of 3,575,783 who voted in that election. Winning or losing government for both sides of politics was that close. And it just happened to fall our way.

As soon as the local returning officer had declared the result, I rang Bob Carr who was in his Opposition Leader's office surrounded by his personal staff. They put him on the phone: "Congratulations Bob, you have won the election. We have just this minute won Badgerys Creek by 107 votes. We are going to form a government and you are going to be Premier". He was pretty excited to say the least. I assume others were also ringing him with the news, but I like to think I was the first. It was a very emotional time and the significance of what had occurred in a small hall in a suburb of South Western Sydney was not lost on anyone. The baton had passed and would not be passed back for 16 long years of Labor Government.

My time for executive power had arrived.

In one sense, as tough as it was, the election was the easy part. If Bob Carr thought the selection of his Cabinet would be smooth sailing, then he would be soon disabused. In later elections, as the dominant political player of both the ALP and the community, he would have much greater sway in his choice of who would be ministers in his Cabinet, than he ever had after that first election win.

Maybe Carr had not expected to win in 1995 and having lost the two-party preferred vote but just won the last seat by 107 votes for a 1 seat majority, he may have felt his grip was tenuous and needed to bring the factional players with him. He was probably

Chapter 7: Winning government

right. The time for announcing who would be in and who would be out of Cabinet would come later, not now.

Under the New South Wales Constitution, the Cabinet was made up of 20 ministers. Under the rules of the New South Wales Parliamentary Labor Party, a meeting of a caucus of all Labor MPs after an election elected those 20 ministers and then the Leader allocated portfolios.

Factional convention provided that the 20 positions be split according to the relative strengths of each faction in the Parliament. This meant by agreement, the right would have 14 positions and the left would have six. The real battle would be within each faction as to who would get those spots allotted to each.

Knight and Lo Po were already in the Shadow Cabinet and Carr wanted Craig Knowles in and both the Trogs and the new Premier were supportive of my election as well. It was all done and dusted except for one point. The Trogs, the Terrigals and the Premier and his acolytes such as John Aquilina, could not agree on the 14th and final position for the right faction position in Cabinet. The Trogs were pushing hard for Bob Martin, an uninspiring toiler from the marginal electorate of Port Stephens and the Terrigals were pushing just as hard for its sub factional leader, Eddie Obeid.

Neither side would shift. The new Premier-elect seemed to have his initial euphoria of winning just ebbing away as this intransigent discussion wore on and on. It was an impasse which was not going to be altered by discussion. I was confident that we had the numbers in the right Caucus, if not a little overconfident. I assumed that in an ALP right faction ballot with 50% of the votes, we could pick our own team, so a ballot for one position should not be too much trouble for us. I took the initiative in the joint right faction delegation meeting with the Leader that we should agree on the 13 positions and have a ballot for the 14th position.

I was chuffed when this was immediately accepted by everyone in the room. I thought I had provided a way to settle the impasse, ensuring that our bloke got up and the Trogs were bested. If only life was that simple. Iemma and Obeid were boasting that the Terrigals had a guaranteed 25 votes which in a right caucus of 44 members would be a solid majority.

I was feeling very proud of what Obeid, Iemma and I had achieved. We had created from scratch a new sub faction which was already bigger than the New South Wales Parliamentary National Party. We had already secured two of our group as ministers, I had just been endorsed by the joint faction meeting and we were only a formal ballot away from getting our sub-faction Leader up as well. It had been a very good four years' worth of work. But a glitch in all that was soon to appear.

The Trogs and Bob Martin must have done the same assessment of numbers for the right caucus ballot as we had, and must have come to the same conclusion we had: Eddie Obeid was going to be appointed as a minister and Bob Martin was not. And then he and the Trogs threatened a scorched earth policy to their own party about to form government.

Bob Martin let it be known to us through back channels, that if he was not elected in the caucus ballot then scheduled for the next day, he would resign from Parliament. I was gobsmacked. I could not believe what I was hearing: That a fellow Party member, a fellow Labor MP, was so devoted to his own advancement, that he would threaten to blow up the whole place if he did not get what he wanted. I thought it had been tough in my years playing ALP politics, but this was something else. This was not the

Russians burning Moscow before it was taken by Napoleon. It was more like Napoleon having taken the enemy's capital unscathed and then being threatened by one of his generals that if he wasn't promoted to Field Marshall he'd burn the capital.

Knight, Iemma, Obeid and I met in Parliament House that night to consider this new development. Was it an idle threat? Did he really intend to defeat the Government before it was even sworn in? We assumed he was making a serious threat.

As much as it pained me, I decided on a course of action which whilst a very poor outcome for me politically, would remove all risk – that was to give the Terrigals a good outcome and still get Bob Martin up as a minister. I called my wife Ann and told her of my predicament and that I thought the only way through such dangerous territory was to give up my ministerial position to Obeid. I had come to the view that I was young and had time on my side. I was also fully aware that a ministerial spot given up was one which may never be available again.

I announced to Knight, Iemma and Obeid of the decision I had made, that I was withdrawing from the field so Eddie could take my place, thereby avoiding a ballot and the consequences it might cause. I was a little surprised by Obeid's very quick dismissal of my plan, almost the immediate moment I had uttered it. "Do you think that after all the years we have put in together, all the hard work we have undertaken that I am going to allow you to pull out in my favour? You have to be kidding. It's not going to happen. We will go into the ballot and see where it ends up."

I can't describe how relieved I was. I honestly assumed he was going to accept my offer to pull out. It was a very emotional evening for the four of us. Knight informed Carr of the threat and to his credit the future Premier asked that we stare it down.

We went over all our numbers late that night and again early the next day. We were very worried that with the threat having got out, that a few of our troops might be panicked into voting for Martin. Carr had indicated he would vote for Obeid and we were quietly confident we had the numbers.

When the faction met, a motion was moved and carried nominating 13 MPs to ministerial positions and calling for a ballot for the 14th position. Kevin Moss, the MP for Canterbury was the faction returning officer and there were three nominations: Eddie Obeid, Bob Martin and Franca Arena. Poor Franca had been told by Carr that she was going to be a minister and she had rung half of Italy to tell her relatives of the great news, but when the Terrigals put in a fierce protest, Bob Carr had to retract what he told her. It was a classic example of not counting your chickens before they hatch.

Moss announced the ballot as follows:

Obeid: 22
Martin: 16
Arena: 6

He then distributed preferences and announced the result:

Obeid: 22
Martin: 22

This was hardly the result any of us had been contemplating. We were sure that some MPs had voted differently to what we had been either told or expected. Carr had voted for Obeid and made a point in true ALP tradition of showing us his ballot paper, so there could be no doubt about where his loyalties lay.

Chapter 7: Winning government

Under the rules of the faction and the Labor Party, where there is a tied vote, the names of the tied candidates are placed in a hat and the winning one is drawn out by the returning officer. And that is how Bob Martin became a minister in the first Carr Cabinet, and Eddie Obeid had to wait a further four years. We were all utterly shattered by the whole experience and the final result. Obeid then devoted himself to 'getting' the Trogs whilst the rest of us had to prepare for our new ministerial lives.

Once the full parliamentary caucus formalised the appointment of the full Cabinet, it was then for the new Premier to determine what portfolios would be allocated to which new ministers. Not surprisingly, Bob Martin was told late and last, that he was getting the hardly mega influential portfolio of Fisheries. It was a small consolation to us that whilst he was in Cabinet, he at least would be barely noticed.

Carr called me in for 'the chat' and advised that he was, amongst other things, considering giving me the ports portfolio and wanted to know if I had any difficulty in pursuing the corporatisation of the three port authorities in Sydney, Newcastle and Wollongong.

He then advised me that he was thinking of giving me State Development, but he had to talk to the new Treasurer, Mike Egan, about it, as traditionally that portfolio had always gone to the Treasurer no matter which side of politics had been in government. Egan at first was supportive of me taking the job, but the department head, Alison Crook, convinced him that it needed a more significant minister than my lowly and humble self, so he recommended Carr appoint me instead as his Assistant Minister for State Development.

Carr said he wanted me to do that for a year by which time he would consider appointing me fully as the sole Minister for State Development, but in the meantime, he would add to my duties the portfolios of Small Business and Regional Development. To say I was ecstatic with all that, would be an understatement. I would have taken even minister without portfolio and still been floating on cloud nine, but to have a number of roles where I could contribute was just gold on a silver lining.

I was commissioned as a new Minister in front of my wife and two very young kids on my 38th birthday, the 4th of April 1995. I still think it is probably the best birthday I have ever had.

Transition from Opposition to Government is not as smooth as the public might think. Straight after the swearing in at Government House, I went up to my new temporary office in the Westfield Tower near Kings Cross of all places. Temporary because the previous Government had spent millions of dollars in their last budget fitting out several floors of the new Governor Macquarie Tower which they planned to have ready for themselves a few months after the 1995 election.

My office was a bit of a shock. I had no personal staff at that stage, so my new host department lent me someone to act as my Chief of Staff and another as a receptionist whilst I selected my own. Apart from a few chairs and tables, the only thing my National Party predecessor, Ray Chappell, had left me, were huge bags of shredded paper. It looked like they had left in a rush almost like the last days before the fall of Berlin. No briefing notes, no handover, no suggestions on the best way forward, just piles of shredded paper. I even answered the phone myself until the receptionist was set up.

Chapter 7: Winning government

My first task as Minister was to get cracking on the ports corporatisation process, but my role and contribution on the task was almost derailed by Treasury from the start. Within six days of being elected, the first Cabinet meeting was symbolically held in Newcastle and Treasury had Mike Egan sign and put on the agenda a Cabinet Minute recommending the corporatisation of the three port authorities. That was all ok, but the sting was that the Minute also recommended that the Treasurer, not the Minister for Ports, have carriage of the process. Knight advised me quietly: "The time to speak up is now or you will lose any role on this at all". I protested and Egan quickly conceded it to me.

Just a couple of weeks into my new job, I called and chaired a council of stakeholders to get the corporatisation process up and running. The previous Government had left the 100-year old Maritime Services Board (MSB) in place and underneath it, had created separate port authorities with their own boards. This looked very much like structural limbo between a government department and an independent corporation.

I held two separate meetings which both went for over three hours with representatives of the unions, the Labor Council, the MSB and the maritime advisory unit in my department. There would have been 15 people around the conference table with the Lead Union Negotiator, Paddy Crumlin from the Maritime Union of Australia (MUA) sitting next to me. For almost the whole of the nearly six hours of discussion, only Paddy and I spoke as we nutted out enough details so I could confidently proceed to legislate the demise of the MSB and create three separate port corporations. I loved the process and thought if this is how the big guys operate, then I will want to do this for a very long time.

Many in the business community and in the media, have made adverse comment about how difficult the MUA can be, that it is controlled by communists and that it is more concerned with wrecking than creating. I am sure they can be tough when required, but from my own experience of dealing with unions across most of the New South Wales public sector, I found them robust but honourable and when they shook hands on a deal, that was it.

My first significant reform to the public sector was introduced into the New South Wales Parliament before my new Chief of Staff, John Richardson was even on board. The process had required burning the midnight oil, using all my negotiating skills and tact, and a fair degree of patience and perseverance. When it sailed through both Houses of Parliament, the Clerk of the Legislative Assembly presented me with a bound copy of the new Act, which is the tradition for ministers when their first piece of legislation is passed. The unions were happy, I was happy and both the Treasurer and Premier expressed their pleasure at how I had steered it all through. I was as pleased as punch.

But we did wonder if the MSB had either a sick sense of humour or wanted some kind of light revenge. The day it ceased operation in 1995, my Chief of Staff rang the main switch and got: "Thank you for calling the Maritime Services Board. Good Bye!" Priceless.

I threw myself with gusto in to my new roles covering both small business and regional development. When I look back, it was probably too much enthusiasm in terms of impact on Ann and the kids. I was away from home a lot.

I had decided that in each region of the State, I would stay three or four days and not just blow in and blow out. I was confident that on a first trip to a particular region, given that we had only just been elected, that it would mostly be pleasant meet and greets. If only! I soon found that any issue of the day which affected rural towns and communities, quickly landed in my patch.

I did have some fun on my trips and I found it fascinating to be able to meet people and places I had never before visited. My new job was taking me to Broken Hill in far west New South Wales, to the Murray River on our far southern border and to the far north coast of the State right up to the Queensland border. I was away from home a lot but I was learning much about our State's people and organisations. It was exhausting, but I found it very interesting, not to mention that country media was so much more pleasant to deal with than any of their Sydney counterparts. A mere arrival was enough to get TV and front-page billing.

In Dubbo and Port Macquarie, the two National Party MPs, Gerry Peacock and Wendy Machin were both former ministers and gracious hosts. When I met their separate local regional development boards and was asked by some big local Nats why we seemed to get on, they didn't seem to mind my response: "The National Party and the ALP both have strong histories and identities with the country which has driven one clear thing we have in common: We both hate the Liberal Party." I loved it, they seemed to love it and it worked a treat in a room full of card carrying members of the National Party.

I even used the line on John Anderson, the National Party Federal Member for Gwydir, when as the Commonwealth Minister for Transport and Deputy Prime Minister in a room full of ALP State Ministers for Transport, he had expressed surprise at something upon which we had just agreed. Anderson feigned embarrassment at the suggestion he 'hated' the Prime Minister's political Party but all the Labor guys and their staffers loved it.

One of my highlights during these trips was when I officially visited Wollongong, an hour's drive South of Sydney, and its local Illawarra Regional Development Board. My ministerial predecessor Ray Chappell had appointed the board and had included the former Liberal Premier Tom Lewis, who had held office in the mid-1970s. I was surprised to be met, as the lift door opened on the designated floor for the scheduled meeting, by none other than the former Premier himself. I had never had the pleasure of meeting him, but I instantly recognised him. Straight as a flash he said to me: "Minister, may I have a quick word before the meeting" to which I responded: "Yes of course". He said out of ear shot of anyone else: "I understand fully that when a new government comes in, it will want its own people in place. All I'd like to ask is that if you would prefer me not to be on the board that you allow me to resign beforehand." I was rather taken aback with the frankness and candour and I told him: "You are a former Premier and as far as I am concerned it would be an honour for me to have you continue to serve on this board." I think he was more relived that I was not going to humiliate him as a former Premier than necessarily wanting to stay on this body.

And to add to the surprise, I received a call from the same former Premier the very next day, whilst I was in the middle of constituency interviews. He said: "Thank you again for your decision to leave me on the board, which I very much appreciated. But there is something you should know about the rest of the board members. You better take a note of this." He then gave me chapter and verse on all the Party and political loyalties of every member of the board. Needless to say, there was not one Labor supporter on the list. Politics often provides unexpected surprises and this was certainly one of them.

Chapter 7: Winning government

I had already been appointed as Assistant Minister to Egan on the State Development Portfolio and a few weeks into the new Government, Egan secured approval from the Premier to appoint me as Assistant Minister for Energy. I loved it.

All electricity assets in the State were owned by the State and I was suddenly introduced into a whole new area of Government. I visited a huge generation plant on the Central Coast, took a long helicopter flight with the Chairman and CEO of the Transmission entity from the far north coast, opened a new power line in remote far western New South Wales and was included in meetings with stakeholders, as well as in briefings on issues from Treasury. It was great stuff.

But it all came quickly crashing down over a discussion with an Egan staff member rather than with Egan himself. One of the big tasks that the Premier had set for Egan was to dramatically reduce the number of electricity authorities which were operating across the State on the distribution and sale of electricity. It was inefficient, unwieldy and unnecessarily costly. A reduced number of new entities were formed and boards were being filled by people Egan had taken to Cabinet for approval.

I noticed that just about all the new board members being appointed, lived in the Eastern suburbs of Sydney and on the slightest of enquiry were certainly not what anyone would call friends of the ALP. I was very concerned that Treasury was dishing up business talent without any due regard for the fact that there had been a change of Government.

I rang Mark Duffy who was working in the Treasurer's private office and said: "I've had a look through some of these recent appointments and I've noticed that they are mainly 'big end of towners' who have no connection with our Government. I know a few solid, impressive businessmen who are not Party members, but who would be a lot more committed to our cause." I was simply floored at the response. He was immediately angry that I had dared to question who they had put on boards and made it pretty clear it was none of my business. In my nearly 12 years as a Minister, no other staff member would ever speak to me like that or even raise his or her voice in making a point. It still astonishes me that he felt sufficiently important in the Government to treat a Minister that way.

Duffy must have quickly relayed his disgust at my unwanted intrusion into their decision-making process to Egan himself, because very quickly afterwards, I was completely frozen-out of anything to do with the Energy portfolio. Every week, the Minister's office used to send me lots of correspondence to sign on behalf of the Minister. That now dried up and to rub salt into the wound, Sandra Nori, MP was suddenly appointed Parliamentary Secretary to Egan and was now signing all this correspondence on Egan's behalf. It got that puerile.

To me it was unexpected, unfair and unnecessary. I thought I was helping. But how naïve I was in not properly appreciating the vassalage expected of ministers by both Egan and his staff. My time as a minister became a whole lot harder as a result of 'falling out' with the guy who could make a minister's life a lot easier with the allocation of funds. Egan did like to play favourites especially when it came to allocating funds to either Della Bosca or Knowles, both of whom Carr and he liked and respected very much, and both of whom at different stages, Egan saw as potential future premiers. And when the dollars were numerous in health and very lean in transport, I had to cop it sweet, take the brunt of the blame for anything which lack of investment may have caused, and never

ever reflect that the Treasurer or the Premier would not give me enough funds in the budget.

By the end of 1995, Carr moved me to the Public Works portfolio and the promise of taking on the full role of Minister for State Development disappeared. Michael Knight had requested to be relieved of Public Works as he was so busy with planning for the Olympics and requested Carr transfer it to me. I still kept the Ports portfolio. Throughout 1996, I set to work on expanding the work and role of the Department which I saw as the contracting arm of Government. This included a much greater oversight on what all departments were spending on advertising and how they were managing property.

Having both Public Works and Ports allowed me to take charge and deliver the new Finger Wharf at Woolloomooloo which remains to this day, a wonderful harbour side precinct. It complements the 'Art Gallery Cover' we built as part of the Eastern Distributor and later still, the $10M installation of lifts and a viewing area overlooking Circular Quay from the Cahill Expressway. All solid legacies of which I am very proud.

But during my time in Public Works I did over reach on one occasion. The department wanted to extend these oversight roles to scrutinise how departments and agencies consumed electricity. At that time, efficient energy consumption was just emerging as an issue and it was deemed important that the Government lead by example. The public works officials presented me with a draft of a Cabinet Minute seeking approval for this initiative. They had proposed that it be a joint Minute with Egan as Energy Minister. I could see no good reason why I needed his imprimatur. He was the Minister for Electricity Assets we owned and operated and I was merely seeking to be the minister for reducing the consumption of electricity by every agency across Government. I was right, but again a little politically naïve.

Egan's Department of Energy would have been consulted about the Minute including it being a joint one with their Minister long before I had been briefed on it. My officials, no doubt, would have quickly informed them that our joint Minute was now mine alone. For me, this was about asserting my independence on a patch I did not think belonged to Egan, but for Egan it became a 'must win' battle in Cabinet against what he now regarded as a recalcitrant minister. I was soon informed that Egan was on the war path and that he had had a meeting with the head of both Treasury and the Department of Energy demanding that my proposal be defeated. I spent the weekend ringing every Cabinet Minister to win their support in the face of the opposition of the Treasurer. None committed and all were fully cognisant that taking on the Treasurer in open Cabinet was ill advised.

This was a rare occasion when one of the scores of Cabinet Minutes I submitted throughout my time as a Minister, was rejected.

Egan had won the day on an issue that should never have mattered to him. Quite the contrary, the policy made a great deal of sense for better managing how the agencies of Government consumed electricity.

From here on until Egan retired from politics in January 2005, he was implacably opposed to just about every funding request I put in over and above the normal operating functions of Government. His opposition to all and every funding request I would pursue in time included implacable opposition to me succeeding Carr as Premier. The lack of investment in rail certainly

Chapter 7: Winning government

played a part in my political challenges and did give a script for others much later to argue against my case for the premiership.

In the face of significant funding hurdles from Egan as Treasurer, I still managed to deliver more motorways and rail lines than any other Transport Minister had in decades. I have often wondered what it must have been like, for say Craig Knowles, when as Minister for Health, he had billions poured his way, whilst most of my requests for extra funding were met with World War Three.

I had never had a direct argument or confrontation with Egan nor up until my freezing out by him ever uttered a negative view about him. The only thing I could ever point to, was that I dared to express an opinion that maybe we ought to be putting more of our business friends on our electricity boards and a lot fewer supporters of the other side of politics. Perhaps I had touched a raw nerve with him. Maybe there was another explanation and if there was, it was never conveyed to me.

If I had known then that such a small thing would have resulted in making an enemy of such an important figure in Government, I certainly would have given it a second thought. But, I would not have taken a back step from my view from the start that as a Minister, I was only second to the Premier.

One of my good business friends who knows Carr quite well, recently reflected on my nine years of hard fought battles with Egan, as partly not giving him the fealty he expected, but also that Carr had effectively appointed him as the Government's Chief Operating Officer, whilst appointing himself as non-executive Chairman and I had not behaved accordingly in my dealings with the COO. When I look back over the years of the Carr/Egan

Government, I think that there may be a bit of truth to my friend's assessment.

Some years after my 'falling out' with Egan, Duffy was working on the staff of Michael Costa and I said to him: "You were the cause of me falling out with Egan" and I was just about left speechless with his response: "Was I? Why? What happened?" It still astonishes me that he could not remember. It obviously was not of importance to him.

I have long held the view that the public expects that having elected a government that it then proceeds to fill all the organs of government with its own loyal people. The Liberal/National Party in government understand this completely, but it would seem the ALP is much more tentative about it. Carr and Egan would usually only support a friend of the ALP going on a board if a Tory appointment was made at the same time to provide balance. They even pushed the unsustainably nonsensical argument that this would give the government insurance in the event of a crisis occurring in a portfolio.

The argument was nonsense then and is nonsense now. Whenever a crisis occurred, it did not matter one jot how the portfolio was structured or who was or was not on the board of a particular State-owned corporation or authority. What mattered was that the media and affected stakeholders wanted to hear very quickly from the Minister, hold him or her to account and if possible, have a hanging by noon the next day.

The Minister was and is front and centre, the only area of interest and scrutiny.

Chapter 7: Winning government

My own experience with a myriad of government boards and chairs during difficult issues, was that they were entirely comfortable staying in the shadows and letting me take the heat.

Kevin Rudd during his time as Prime Minister brought the appointment of political opponents to a whole new level of sophistication and unrequited generosity.

In fact, I counted 12 Tory appointments in a row before the appointment of former Labor Leader Kym Beazley to the position of Ambassador to Washington. When I brought this to Beazley's attention, his response pretty much summed up what ought to have been the attitude of a Federal Labor Government from the beginning: "Well, I'm worth 12 Tory appointments". Priceless!

If Kevin Rudd ever imagined that his extensive list of appointments of Liberal and National Party former ministers to plum jobs would be appreciated and returned in kind, he would be disabused of it in July 2016, when Malcolm Turnbull spurned a request to nominate Rudd for the position of United Nations Secretary General. I do not recall a single beneficiary of Rudd's generosity coming forth to publicly back their patron. If Rudd had in fact assumed whilst PM, that appointing his retired political opponents to plum jobs would help with a future global role, then he got no return whatsoever from the investment. Perhaps he imagined that he would still be PM when the position became available.

It would be nice to think of our first term in Government in New South Wales from 1995 to 1999 as smooth sailing, but it was nothing like that. The failure to deliver on our promise to abolish the tolls on the M4 and the M5 and the clumsy attempt by Carr and Egan to sell the entire publicly owned electricity industry, left the

Government reeling in the polls and left us thinking for more than a while that we may in fact be just a one-term government.

During my short time as Assistant Minister for Energy, there had been whispers and rumours about the Government wanting to make a move on selling electricity assets. There were two main unions which covered the power industry: the Electrical Trades Union (ETU) covered workers in the transmission and distribution part of the power network, and the Construction Forestry Mining and Engineering Union (CMFEU) covered workers in the Generators.

The ETU was closely associated with the ALP right and the CFMEU with the left. The ETU made it known that it would be relatively happy with the sale of a generator, provided we did not move on any of the poles and wires covered by their members. This made political and practical sense, as it would deliver the sale of an asset worth a few billion dollars whilst keeping onside an important part of the dominant right faction.

At the invitation of Egan, I had already attended a couple of regular consultation meetings he had held with unions representing the power industry. The meetings canvassed routine, small beer issues. At the third and last meeting that I attended, Egan pulled out a twenty-something page document outlining the case for the sale, not of one generator which we had all thought he had been quietly working on behind the scenes, but of the whole industry: all generators, the transmission lines and all the poles and wires and retail arms of the three distribution businesses.

As you could expect from someone who probably regarded himself as the COO of the Government, as a mere junior assistant minister, I was neither consulted nor informed of this crazy overreach by Egan. It probably did not occur to him that I may

Chapter 7: Winning government

have had some smidgen of political nous to provide some input on the risks. This was really dangerous, lone ranger stuff!

When Egan's 'privatisation suicide note' thudded onto the table, I was astonished to say the least, and so were all the union delegates in the room. I couldn't understand why a guy as smart as Egan would want to try and bite off the whole of something when a big chunk of it was effectively already in the bag. The Secretary of the ETU announced that the union would support the initiative and he was promptly removed by the members and replaced by the hard-line Bernie Riordan who expressed implacable opposition to it.

Carr and Egan then began to argue very strongly that selling the assets was essential for the economic wellbeing of the State. We would be able to retire debt and invest in new infrastructure. This did not wash with either the wider union membership or its leadership or for that matter the wider party. Eventually the proposal would be defeated on the floor of the Annual Conference of the Labor Party. To overrule a policy position of an elected Labor Government was a very rare thing indeed and one not taken lightly. Carr took the sensible course of action and withdrew the commitment to sell, averting what would have been a great crisis in the party.

Life as a minister was certainly a very different life to that of a backbench MP. I worked hard over many long hours most days of the week. Even when I was with the family, it was often hard to switch off. When the kids were still quite young, we went away one year just after Christmas to Port Macquarie, but the work of a minister still grinded on. I was under a spousal expectation of total focus on the family and not my work. But one morning whilst I was huddled under a palm frond on the ground floor and glued to a phone call with my media advisor, I could hear my young son

James bellow from our 3rd floor balcony: "Mum, Dad's on the phone." Busted! Again!

A day in the life of a minister – what is it really like?

Over the nearly 12 years as a minister, I worked an average of 250 working days a year, not including weekends. This meant over all those years of service that I covered in the order of 3000 working days at the office or wherever I was carrying out ministerial duties and responsibilities. That is a lot of time at or near the peak of the political game.

Whilst every weekend almost always involved reading briefing notes, attending daytime and evening functions, satisfying the 7 day a week news cycle and attending more often than not a Sunday news conference, I could at least for part of the weekend wear casual clothes and pretend that I was not working. The weekends were breathing space to absorb the past week and think about the week ahead, and catch up on essential signing, approvals and urgent decisions. Weekends were my critical thinking time. But usually I did not have to go into the office.

As an MP representing a seat in South Western Sydney, I lived in Edensor Park within my electorate, which was an hour and half drive into the city in the morning and about an hour home in the evening. My car was a mobile office where I would spend the equivalent of a day and a half a week to and from the office. I got a lot of work done in this time, on the phone or buried in paperwork. The relationship of trust between a ministerial driver and the minister is critically important. Joel Donaghy drove me for 10 years and Wayne Leach for the remainder of my time as minister. I could trust my life on them, which meant there was nothing I could not say on the phone in their presence. This made

Chapter 7: Winning government

a huge difference in being able to make the most of my long journeys in the car. They were also great company.

Every single day of my life as a minister was different, but there was some routine to it. Cabinet would meet on a Tuesday morning in non-sitting weeks, and on a Monday during sitting weeks. Almost every day would require preparation and response to media enquiries of varying degree of difficulty. There were always countless meetings necessary to stay in touch, to meet stakeholders, be briefed by staff and most importantly to keep on top of the many government agencies for which I was responsible.

On most weeks, I would have a couple of important news conferences to either launch something new, announce a new project or take the heat on a difficult issue. It may surprise some of the more cynical members of our illustrious press galleries around the country, to learn that all of these took a lot of time and effort in preparation. I was astonished one day in my office, to hear a recent media recruit from the press gallery say after a three-hour meeting with the Roads and Traffic Authority major projects team: "Carl, I can't believe how much effort and how much time goes into to these big projects. In the press gallery, we always assumed that whenever one of these were announced that you had pulled it out of your back pocket as a distraction."

In fact, most of my major projects had hours and hours of meetings, deliberations, research, consideration, Cabinet approvals and then media preparation before it was actually announced. Most journalists never get the opportunity to run anything and for the very few who do, it is usually just to run a newspaper. It never seems to dawn on them or for that matter, most people in the community, that only a smidgen of time is spent fronting cameras and Parliament compared to the long hard slog of actually running a major administration. In fact, over 90% of my time as a minister was spent in effectively being the CEO of my portfolios, managing and holding to account the many organisations for which I was responsible. In Transport and Roads, this was a huge daily task and more often than not, a huge daily grind with little joy and thanks. Most of the job involved countless hours of meetings where I would question, probe, nudge and demand from my heads of department and senior public servants on the countless issues before us at any particular point in time. At the same time, stakeholder management, meetings and resolution were always a big part of the week.

To give a flavour to all this, I decided to pick a day just after the Olympics, when I was still Minister for Ports, Transport and Roads – Monday, 23rd October 2000.

That day was busy and typical of what I had to do on nearly 3,000 other occasions. This is what my diary and recollections record for that day:

6.00 am: Wake up, read reams of press clippings faxed to home of all relevant stories in the four morning papers, consider any need for immediate radio response, call senior media advisor for discussion on morning and day ahead, peruse on-time passenger rail performance for the previous evening peak

6.45 am: Shower, shave and suit up

7.15 am: Make school lunches for the kids and grab a few pieces of fruit for breakfast in the car

7.30 am: Long drive to the office in the CBD, peruse briefing notes for day's meetings, speak to Chief of Staff on

Chapter 7: Winning government

	day ahead and read all four daily newspapers, return all outstanding calls from the day before
9.00 am:	Meeting with senior personal staff
9.30 am:	Meeting with CEO and Chairman of Rail Services Corporation re: rail maintenance issues
11.00 am:	Meeting with the CEO of National Rail re: national freight rail issues
12.00 noon:	Meeting with the CEO of Rail Access Corporation re: track condition and performance
1.00 pm:	Quick sandwich over a diary meeting with private secretary to discuss all requests for meetings both internal and external.
1.30 pm:	Meeting with the CFO of the State Rail Authority re: recurrent budget for passenger rail operations and need for supplementation from Treasury
2.30 pm:	Pre-briefing from CEO and Chairman of State Transit Authority (STA) re: meeting with Treasurer
3.00 pm:	Meeting with Treasurer re: settling financial statements and corporate intent statement for State Transit Authority
4.15 pm:	Meeting with the Deputy Premier
5.00 pm:	Pre-Board meeting with CEO and Chairman of the State Rail Authority re: Monthly Board Agenda

6.15 pm: Meeting with Chief of Staff re: discussion on the day and what to expect for the next one

7.00 pm: Long drive back to the electorate, peruse traffic fatality sheet of persons killed in road accidents the day before and why, peruse rail on-time running figure for the morning peak and consider causes of any problems and steps taken to address them, return all calls made by MPs during the day, peruse all press clippings from across the State and all radio transcripts of the day relevant to my portfolio, sign urgent papers, peruse briefing notes and draft press release for media event the next day on road safety with the NRMA on "Don't leave children in parked cars"

8.00 pm: Attend and address Smithfield branch of the ALP re: monthly meeting

9.15 pm: Arrive home for a quick dinner and chat with Ann and the kids, check fax for any urgent notices or media advice, take calls from media team and Chief of Staff, replay VCR recording of Channel 9 and Channel 2 news, and watch some television with Ann

10.30 pm: Off to bed, but if there was even a hint of bad news coming our way, I would wait up until quite late to get the early Sydney Morning Herald and Telegraph editions sent to me over the fax about midnight. That happened countless times in my journey as a minister.

11.00 pm: Hopefully, asleep!

This was very much my usual daily routine throughout my time and life as minister. 15+ hour days were the norm and usually another 5 to 10 hours over the weekend. If a tough issue blew up, then the hours just lengthened and became a whole lot more intense and exhausting. It was not possible to do the job properly without putting in this sort of effort. It is the main reason why I survived, long after a ministerial career would have normally been extinguished.

On the 23rd of October 2000, I had been a minister for over 5 years and Minister for Transport for nearly 3 years. My life and my diary over my years as Transport Minister were consumed by rail issues. They were tough years, but I still found time and energy to build motorways and run the Ports portfolio. On that particular day, I had exactly 6 years and 2 days left in my ministerial career. A lot of water would go under the bridge in the intervening years.

CHAPTER 8

The Sydney Motorways – what it took to build them

When a 90-year old woman resident of Bardwell Park lamented to commercial TV news one evening in mid-1997 in relation to chimney stacks proposed for the M5 East tunnel right on top of her home: "I moved here in the 1920s as a new bride with my war veteran husband and I can't believe what is happening to me. Carl Scully is going to kill my lawn, kill my pet cat and then kill me", I quickly called my Chief of Staff and said; "Did you just see that, I have to fix this real soon or this whole project will be too hard to deliver". I already knew from the Eastern Distributor how tough it was to try and build a new motorway through a major urban centre like Sydney. And the M5 East proved to be just as tough as the rest of them.

The Goss ALP Government in Queensland had fallen in 1996 because of an attempt to push a new motorway through five marginal seats. The Fahey Liberal NP Government in New South Wales lost the marginal seat of Gladesville primarily because it had rammed the new and much needed M2 Motorway through homes, schools, churches and public open space. It was one of the three seats we had won in 1995 to form government by no more than a finger nail.

Chapter 8: The Sydney Motorways

In the first few months of the Carr ALP Government, we were battered by the media and the public from pillar to post on not delivering on our promise to remove the tolls as promised on the M4 and M5 Motorways. But being candid in Cabinet about our intentions on some of our pre-election promises was not always welcome.

When Michael Knight as the new Roads Minister, brought to Cabinet the bad news that the promise could not be delivered because "the tax implications for the Government are far greater than we had imagined", few were surprised by us backing out of the promise and fewer still, believed the reason he was giving, as the true justification for doing so.

I was a new minister still pretty wet behind the ears and silly enough to enunciate what I am sure everyone in the room was thinking: "We never really intended to deliver on that promise". It was one of the rare occasions in Cabinet when Carr jumped down my throat and emphatically denied that he had intended to do anything other than implement his commitment to abolish both tolls.

This was my first realisation that Carr had to be very careful, even in Cabinet that anything he expressed anywhere could or would be reported as a contrast to his official line. There would never be a frank exchange with Cabinet colleagues about his real thoughts, if it meant an unpleasant slant in a media story contrary to the message. But that day, as we discussed Knight's recommendation that we dump the toll abolition promise, I did think that the Premier's rather strenuous denial was a little like what Shakespeare might have said: "He protesteth too much".

The reversal of the commitment to abolish the tolls, hurt the Government a great deal, particularly at such an early time in the life of the new administration. It quickly became a character question well beyond the borders of those communities still having to pay the tolls. We had promised something and almost nonchalantly reneged on it. Like Rudd's almost flippant dismissal of his "great moral challenge of our generation" on climate change, this issue quickly became one of integrity and good character, rather than just a road revenue issue. It was hurting us so much, that Knight had to come up with something relatively good, or we may well be a one-term government. It got that bad.

The Cash Back scheme where privately owned vehicles could claim reimbursement for tolls paid on the M4 and M5 was the circuit breaker the Government needed. It was well received and quickly got the toll promise off our backs. Additionally, because the scheme was limited to private cars and had a degree of complexity to it, the cost turned out to be relatively modest.

As mentioned, Knight was too busy planning for the Sydney 2000 Olympics and by the end of 1996 asked Carr if I could take over the Roads portfolio. It was one I would hold for 8 years, 1 month and 25 days. It was certainly the most rewarding of all the portfolios I would hold, but at times very tough in steering much needed infrastructure to fruition.

I certainly learnt the hard way that having plans for motorways was a whole lot easier than actually trying to have them constructed and open for business: funding issues, environmental approvals, stakeholder resentment, local council obstacles, Treasury opposition, constant media attacks, tough tender processes and the oversight of challenging construction. For the six motorways (five plus the $800M Bus-only Transitways) I was responsible for delivering during my eight years as Roads Minister, it was these sorts of issues and more, which made the long challenging task of delivering each one of them very difficult indeed.

Delivering motorways, financing them from new tolls and developing motorway policy was not for the fainthearted in this tough environment. It would take a lot of nerve, resolve and poise to push through in the face of those very tough challenges to deliver major road infrastructure that was so essentially needed by the people of Sydney. The Eastern Distributor motorway was the first and toughest, the M7 the most rewarding and the Cross City the last and most damaging. However, I like to think that they have all made a great difference to the mobility and quality of life of the people of Sydney.

The Eastern Distributor

The Eastern Distributor now provides divided dual carriage way without traffic lights or intersections from the CBD of Sydney all the way to the airport and beyond. Plans and ideas for building such a link had been around for over 40 years. There had been a lot of talk, but no action taken.

A large urban metropolis like Sydney needed a motorway network running around it and through it, but when I became Roads Minister, this was far from a reality. The Wran Labor Government had built the Southern Cross drive from the airport towards the city, which then petered out into enormous traffic congestion on South Dowling Street. The M5 built by the Greiner Government disappeared at Hurstville leaving a 10 km missing link to the city, and the much trumpeted M2 just ended at Lane Cove River without a care or thought on what was supposed to happen then. Across Western Sydney, it was no different with a 40 km gap between the end of the M2 and the beginning of the M5. There was much work to do in filling all these gaps and it would take all of my 8 years in the job and all of my energy and capability to fill them.

Motorists would struggle now to remember just how hard it was to get from the Sydney CBD to the airport. It involved a tortuous path down city residential streets onto Southern Cross Drive and then onto residential streets in the vicinity surrounding the airport. It was congested. It was tough. It was hard to endure even for more resolute motorist. A plan had been brought forward by the RTA to build a freeway link by a mix of short tunnels under very busy intersections with a surface road as well. It was ambitious and essential to the future of Sydney.

Prior to handing me over the roads portfolio, Michael Knight had brought the process as far as announcing the preferred consortium to deliver a new toll funded $700M Eastern Distributor motorway lead by Macquarie Bank and Leighton Contractors. But that is as far as it had gone. I was astonished to quickly learn on being commissioned as the minister that no planning approval had been given before determining which bidder would be given preferential bid status.

This meant that if changes were required to both win community support and to gain planning approval, we would have to negotiate the cost of those changes, not in the environment of a competitive tender, but having to go cap in hand to the winning consortium and ask for their best price. This was the worst possible place to be in with a road building contractor and a bank like Macquarie. I was surprised that both Knight and the RTA had allowed this to occur and was certainly something which I ensured was to never be repeated.

The CEO of Leighton Holdings was asked on his retirement after 23 years at the helm, how he wanted to be remembered. He

Chapter 8: The Sydney Motorways

replied: "As a great contractor." And any great contractor will tell you that it is their job to pursue claims for variations as vigorously as possible with the client. Once the government committed to building a major project and then announced who was going to build it, meant that its only negotiating position on variations to the original scope of work even before signing a contract, would be 'please be kind to me'.

And it very soon became apparent that to win a reasonable degree of community support and planning approval, the Eastern Distributor would require not just a few changes, but a wholesale overhaul of parts of the scope of work for the proposed motorway. On day one of my long term as Minister for Roads, the Eastern Distributor Motorway was undeliverable as a major project and it very quickly consumed both me and the leadership of the RTA to turn that around.

There were two serious, but separate and distinct community issues, which quickly emerged as strong enough to threaten the likelihood of the motorway project actually proceeding: The Art Gallery in Sydney and the residents of South Dowling Street.

The Art Gallery of New South Wales is in a purpose-built building set amongst an attractive tree lined street nestled next to the large CBD parkland known as the Domain and right next door to the Sydney Botanical Gardens. It is a beautiful part of the city and a great setting for such a cultural icon.

And then came the Eastern Distributor.

What was proposed by the RTA was no less than ten lanes of motorway traffic to manage, disperse and redirect a huge roadway, which was to be built right under the nose of the Art Gallery building. Not surprisingly, the cultured in the city and senior gallery personnel started to make a strong voice in opposition to the whole project. Not only did the 'friends of the gallery' weigh in to support the Art Gallery Director, but so did some very famous Australian actors. I quickly formed the view, that such a devastating attack if unresolved, would probably kill off the project. I needed to act and act in a substantial way.

I came to the view that whilst the cultured representatives of the city were vocal and angry, it was not against the project per se, but how ugly it was going to look in front of their art gallery, which troubled them. I surmised that if the eyesore became unseen from their vantage point, then they would go away as an issue. This proved both correct and expensive. I decided that the best way to do that was to construct a lid over the ten lanes of motorway below the gallery area and to cover it with grass lawn, shrubs and garden furniture. The changes came at a cost of $41M with the RTA contributing $21M of that cost at my request.

In January 1999, Bob Carr and I opened the new mini park next to the Art Gallery of New South Wales as a very welcome addition to the Botanical Gardens. It meant that for the first time, the Domain would be connected by open space to the Botanical Gardens. In an astonishing act of irony, in 2013, the new Director of the New South Wales Art Gallery, Michael Brand, proposed a $450M Pharaonic redevelopment right on top of the open space I had proudly left for the people of Sydney. This is land still being paid for by Sydney motorists every day through tolls and was never intended as a site for Art Gallery dreams of expansion. Former Prime Minister, Paul Keating, was right to call the proposal a 'land grab'. Thankfully, since well-known corporate heavy weight, David Gonski, became President of the Art Gallery Board of Trustees in January 2016, nothing further has been heard of this proposal.

Chapter 8: The Sydney Motorways

After the Art Gallery of New South Wales issue, it was the residents of South Dowling Street who started protesting. The terraces along this road on the southern edge of the Sydney CBD had been built over 100 years ago. They were only on one side of the street, which faced a very busy four-lane road to the large expanse of the Moore Park playing fields. Even though the traffic noise and congestion must have been unwelcome, I thought it did seem like a nice outlook to live amongst.

And then came the Eastern Distributor.

The RTA's plan provided for an additional surface level four-lane freeway on top of the four lanes of traffic already in place. In order to enable entry and exit lanes, the number would swell to ten lanes in some parts along this stretch. This was too much for local residents and the local MP started a loud orchestrated campaign of protest.

Talk-back radio and the main stream media started to run on how this project was about to ruin the character and ambience of this neighbourhood. Like the area in front of the Art Gallery of New South Wales, a couple of kilometres away by proposed tunnel, I realised that I had to deal with a multi-lane eyesore which was going to be built in front of the terraces of South Dowling Street.

I asked for options from the RTA on how they could deal with the issue and one amongst a few was to lower the motorway well below the eyesight of residents and build a few road and pedestrian bridges over the sunken motorway. This worked a treat with local residents, the local MP, the shock jocks and the general media. But at an even more substantial cost of $91M.

I had now found a way through the enormous social, political and environmental challenges facing the project. It was a relief, but the hard yards now commenced in negotiating with Macquarie Bank as the financier of the consortium, on how Leighton Contractor's agreed extra construction cost of $132M for both major variations were going to be paid for. The toll period was extended to 48 years and the method used to calculate toll increases was altered in favour of the bank.

It had taken over 6 months of hard, relentless work.

Incredibly, the Department of Planning under Gabrielle Kibble, started to claim that it was not yet satisfied of the need for the project and that it may not get approval. I was astonished that this could occur when the Government had made it abundantly clear it wanted the project. My view of the role of the Department of Planning was to approve the project or get out of the way. As I could not be sure it would do either, I met with the Leader of the Opposition and most of the Shadow Cabinet and secured support for the carriage of legislation authorising the use of a strip of land in Moore Park for the new motorway. This was enough of a parliamentary prod for the Department of Planning to fall into line and allow the project to proceed.

We now had an approved, legislatively authorised, contractually agreed, and funded major road project for Sydney. I was exhausted. It had been a long hard road of considerable hours and anguish over many months. More than a few times, it looked like it was going to fall over in front of what looked like yet another insurmountable obstacle. But, it had been a great journey with the RTA senior personnel and its trusted consultants and advisors. This was the start of a team which would go on to deliver more motorways and major road projects than at any other prior time in Sydney's history.

Chapter 8: The Sydney Motorways

At that point in my ministerial career, I really did feel like I had been through a major battle and had come though victorious. The real winners were the people of Sydney, as it is impossible to now imagine Sydney without the Eastern Distributor. I doubt very many motorists when travelling on it, even give it a moment's thought to how close it went to not being at all.

It is not usual for a minister to get to open major projects. We plan and deliver them, but it is the role of the Premier to open them. And so it should be, as without the support of the Head of Government, projects like this would not happen.

I just assumed that Carr would want to do the opening of the Eastern Distributor, but when the date was announced for the end of 1999, he called to say he would be on leave in Europe and asked that I stand in for him. I had to feign respectful agreement but thought: "You little beauty". I had put so much of my life into getting the project up and had drawn on all my political skills and more to steer it passed troubled waters, I did think it was nice that I could actually do the opening itself. I didn't expect it, but it was a nice reward to be asked to do it.

The opening of a new motorway right in the heart of the Sydney CBD was always going to have a major impact on the way motorists had been used to driving in that part of the city. There had been no such project causing and requiring such major changes to city traffic that anyone could remember.

The RTA had allocated $6M to the Sydney Council to pay for the cost of local area traffic management necessary with the introduction of the motorway and had also implemented major changes to the directional flows of two major one-way streets.

Difficult media management – Competent vs Incompetent

The public's reaction after the opening of the Eastern Distributor was similar to the public reaction after the opening of the Cross City Tunnel Motorway nearly six years later. As with the Cross City Tunnel, motorists and local residents started complaining long and loud about the changes to street flows, restriction of access to certain roads, and all manner of complaints about the new project. As is often the case with large community complaints, the Daily Telegraph loved reporting it and talk-back radio lit up with irate motorists demanding that the government do something about it.

When I ask the Negaholics of the Cross City Tunnel to put on hold their negativity on that project and to read the press clippings, which reported story after story in the first few months of the opening of the Eastern Distributor, they always come back to me with a comment on how the stories and complaints are almost identical. Few have bothered to undertake the exercise and anyone who has an opinion on the Cross City Tunnel should first test that opinion by considering just how similar the issues were on that project with the post opening issues of the Eastern Distributor and how very differently they were handled by the Premier and Minister of the day.

The only real and lasting difference between the management of the post opening of the Eastern Distributor and the management of the post opening of the Cross City Tunnel was that the former had an experienced Premier at the helm and a Roads Minister who didn't flinch at the first sight of media grapeshot. And Carr and I certainly did not say of the Eastern Distributor that 'too many compromises had been made' à la Tripodi. We didn't sack the CEO of the RTA, we didn't reverse any local traffic measures and we certainly didn't trash our own project. These are the things which Iemma and Tripodi did on the Cross City Tunnel and which Carr and I did not do on the Eastern Distributor project.

Carr and I did what a Premier and a Roads Minister should do when faced with difficult media reaction, talk-back shock jocks on the warpath and less than happy motorists. We used calm resolve to explain the benefits, we argued the case for the project and the great benefit it would be seen as in time for the people of Sydney. Most importantly, we asked the people of Sydney to be patient with such a massive change to the traffic dynamics of Sydney and to bear with us as we all got used to its impact. And just as importantly, I informed the community that if after six months, these expected teething problems were still causing heartache, then I would make changes. This is how transition to a changed environment is properly managed.

No changes were needed in the end on the Eastern Distributor, as before the six months were up, motorists had got used to the new arrangements, and understood how to access and use the new motorway. Gradually, all the complaints and negativity drifted off into the sands of time. Nobody remembers the angst and anguish following the opening of the Eastern Distributor, but many still remember what followed the opening of the Cross City Tunnel. The latter was an attempt to differentiate Iemma from Carr by attacking the credibility of a Carr Government project, as if Iemma had arrived with no ALP colours. It did not work!

The community reaction post opening of each motorway was the same, but the Government's response to that reaction was palpably different. The response to reaction on the Eastern Distributor enhanced and protected the Government's reputation and record on major projects, whereas the response to reaction on the Cross City Tunnel irreparably harmed it.

There is no better contrast of Carr and Iemma than on the massively contrasting ways in which each handled the opening of their first motorway. It is no accident that for Carr, there would be four more motorways planned and delivered, but for Iemma, there would be no more. What ought to be remembered on the Cross City Tunnel post opening debacle, is not how awful the project was, but how an image in the public mind of it being an awful project, was self-inflicted by the very government which planned and built it. Just extraordinary and contrary to even the most basic manual on how to manage difficult public issues.

Delivering a motorway through a large urban metropolis is a very tough business. It takes nerve and determination to do it, and so it also does when confronted with an adverse post opening reaction. Iemma and Tripodi never bothered to ask Carr or me how we had handled the Eastern Distributor and then stumbled into difficult waters. It did not need to be so.

The Cross City Tunnel

Of all the motorways to cause the RTA and me the most grief, it was the last and shortest of them all, the Cross City Tunnel. I was in a hurry. I wanted to get as much built in the city as I possibly could in my time as Minister for Roads. I wanted to make a difference for the motorists of Sydney.

Delivering the Cross City Tunnel brought me my first introduction to the legendarily temperamental Lord Mayor, Frank Sartor. He was not known as 'Cranky Franky' for nothing. And when I met with him and told him that it would be a short tunnel, rather than his preferred longer version underneath William Street, he went apoplectic: "Minister, I don't blame you for this as you are just following what the RTA has dished up to you" and then turned towards CEO Paul Forward and Head of Road

Chapter 8: The Sydney Motorways

Network Infrastructure, Mike Hannon and let it rip: "But as for you two miserable pricks, you would have to be the pair of lowest...that ever had life breathed into them" and so on, and so on for several minutes. It was great theatre and the sort of performance which Sartor loved to unleash whenever he was not getting his way.

Despite the theatrics, I did think he had a point and so I asked the RTA to quietly rethink the project with a view to continuing the tunnel all the way under William Street and Kings Cross. He was a whole lot happier the next time I briefed him, but he did ask that we protect the view corridor of Cathedral Street. I had not been familiar with this small street located below St Mary's Cathedral. It had been called Cathedral Street because it had a great view of the cathedral all the way along its relatively short length. The proposed exit point of Sir John Young Crescent, to enable traffic to enter the city or the Sydney Harbour Tunnel travelling north, was slated to come out just before Cathedral Street. This would mean that the view of the cathedral would be impaired, if not destroyed, and Sartor asked us to do what we could to extend the exit point of the tunnel just a little further to protect it. I was able to do that at an additional cost of $25M and Cathedral Street was saved, or so I thought.

After the design and tender for the Cross City Tunnel Motorway had been concluded, Sartor in his capacity as Lord Mayor of Sydney, undertook a major redevelopment of Cook and Phillip Parks, located right next door to the iconic St Mary's Cathedral. This provided a CBD pool leisure centre right in the heart of CBD Sydney together with a restaurant and an upgraded park area. It is a valuable legacy which I believe Sartor can point to as being delivered during his period of stewardship.

However, when I pointed out to Sartor some years later, that this major redevelopment around and in front of the Cathedral, had in fact substantially blocked the Cathedral Street corridor view he had asked me to protect, he did not even remember the request he had made in the first place. I was not impressed.

A lot of ignorant comment was made in relation to the Cross City Tunnel in the months after it was open to traffic. This was almost entirely fuelled by the tabloid press and shock jocks, following motorists being upset by a number of changes to traffic conditions, as well as the private consortium making a loss on the deal. However, it was well built, fully funded by the private sector, at no cost to the budget, and continues to provide a great service to the motorists of Sydney. Even well after I had left politics, I had to listen to an uninformed PPP banking expert at an infrastructure conference in Brisbane, using the project as an example of how not to deliver a PPP. That he was 'spruiking' himself as a financing PPP expert, whilst drawing not on his personal experience of the project, but on what the daily tabloid press had said about it, considerably irritated me. I did use the Q and A conference session to correct the record, mention my role in delivering this very good piece of privately financed infrastructure and hopefully, left the banker feeling a greater need to rely on his own experience on a project, and perhaps draw a little less from the Daily Telegraph and a lot more from the Australian Financial Review or other more reputable sources.

In the daily hurly burly of political contest, most folks expect claim and counter claim, attack and defence, as their daily diet of democracy, and do not take much notice on a day-to-day basis of any particular issue of the day. However, if a government stops that process and joins with the opposition, the media and the public and begins to attack itself and its projects, then folks take very close notice and interest in what is going on. It is so rare for a government to start pouring bile upon itself, that when it does happen, the minister delivering it, will have no difficulty in getting attention. This is precisely what happened on the Cross City Tunnel, which considerably undermined the Government's strong record of successfully building public infrastructure and directly led to a loss of confidence and willingness to pursue more much needed large projects.

The period 2005 to 2011 was a sad, wasted six years of non-delivery of any new motorways and no new rail lines or bus-only transitways. The contrast with the huge public infrastructure projects being delivered now in rail, light rail and roads, by the current Liberal state government is, in my view, simply embarrassing.

The roads portfolio was Joe Tripodi's first experience of a senior portfolio. He had only been a minister for six months, had never built anything in that time and had no experience in dealing with major adverse media reaction to government decisions. Once the ghouls of the press were let loose on whipping up as much negativity as they could of the public angst on the Cross City Tunnel, the new minister struggled to cope, and then took the lazy, easy option of attacking the project itself, the department which managed it, its CEO and finally, his ministerial colleague who had delivered it.

Tripodi got a great run in the Daily Telegraph saying "compromises had been made" in building the motorway.

I asked Tripodi for a meeting in my Leader of the House office in Parliament House just before Question Time one day. I said to him: "Joe, why on earth would you give the impression that something wrong was done in delivering the Cross City Tunnel by claiming that compromises were made. It is obvious compromises are made to get a big project up, but you are making it sound like we did something we shouldn't have."

The conversation then went as follows:

Tripodi: "They're fucked"

Me: "What's fucked?"

Tripodi: "PPPs."

Me: "Do you mean this PPP or all PPPs?"

Tripodi: "PPPs are a terrible way to deliver public infrastructure"

Me: "Well if I had not delivered them as private tollways, then none of them except the M5 East would have been built. You know that Egan and Carr wouldn't give me a dollar for any of those projects. The only way they were ever going to be built were as PPPs or not at all."

Tripodi: "Then they should not have been built."

Me: "Are you kidding. I can't believe you think that let alone actually say it. You are supposed to be the Roads Minister. Are you really telling me that the people of Sydney would be better off not having the M7, the Eastern Distributor, the Lane Cove Tunnel and the Cross City Tunnel if the only way to build them was from private finance as PPPs? Are you really saying that?"

Chapter 8: The Sydney Motorways

Tripodi: "That's right. Yes, I am."

Me: "I just can't believe you really think that. Joe, I built five motorways across Sydney and four of them were PPPs."

Tripodi: "I know that. Everyone knows that."

Me: "Well then, you seem to be such an expert on this stuff, could you name the driveway you have actually poured concrete on which gives you this mega project experience to be able to so authoritatively pass judgement?"

Tripodi: "You're a fucken smart arse."

I must have upset young Joe with my last remark, as he stormed out of my office and into the chamber for Question Time. When the Opposition asked the expected question on the Cross City Tunnel, Tripodi unexpectedly converted his words of the previous day from "compromises were made" to "too many compromises were made". To this day, I do not know if Tripodi was consciously upping the media angst towards me, the RTA leadership and the project by simply adding the word "too". Perhaps he was just careless and clueless about how devastating words, or even a single word, can be in a situation like this. I am inclined to think that he was so upset with our conversation that he deliberately set out to inflame the situation.

Either way the result was major public and media grief for me, the RTA and the reputation of the project. The next day, the Daily Telegraph ran a front page with a picture of me and a nasty story accusing me of causing all manner of evil things upon an unsuspecting public. Good for Tripodi, bad for me, appalling for the project and a terrible way for a government to deal with itself. It would not be the only time post Carr that amateur hour would arrive at Macquarie Street.

But Tripodi's work was not done on the Cross City Tunnel. He and his Chief of Staff, Aaron Gadiel, were upset with RTA CEO, Paul Forward, about a couple of important documents being inadvertently not included when over 30 boxes of material were delivered to the Legislative Council, in compliance with a Notice to Produce Documents. The Tripodi/Gadiel duo issued Forward with a Notice to Show Cause and sacked him the next day. I rang Iemma at home that night and pleaded the case for Forward's retention and when all Iemma could muster was: "He's the minister", I had to remind him to no avail: "Yes, but you are the Premier". It was an outrageous decision. Forward in my view, was the best CEO in the government, had done all that he had been asked to do on a difficult project and had done nothing even slightly resembling a justification for his removal.

At least much later, Iemma would say to me: "That was not our finest hour". Even Egan called me to say: "This is just oops on the part of the whole organisation. You can't sack a CEO for that."

Iemma had wholesale swallowed the advice of his mentor, Peter Barron, that the new Premier needed to differentiate himself from Carr, by attacking a Carr Government project. The advice assumed that people are stupid and would behave as if the denigration of a new motorway was not from the same long term Labor Government which planned and delivered it, but from a new administration in a transition from the bad old Carr days to the wonderfully new and invigorating Iemma ones. Arbib loved the advice and encouraged both Iemma and Tripodi to not hold back in heaping abuse on a Labor government public infrastructure project. The advice directly resulted in the trashing

Chapter 8: The Sydney Motorways

of our terrific record on delivering infrastructure and lead to infrastructure atrophy under Iemma, Rees and Keneally. So far as I am aware, neither Barron nor Arbib have ever acknowledged the damaging consequences of their advice to Iemma that he should launch a Labor government in a bitter attack on itself.

There were still a couple of amusing things to come. Just as former Premier, Bob Carr and former Treasurer Michael Egan were about to give evidence in the Upper House inquiry on the Cross City Tunnel, Egan called to get my approval for the lines: "I want to complain about Carl Scully getting all the credit for the Cross City Tunnel. I was up to my neck in approving this project and I deserve some of the credit." It worked a treat in the media. Carr and Egan were terrific in the box defending a project I was stymied from defending, because the then Premier and Minister wanted to attack it at every opportunity. Iemma even pulled me aside during this and said: "These two clowns don't get it." What he didn't get, was that he and Tripodi were the ones not getting it.

A great project was attacked by the very government that had built it, the CEO who did as he had been asked was sacked for the most spurious of reasons and the Government and the RTA just lost their desire to build any more motorways. It would take a change of government to get the ball rolling again on building major new road projects in Sydney. It did not need to be so.

The three other motorways I planned and delivered: The M5 East, The Lane Cove Tunnel and the huge M7 across Western Sydney were all tough and at times provided what looked like insurmountable challenges. Only the M5 East was built as a freeway because Egan and Carr were not prepared to put a dollar into any other major roads across Sydney for one simple reason: they were not a funding priority for them. So, the remaining four had to be tollways funded by banks as PPPs. Otherwise they would not have been built.

The challenges of them all were many.

The M5 East

On the M5 East, it was trying to find an additional $300M of funds from within the RTA, after Knight had announced that the project would only cost $480M when it actually cost nearly $800M. Also, a protest rally of over 2,500 local residents complaining about the location of three exhaust stacks, and their homes being devalued by living on top of a road tunnel, spurred me into action.

The irony of the M5 East is that very few in Sydney know that the exhaust stack for the Sydney Harbour Tunnel is in one of the four sandstone pylons which provide grace and texture to a wonderful Sydney icon. Whoever came up with the idea of pushing vehicle fumes up a hole in a pylon and into the surrounding air shed ought to be given a medal for services in avoiding adverse publicity for a project. I do not ever recall a single resident complaint about the issue when the project was being planned and delivered in the early to mid-1980s.

Likewise, on the Eastern Distributor, nobody knows how or where the exhaust is emitted from the long tunnel which commences just past the art gallery on the edge of the CBD. Nobody complained and it was never an issue.

The M5 East project was on another planet by way of comparison. Not only was air quality and the location of exhaust stacks a very significant issue, it soon emerged that if not properly managed, it could become a project destroying issue. That is why I stepped in and directed that only one stack be built, instead of

Chapter 8: The Sydney Motorways

the planned three, and that it be built on the only available land in a relatively lowly populated area, next to the railway line, about a kilometre away from the project.

I announced my solution to acclamation from affected residents, local media and the shock jocks. It had been another tough 15-round fight in the sun, but I had managed to find a way through. It still caused lingering angst amongst some of the residents newly affected, but this was just standard irritation for a project of this size which was now politically buildable. On the nonsensical claim that homes would be devalued by having a tunnel built under them, I also made a call that I would direct the RTA to purchase every home affected if required to do so at pre-project announcement values. The RTA leadership almost collapsed from cardiac arrest at the thought of having to find an additional $150M. I was convinced that the claims were bogus, that few would want to move and of those that did, we would make a handsome profit on resale. And that is how it all played out.

Power and consent

By the time the Eastern Distributor and the M5 East were delivered and opened to traffic, I had learnt a lot indeed about community power and stakeholder engagement and that government authority was more ethereal than substantive.

As a young party activist and law student, I thought that an elected government was by virtue of that election, able to exercise power and authority within the community only subject to statutory and constitutional constraint. How naïve I was in retrospect.

Except for the legislative amendment I needed to vest some Moore Park land into the ownership of the RTA, there was no statutory or constitutional restrictions to the Government running a tender process, and signing up a consortium to deliver a big tollway. It was a good position to be in, but not as good as it sounded on paper.

I had been confronted with such strong community protest on both the Eastern Distributor and the M5 East, that it nearly put them on the brink of being cancelled. This was not an elected government exerting its mandate to govern in the best interests of all the community, but a new government finding its way through the ebb and flow of community consent. My blowtorch to the belly christening on two major projects made me ponder how power, consent and authority really worked in practice between a community and its elected government.

Some of the more naïve political scientists and many MPs assume that general elections held at regular intervals, settle who has power and who does not. But it is a whole lot more complicated than that. It is true, if not obvious, that governments in a democracy like ours must receive the consent of the people at a general election to give it the constitutional and statutory authority to hold office and to exert relative and situational power. In a genuine democracy with demonstrably free and fair elections, power is vested at elections only to a degree. Community consent can be withdrawn at points of time or in relation to specific projects or policies or regions.

The second failed attempt in 2008 to privatise the New South Wales electricity assets unleashed a loud and bitter union and party war with its own Labor Government over many months. This was fought out publicly with little or no regard for the political consequences. Not surprisingly, the Party and the Government it had spawned, soon appeared to be at war with itself and completely distracted from governing on behalf of the

Chapter 8: The Sydney Motorways

folks who elected them. The polling in due course reflected this sentiment and never recovered. It was well prior to the 2011 election when the Labor Government no longer had the consent of the community to govern.

Whilst the long drawn out battle within the ALP Party and caucus over electricity ownership was the catalyst for a long major and eventually irreversible decline in poll after poll, the hint of what might come, began with the decision not to support and argue the case for the Cross City Tunnel Motorway, but to side with its detractors, with talk back radio, with the populist press and with the political opposition, and attack it.

At least for the first 10 years of the 16-year Labor Government, the complete opposite occurred. Olympic infrastructure was built, major hospital upgrades occurred, and more road and rail projects were delivered than at any other time in recent political history.

I learnt the hard way on my own projects, that if I did not bring the affected community with me, then the government's power and authority to deliver it could be withdrawn. It had been real 'school of hard knocks' stuff, but something I would take with me for the rest of my time as a minister. It taught me a lot about leadership being conditional on consent being granted to the leader.

Nowadays, the private sector loves to use terms like 'licence to operate' or 'social license' to indicate the broader project-destroying potential of community protest. Then, it would have been called 'stakeholder engagement', but now, it is formally recognised that government does not have the only or final say on whether or not a project proceeds. Back then, not much of this was talked about and it was assumed that government could just get on with the job even in the face of loud and deafening protest.

The M7 Motorway

I sometimes still get asked what my favourite project was in my many years spent in the New South Wales Cabinet. It is an easy question to answer: The M7 Motorway. It had its challenges but when I look back, I think that this one made the most difference to the people of Sydney and was one of the most satisfying projects I had the privilege of being involved in.

Western Sydney had been long neglected on public infrastructure by the time I came to the roads portfolio in the mid-1990s. I decided to do something about it. This required the building of four lanes for cars and trucks along Windsor Road and Old Windsor Road, a two-lane bus-only transitway from Rouse Hill to Parramatta and Blacktown and then Parramatta to Liverpool, as well as the 40 km M7 motorway. With an investment of public funds in excess of $2.5B, the length and breadth of Western Sydney had never seen so much transport construction in its entire history. It all made a huge difference to a massively congested and historically ignored part of Sydney. And the jewel in the crown was the M7.

But the M7 was considered a national highway project and three successive Howard Government ministers had made it quite clear that there would be no funds for such a project in at least the next 20 years. I decided that the only way this critical road for Western Sydney was ever going to be built, was as a privately funded PPP tollway. That would be a first for the national highway and was going to be a tough sell. I did not even bother asking Carr or Egan about funding from the budget, as I already knew what the response would have been.

There was much work to do to get a toll project across, through and past the Federal Government, State and Federal MPs,

Chapter 8: The Sydney Motorways

the NRMA, the trucking industry and the many motorists who would be paying for it. The RTA came up with a scope for a four-lane freeway running for 40 km including a huge M4/M7 motorway to motorway interchange and a grade separated cycleway along the whole route. The estimated cost was $900M which I rejected out of hand as way too low to build a project of that size. I had been burnt a few times by media reaction when projects ended up costing a lot more than originally estimated. So, I told the RTA to add $300M to the estimate. I was confident that the end cost would be well in excess of the $900M estimate, so I just added 30% to that figure.

I asked the RTA to assume a project cost of $1.2B and to advise me on what might be the possible shortfall of funds from the private sector delivering it as a PPP tollway. They came back and said that we would need $350M from the Federal Government to enable it to be a viable PPP project. I then met with Deputy Prime Minister John Anderson and gave him an offer I knew he could not refuse: "Give me $350M and I will cap the liability of the Federal Government to that amount. If it is not enough, then New South Wales will make-up the shortfall."

Anderson took my proposal to Federal Cabinet and came back to me with advice that Prime Minister John Howard would support the M7 on the following basis:

1. M7 to proceed as a PPP Tollway.

2. The liability of the Commonwealth be capped at $350M.

3. The New South Wales Labor Government undertake to ensure there is no protest from the ALP anywhere about a toll on the national highway.

4. That the RTA and the Federal Department of Transport carry out a joint study of the options for a motorway link between the F3 Freeway and the M2 Motorway.

5. That the price for trucks using the tollway be capped at an agreed amount.

I had a good meeting with Anderson, and gave him all the commitments and undertakings that he and the Prime Minister had sought as a condition of them supporting a tollway and part funding it. After the meeting, I punched the air with exhilaration as I was very confident that with the deal we had just agreed upon, I would now be able to deliver the M7 to the people of Sydney. It was a great feeling.

It was a calculated risk in letting the Federal Government off the hook with such a modest contribution of just $350M towards the cost of a major project, which should have been fully their responsibility. However, I knew they would never fully fund it or even substantially fund it, and that if I haggled for more funds or even a more open-ended commitment from them, the endless negotiating would have gone on for months and possibly longer. I was in a hurry and the dangle for them of getting a $1.2B piece of national highway for a quarter of that amount was just too good to turn down.

I had locked in the Federal Government without any absolute certainty on what would be the final construction price submitted as part of a full PPP tender bid. I took the deal I had done with the Deputy Prime Minister to the New South Wales Budget Committee and it was approved with the proviso from Egan: "If the $350M from the Feds is not enough, you are on your own. You will have to fund the shortfall from your own RTA Capital programme." I had come to expect no less from the Treasurer. It would mean that for every dollar needed to subsidise the PPP above and beyond the Commonwealth's $350M, I would have to take a dollar from other road projects around the State.

Getting Egan's approval for such a deal with the Federal Government and approval to commence a tender process on a $1.2B road project was still a milestone which I much appreciated. You could never take him, his department or the budget committee for granted on these things.

I had now put myself and the RTA between a rock and a hard place. If the best the private sector could do was to contribute say $750M to the cost of the $1.2B project, then all the Feds had to do was pitch in $350M and I would have to find the balance of $100M from somewhere in the RTA forward road programme. That would be very hard to find and would create a whole range of difficult conversations with communities as much needed projects were postponed.

However, it was not a silly or wantonly reckless risk I had taken. But it was a risk nevertheless and the RTA and I were the only ones in the game to take such a risk. All the other players: The Feds, the State Treasury and even the private sector all knew what they would be exposed to in funding the project. Except the RTA.

In committing both the New South Wales Government and the RTA to this risk, I had gone, not on the advice of endless briefing notes and consultant's advice, but on gut feel for what was the likely outcome. I had lived in Western Sydney by then for over 15 years and I had a good idea, I believed, on just how many motorists would want to use the M7. I figured that the smart guys putting bids in, would reflect on that fact and in the deal, they would be prepared to put on the table. Some of my best decisions were made on gut feel, but it did not always work out for the best. However, on this one, it did in spades.

When the bids came in, the successful bid pitched the price of construction at $1.5B and would cover all the cost of that with the proposed user charge on motorists. This would mean that the Federal Government's contribution of $350M was not actually needed, but they delivered on the funds as promised and we spent it on State road connections across the length of the motorway. One of the reasons the M7 motorway is still the flagship motorway in our Sydney Orbital Network is because so much money was spent on all the surrounding network connections.

The State Treasury officials noticed this and raised an eyebrow or two about it, but we were able to fob them off with the argument that we needed to comply with a Federal State agreement. I like to think they scuppered away on that, because they knew that if they had initially accepted liability for any shortfall then they could have conditioned it on keeping any unexpected surplus federal funds. But they didn't do that, and I ended up getting a great deal indeed. The people of Western Sydney were the real winners on that one.

Anderson and Howard had been quite serious in seeking an undertaking from me that I would ensure that there would be no protest from the ALP at any level in return for them supporting the M7 going ahead as a PPP Tollway. I fully understood their position which was both reasonable and smart politics. They did not want to be making an important commitment like this to a New South Wales Labor Government only to have the Federal ALP Opposition start what would have been a very effective campaign against what could have been labelled as 'the shocking decision to put a toll on a national highway.'

I did have to put in a lot of effort to shut down any potential ALP protest, which I was able to do with pragmatic help from Martin Ferguson federally and Paul Lynch at the State ALP level. Only Blacktown Council held out and despite them being the venue of the great campaign launches for Gough Whitlam in 1972 and 1974, I decided in the end to ignore their protests.

Opposition to the toll had now been silenced, stymied or ignored. The deal with the Federal Government and the project itself could then proceed unhindered by the sort of devastating toll protests which had appeared when the Greiner Government announced the M4 and M5 Tollways in the early 1990s. I was very happy and I knew we were going to make a lasting difference for the people of Sydney. And not just for motorists.

How the M7 funded the Abbotsbury Parklands

The M7 Motorway provided an unexpected opportunity to do something for my electorate which would never have been funded in the normal course of the State Labor Government's budget processes.

I lived not far from the Fairfield City Farm which was on land owned by the Department of Planning and formed part of the huge Western Sydney Regional Park, which Carr had delivered after being elected in 1995.

On Sundays, I would often go for a long walk around the ridge which had a panoramic view of the farm and surrounding hectares. On a clear day, you could see as far as the city in the east and as far as the Blue Mountains in the west. And I could always see where the M7 alignment would be aside Wallgrove Road.

I would use the time to ponder alone on the usually many intractable problems before me, and work through in my mind what might work as solutions. By the time Chris Bowen had become my Chief of Staff, he was so used to it that on a Monday morning he would often ask: "What have you got for us." On every walk, I would pass by an area of land several hectares in size, which had previously been the site of a very run down and sad looking horse agistment area, known as the Plough and Harrow. It looked even sadder still by the time I became a regular weekend walker through the area.

But, I had long stopped seeing a run-down horse farm and could now picture a terrific picnic area for the local community. It was just a pipe dream of mine as the local MP until delivering the M7 came along.

To build the M7, a small sliver of the Western Regional Park along its boundary with Wallgrove Road had to be excised and vested into the ownership of the RTA to enable the project to proceed. The National Parks and Wildlife Service (NPWS) had assessed the cost of mitigating that damage at $7M, which would require payment of that amount by the RTA before they would agree to the necessary excision.

Paul Forward and the RTA Head of Road Network Infrastructure, Mike Hannon, handed me one day a short briefing note seeking my written approval to the payment. I think I surprised them somewhat when I said: "That is not nearly high enough. I want to pay a whole lot more for a major upgrade in a section of that regional park."

The following Saturday, I met on site with Mike and my Deputy Chief of Staff, Brent Thomas. We spent about three hours bush bashing our way around the several hectare site. I showed

Chapter 8: The Sydney Motorways

Mike and Brent where I wanted well maintained grass lawn for families to picnic on and play ball with their kids, where I wanted walking tracks built and cycle ways, as well as toilet facilities, clusters of BBQ areas and a reasonably sized conference centre. I told the two of them: "These are the things which are going into to this park. Don't take any of this stuff out when you do the design. I don't care what it costs, as I want to leave a lasting legacy for my electorate from the M7."

They got the message, as the draft plan from our consultants looked very impressive. I met again on site with Mike and Brent to meticulously check that the plan was setting out all that I wanted, and in the places that I wanted them. With a few changes, we had the makings of one of Western Sydney's best picnic areas and right in the heart of my electorate. Mike Hannon was worried about the $18M price tag, but gave me very useful advice that we would be able to take that from the $350M Federal contribution as it was an untied grant with no special conditions attached. If it was a condition of the NPWS that we undertake the work, then the Feds would simply release the funds for payment.

I then instructed Mike to present to the CEO of the NPWS, the park upgrade that I wanted the NPWS to demand of us in addition to the already requested $7M. The CEO must have thought Christmas had arrived early, as the RTA very quickly received a written request for payment of $25M as a condition of their consent to the impact of the M7 on the local regional park. The Feds soon ticked it off and allocated the funds and a fantastic addition to Western Sydney parkland was achieved.

By the time of the opening, Di Beamer was the relevant minister and appropriately had her name on the plaque. I don't apologise for manipulating the system in doing what I knew would be a wonderful thing for my electorate and the people of

Western Sydney, which would stand for decades to come. This is not a project either Egan or Carr would have ever financed and the Federal Government would normally scoff at a request for such a project. It would have also been beyond the funding capability of Fairfield Council. It was done right under the noses of both the Federal Government and the State Treasury and neither even noticed. I am delighted I was able to do that.

Joe Tripodi, the MP for Fairfield, lived near the park and I delighted one day in telling him about how many hundreds of locals I had witnessed the previous weekend enjoying the new facilities. His response just about floored me: "It was a waste of money. We already have plenty of parks in the area." I really did not know why this man ever became an MP. Providing much needed public infrastructure, installing a large leisure area for families and advocating for your local community were, in my view, some of the essential characteristics of being an MP, but not for Tripodi. In the Tripodi world, building four major new highways in Sydney for $4.5B as tolled PPP motorways was "fucked" even if not to do so, would leave them unfunded and unbuilt; creating a huge parkland and picnic area was "a waste of money", and my favourite from when he had been an MP for only a couple of years: "Don't you just hate doing constituency work." What more need be said?

The M7 Cycleway

Despite the negativity of my neighbouring MP, I was then and I am still now, delighted that the M7 delivered this wonderful huge area of parkland for the local community. It endures to this day as a very popular destination for Western Sydney families. In addition to this, I was also able to include in the M7 scope of work, a 40 km off road cycleway, separated from traffic for its entire length. Whenever I travel the M7, I get enormous pleasure in seeing this huge addition to the city's cycling infrastructure.

As I expected, the cycle way is now a well-known and valued part of Sydney's off-road cycling facilities. But even that wonderful addition to the scope of the M7 would probably, in my view, have been deleted by Michael Costa. I am reliably told that within days of being appointed Minister for Roads, Costa demanded to know what it had costed. When informed by senior RTA personnel that the cycleway on the M7 cost $65M out of the $1.5B project, I am told Costa went apoplectic, storming about his office lamenting to every available staff member, at what he considered was a complete waste of money. I do wonder how Costa would have reacted when years later, I was told by the Leighton Contractors State Manager, that the figure of $65M was just an RTA estimate and that it had actually cost the company $140M to build. "We made money on the project, but we lost money on the cycleway" was his lament. But in my view, it was worth every dollar of the expenditure.

Final approval of the M7

The last hurdle to get the M7 built was what I regarded as a formal sign-off from the New South Wales Budget Committee of Cabinet. But the State Treasurer was having none of that.

Paul Forward as CEO of the RTA, Les Wielinga as Director of Motorway development and I, would never take for granted the approval of a major project tender by the Budget Committee and the M7 was certainly no different. We had put a Treasury representative on the tender assessment panel and he had helped us steer it through the senior leadership of Treasury. I met with the Secretary of Treasury and with his nod of approval, I formally submitted the Cabinet Minute for the next meeting of the Budget Committee.

I made one mistake here in assuming (usually correctly) that if the Secretary of Treasury was OK with something, then the Treasurer would automatically tick it off at Cabinet. Just as I started in to my well-prepared spiel which included: "Treasury has been fully briefed including the Secretary and they are in agreement with the recommendations" Egan leaned over to John Pierce, the Treasury Secretary and said: "Who the fuck do you think you are? Just because you say it's OK doesn't mean I'm going to." Egan then turned to me and the RTA and said: "You may have briefed Treasury, but I am not yet satisfied that this should be given my approval." As always, the ever capable Les Wielinga had brought with him every morsel of documents and diagrams. The Budget Committee adjourned for 45 minutes whilst the motorway guru convinced the Treasurer that approving the massive M7 motorway was a good idea.

I am convinced that Egan was just playing with me and would have had every intention of approving the project. He never went near a Budget Committee meeting without being fully briefed by Treasury, so I think he was just having some fun at our expense. Either way, we just about lost our breath when Egan threw a spanner in the works. It was approved that same afternoon, I was able to call the CEO of Leighton Contractors to inform him that his consortium had won the job and with that, my favourite project was off and running.

The M7 motorway weaving across the length and breadth of Western Sydney was a step change in the way thousands of people travel about their daily lives. It provided the catalyst for a dynamic growth in employment generating activities along its route, as well as a wonderful new park and an extensive addition to Sydney's cycle way network. It is a piece of infrastructure which will have lasting benefit for the people of Sydney for decades to come. It is my proudest legacy.

Costa kills off the M4 East Motorway

If the delivery of the M7 gives me the greatest pleasure out of my eight years in the roads portfolio, it was the decision of my ministerial successor to kill off the proposed M4 East which gives me the least pleasure.

The M4 East provided for the completion of the widening of the existing M4 to four lanes and to then extend it in tunnel to bypass at least seven sets of traffic lights on a very congested Parramatta Road.

By December 2004, I had spent nearly three years working up the M4 East as a serious PPP tollway project. I had worked closely with the RTA leadership, local communities and MPs, stakeholders and the agencies of government, over a sustained period, to get this project to the point of being able to release an Environmental Impact Statement (EIS), and to start a tender process by early 2005. Michael Costa was appointed Minister for Roads in late January 2005 and scuttled the whole project within one month of being appointed. And with it, went the last motorway of Labor in government.

When I heard Costa's announcement on the radio, it was the one and only time I was so upset with Carr, that I rang him and let rip for a full 20 minutes. Allowing Costa to kill off the project and the three years of effort put into it was not Carr's finest hour. All Carr could bring himself to say was: "Are you finished". I was, but little did I know then that it would take a full 10 years and a change of government to get this critical project for Western Sydney up and running again.

Costa had also only two years before, cancelled the Epping to Parramatta rail link, within just one month of being appointed Transport Minister. Both the M4 East motorway and the Epping to Parramatta Railway had been approved by Cabinet, but Costa would cancel both these mega projects without any reference to it. At least on M4 East, the Premier received a courtesy phone call which should have resulted in Carr telling his minister to go jump.

Both projects had taken years of careful preparation, consultation and determination to get them to the stage of being deliverable. Several millions of dollars of public money and countless hours of senior public servant time had been invested in working the projects up. They would have made invaluable improvements for both motorists and rail passengers. This was the end of Labor's building programme.

Heads of government usually exercise step-in rights when a portfolio is getting a tough time in the media, but they should also step-in to prevent much needed initiatives from disappearing. Bob Carr brought Costa into the Parliament, promoted him within days of his arrival to the ministry and then left him to his own devices. Carr should have ensured that these cancellation decisions were first put through the same rigorous Cabinet process I had to go through to get them approved in the first place. I am very confident that if Costa had been subjected to the same level of cabinet interrogation on cancelling this important project, as I had been in getting it approved, a very different outcome would have occurred. The community and the government's standing on delivering major public infrastructure, would have been the better for it. Perhaps then Costa may have been less inclined to boast when Treasurer: "The most joy I have had is stopping things from happening". It certainly would have made for an entertaining Cabinet to witness Costa having to justify to his colleagues why critical infrastructure should now be 'undelivered'. Planning and delivering is always much much harder than denigrating and halting.

Battling the Commonwealth Government

On a less serious note, I did have some fun in the portfolio. When Federal Minister for Transport, John Sharp and the seven other Liberal/National Party Roads Minister agreed to let heavier trucks onto our National Highway Network, as a prelude to wider access to State and Local roads across the country, I took them all on and won. I was then the only ALP Roads Minister in the country and had to almost threaten to impound trucking fleets on our borders to get the message through to them. I loved the battle and that they all blinked first in the face of my lone showmanship. But it was for a good cause. The extra weights would have caused a lot of damage to our roads and bridges without any indication of compensation – a typical Commonwealth tactic of coming up with noble policy initiatives provided the States paid for it. I had no intention of copping that and I didn't.

The Sydney Harbour Bridge Toll

But probably my most enjoyable lighter moment came late in my time as the Minister when I put up the Sydney Harbour Bridge toll from $2.20 to $3.00 to pay for much needed additional maintenance on a number of country roads. Whilst I was denigrated by the press, attacked by local Liberal MPs and well-heeled motorists from the much wealthier north side of Sydney, I did rather enjoy the Robin Hood approach of taking from a rich part of the city and giving to a poor part of the State. I would find out a little later, after the media reaction had died down, that a panicky Eric Roozendaal, then ALP General-Secretary, had quietly appealed to Carr to overturn my initiative. That appeal must have been given the contempt it deserved as Carr never raised the issue with me.

My time in the roads portfolio would be my most rewarding time as a minister. Working with the RTA was such a pleasure, especially seeing how responsive it was to the wishes and demands of Government on behalf of the community. The sheer size of the infrastructure we delivered together, fills me with much pride.

I still look back at my time in the job as perhaps the most productive and rewarding period of a long working life. There is not much I can think of during my 8 years as Roads Minister which I would not do all again.

Chapter 8: The Sydney Motorways

CHAPTER 9

Road safety – saving lives

Whilst my day-to-day work as Roads Minister was mostly solid hard work, I did get to do many regional trips to country New South Wales which I enjoyed very much. The communities and their local media were always appreciative when a minister fronted and even more so when funding and projects materialised in their midst.

Roads are the life blood of country towns and villages and there was no end of requests for projects which made a big difference. Life under the scrutiny of Sydney media was unpleasant at the best of times, so sealing dirt roads, replacing timber bridges, putting in place rail safety crossings, and witnessing how it all directly improved the lives of individual town folks, farmers and business people was always a welcome antidote.

Whilst building huge road projects filled a lot of my time, passion and commitment, it was road safety which troubled me the most. Just about every single working day of my entire time as Roads Minister, I was reminded of death, suffering and misery on our roads. I took every fatality to heart and would wonder every time if I had done more, could I have saved that life? Should I have been harder on penalties, spent more on shock and awe advertising, or delivered more infrastructure? I found the deaths of children and young people particularly distressing.

Death and complacency on our roads

At the end of a long day, I would always be given a folder full of stuff to look at on the hour-long drive home. There would be the diary for the next day and associated briefing notes for each meeting. Then a pile of media reports in which I had appeared or in which I had been mentioned during the day, and advice on what to expect on media issues for the next day or so. There would usually be a draft speech for an event, but always on top of the pile was the 'Fatality Tally Sheet'. Tired as I always was, I would always pause and reflect on the grieving families who would never recover from their tragedy and I would think if I was with them now, what would I say to them, and what would they say to me? What more could I have done? What more should I do now?

It is sad just how high community and media complacency has reached on road related deaths. 4,548 people died on New South Wales roads during my 8 years, 1 month and 25 days as Minister for Roads. In my first month in the job, December 1996, 50 died and in my last month, January 2005, 52 died. I only recall two issues which caused notable press, community and talkback radio response. The first involved a six-year old boy, on the last day of school, running across the road to his Mum, only to be run over by a four-wheel drive. It was an awful tragedy that tugged the heart strings of everyone who heard the story. To placate the demands for action and to minimise the risk of it occurring again, I introduced 40 km per hour speeds around schools which are still in force today. I also began trialling flashing lights and signage and ran a $20M Safer Routes to School programme designed to identify the safest way for every primary school kid to get to and from school.

The second involved a small group of teenagers who dropped a sizeable rock from an overpass on the Hume Highway which struck and killed a passing truck driver. A senseless death caused not by road conditions, but by murderous stupidity. The teenagers went to jail and a young family was devastated. I then authorised an extensive and expensive programme to install high wire mesh on all road and rail overpasses.

Apart from those two deaths, I do not recall a single other which was given anything other than passing media commentary. I was never once asked to submit a road safety proposal to Cabinet. No subcommittee of Cabinet was ever formed. And it was never an election issue. Despite hundreds dying every year, I was left alone. What a contrast to the Glenbrook and Waterfall train accidents which each killed seven people. The sky literally fell in when those accidents occurred, Judicial Commissions of Enquiry were established, rail safety and operations restructured and millions of dollars expended as a result. But even that contrasts with the seven rail maintenance workers who died on the tracks during a two-year period whilst I was Minister, barely rating a media mention. Raging white hot anger on rail passenger deaths, a boy on his way home from school and a truck driver doing his job, but almost nothing for literally thousands of road users and seven rail track workers.

To me, all lives mattered. If five to eight people died each week of almost anything else, the Government would be teetering on the edge, as community, media and the Opposition demanded answers and action. When two or three people get killed by shark attacks in a year the resulting media coverage is huge, government interest rises quickly to the highest levels, large funds are allocated and action plans put in place. What a contrast to the current road toll of between 300 and 400 which mostly attracts an annual

Chapter 9: Road safety

December commentary of either a "gee the road toll has gone up a bit' or an 'aren't we doing well to get the road toll down' sort of response.

I am still astonished at the appalling attitude of a very senior tabloid journalist who had been excoriating me for almost personally causing the 7 Waterfall passenger rail deaths. In January 2003, I said to him: 'In the last 50 years there have been 183 passenger rail deaths across the country. Do you know how many road deaths there have been during the same period?' And he replied: 'a million, who cares'. I then said: 'it is actually well above 100,000' to which he left me speechless: 'so what' was his reply. And that alone sums up how and why the community, the media and government are not outraged by the level of death and suffering on our roads. Such an outrage if it ever developed, would demand that cars travelling at 70km per hour or more would never pass another vehicle coming at the same speed in the opposite direction with less than a metre between them and no barrier. It is no accident that our divided dual carriageway motorways are our safest roads. Modern motor vehicle technology with cameras and drones could be used today to control vehicle interactions, limit the speed of vehicles in certain circumstances or render them inoperable with any lack of seat belt wearing, alcohol non-compliance or obvious fatigue impairment. Autonomous or remotely controlled vehicles could be the next silver bullet in driving the road toll down.

However, all this would require such a major realignment of focus on road safety policy, research and expenditure as to be unlikely given the current community and media stupor on the issue. It would also require a New South Wales Government driven national approach with the automotive industry ensuring that New South Wales again became the lead state on road safety policy. This could be effectively done with a joint State / Commonwealth / industry and motoring stakeholder statutory authority with power and funds to drive initiative and change. It would save lives and lift road safety policy and regulation well above and beyond their current sterile and unimaginative bureaucratic domain.

In the late 1940s, Prime Minister Ben Chifley and Premier William McKell established the Joint Coal Board to address the appalling safety record of the underground coal industry. This continues to this day as Coal Services NSW and does great work for the safety of our coal miners.

A similar initiative is needed to deal with what should also be regarded as our appalling road safety record. It would cost billions to do properly but motorists are already across the country, paying billions every year in fuel excise charges, accumulated every time they fill the tank. Only a small fraction of that finds its way back into road infrastructure and black spot remedial action projects. But community anger and a vehement articulation of it would be the necessary precursor to such a wonderful initiative. I doubt we will ever see either.

Bicycle and motorcycle interaction with cars, trucks and buses on a daily basis are simply time bombs waiting for the next unnecessary fatality. In a road safety regime serious about dealing with the road toll, restrictions would be placed on both, not because they ride or drive unsafely, but because there is next to no protection in the event of a collision with a motor vehicle. Banning motorbikes from main roads in peak times and bicycles from all main roads at all times would considerably reduce the 70 bicycle and motorcycle fatalities each year. But, this is unlikely to ever happen, as bicycle rights advocates would go feral leaving these unnecessary deaths to continue. It still perplexes me how

Chapter 9: Road safety

otherwise rational beings can hop on a bike and chance their lives on main roads or in peak hour traffic.

The Glenbrook rail accident of December 1999, killed 7 people. That same month 50 people died on our roads and a further 603 died in the following year. In the same month of the Waterfall rail accident, January 2003, 42 people died on our roads and 539 in the following year. The contrast is palpable and so is the level of disinterest and complacency on our roads deaths.

No-one would suggest that our governments should lower the enormous effort and expenditure on counter-terrorism. However, the likelihood of being killed in a motor vehicle collision is astronomically greater than from an act of terrorism. Perhaps just a small extra focus from government on a far greater killer, might actually bring greater benefit to the community.

Despite the lack of community and media interest and their perplexing level of complacency, I took my job as Minister for Road Safety seriously. I decided that if no one was going to put pressure on me, then I would do so myself. I was determined to do all I could to get the road toll down and to keep the pressure on the RTA to achieve that. And the RTA took the issue as seriously as I did.

Double demerit points

One of the road safety initiatives I am most proud of introducing was the 'Double Demerit Points for speeding offences', which was put to the test over the Easter weekend of 1998. That particular weekend, motorists slowed down and instead of the usual 18 to 20 road fatalities we had always expected, there were just three. That meant that at least 15 people were alive at the end of the weekend than would have otherwise been the case. Of course, we did not know who they were, but they were alive and that was one of the most gratifying experiences I would ever have in politics. It was another initiative I had run with, not on endless briefing papers and policy analysis, but on a gut-feel that it would work and it did. It was this initiative and not monetary fines that saved lives. I had made a real difference. I then decided to make Double Demerits a fixture of every holiday weekend from then on, which in due course would also be implemented nationally.

Digital speed cameras

The police highway patrol cannot physically patrol any more than a small percentage of our roads at any one time. They do a great job but with limited resources. I decided to use modern technology to effectively create 24/7 digital highway patrol officers at certain fixed points known as accident black spots. The introduction of initially 25 digital speed cameras, later increased to 50, had an immediate positive impact. At these locations, dangerous speeding disappeared saving lives and avoiding serious injuries, but drivers still went modestly over the limit incurring enough fines to pay Treasury back the $50M cost and some. My attempts to hypothecate speed camera revenue to road safety were vigorously resisted by Egan and John Pearce, the Treasury Secretary. But the claim they were revenue raising initiatives were irritatingly wrong. I proposed them, the RTA acquired them and the Treasury funded them. Not one red cent ever went to the RTA. But they were effective and soon began to appear around the country.

Graduated licensing for young drivers

Young drivers were figuring far too much in fatalities not for aggressive hoon-like behaviour, but simply because they were inexperienced. I asked the RTA to develop a programme, where young drivers would not be just handed their provisional licence after a road test and a quick knowledge test, and then given a full licence after a year. I wanted these youngsters to have a longer drawn out process of tuition whilst learning, and then be required to show some acquired aptitude before getting their full licence. The Graduated Licence Programme from Learner to Provisional to Full Licence I think has made young drivers a lot safer on our roads. No one asked me to implement it, but I worried deeply about how easy it was for young people to get a licence, and then how easy it could be for them to get into trouble. My own kids were approaching learner driver age and I wanted them to be part of something safer.

When it was all introduced, friends of both my son James and daughter Sarah, when around at our house, would take the opportunity to give me a polite dig for making it harder for them. I would always say: "I think your parents will be glad even if you are not." It too in time would be implemented across other jurisdictions.

The Sea Cliff Bridge

I did have a few more scrapes on major road issues before my eight years in the job was done. One which stands out above all others, was Lawrence Hargrave Drive now much better known as Sea Cliff Bridge. Those who take notice of TV car commercials will now see a modern vehicle zipping around a very picturesque ocean bridge just south of Sydney. Few will know its chequered history.

The Lawrence Hargrave Drive had been originally constructed in the 1870s to allow traffic from Sydney to drive along the coast through Heathcote and on the way to Wollongong. It was not a road which had come much to my attention, except as a scenic route to the next large urban centre just south of Sydney. That all changed when a few years into my term as Roads Minister, there were reports of an increasing number of rock falls onto the road from the cliff face above, which ran along a section of the roadway.

The RTA had commissioned an expert to have a look at what might be causing this and to recommend any necessary remedial action. The report found that amongst other things, water seeped into the cliff face and supporting rock structures after rainfall, dramatically increasing the risk of rock falls.

The report had a clear recommendation that when a certain level of measured rain fell in the area that for a period of time the road should be closed. Both the RTA and I accepted this recommendation and advised the local community of these safety measures.

Not long afterwards, when rain fell, the measurement equipment picked up the offending amount of water, and we closed the road for a short period. Many of the locals were more than a little upset and started complaining loudly about the RTA being unnecessarily heavy handed about it.

My good mate, David Campbell, who was one of the affected MPs asked me to come down and have another look. What we found was alarming. The road looked unstable and in one spot a large crack had appeared on the side of one section of the road.

We met with the locals who demanded that a proper expert review the 'questionable' findings in the consultant's report. I agreed to do this and it became a timely reminder to them: Be careful what you wish for!

The RTA soon after arranged for a recognised expert in the field to review the recommendations on closing the road after certain levels of rainfall. I shared the suspicion that the original report may have overcooked the safety concerns a little and an expert review would probably tone that down somewhat. How wrong we all were. The report found that the likelihood of major rock falls onto the road below was so high that the road needed to be immediately closed.

As soon as the RTA leadership brought this to my attention, I directed the road to be closed and informed the community of the reasons. I also asked the RTA to urgently come up with options on the way forward. As expected, the community was even angrier than before. But I knew I had to stick to the RTA's position. To do otherwise, would have put people's lives and safety at risk and of course, put us all in a very difficult legal position if someone was killed or seriously injured after we had chosen to leave the road open. I wanted to believe that the locals would have known this, but if they did, they certainly didn't seem to care.

On one reckless Saturday morning, a large crowd of locals put on a protest march, pulled away the wire fence across the closed road and marched across in defiance to hold an angry meeting on the other side of the closed section of the road.

Amazingly, just after they had walked through, a boulder the size of a small family car had fallen off the cliff face and landed slap bang in the middle of the road where they had all passed only an hour before.

The media who had followed the protest were incredulous and ran the line that maybe the road should be closed for public safety. The best the leader of the protest group could come up with was: "Carl Scully got the RTA to do this." I didn't even bother to respond. It was clear from this episode that we had made the right call and that the local protest no longer had any credibility.

The RTA looked at all manner of options including bracing and reinforcing the cliff areas, but came to the view that the only way to ensure 100% safety was to build a new ocean bridge away from where rocks could fall and close that section of the road permanently. I baulked at the estimated $47M cost and asked Paul Forward where on earth we were going to get that from, given that we well knew that Treasury would never fund it.

Forward advised that he believed the RTA could take the $47M out of the following two-year State road maintenance funds by slightly reducing the amounts we would normally spend in a whole range of places across the State. I agreed to this and the RTA then went to work in earnest in delivering another first-class piece of public infrastructure. In the design, I added a cycleway/pedestrian walkway that sits underneath the bridge, which I am told is now well appreciated by the local community.

I do look back with pride at what we delivered just south of Sydney. It is a beautiful, safe structure which showed the RTA at its best!

Seat belts and the Premier

During my long stint as Roads Minister, I was always acutely aware of just how senseless and avoidable deaths or serious injuries were as a result of drivers and/or passengers not wearing a seat belt. As a young 20-year-old university student, I had experienced first-hand what that could have been like. One night on my way home from Macquarie University during an awful storm, I hit a large pond which had built up across Lady Game Drive near Lindfield. My car aquaplaned off the road and

Chapter 9: Road safety

slammed into a large tree. The result was that my Dad's much loved and well-maintained Holden was a write off, I suffered a broken knee cap, had to have 17 stitches on my forehead and had deep seat belt bruising across my chest. But, I lived through it for one simple reason – I was wearing a seat belt.

I found the estimated 50 fatalities a year on our roads solely caused by not wearing a seat belt as something I was compelled to do something about. Education, enforcement and fines were the order of the day.

When I berated non-seat belt wearers in the New South Wales Parliament and expressed disbelief that any motorist could be so stupid, Channel 7 ran a primetime TV news story with video footage of the Premier doing just that the night before in a police vehicle doing the rounds with some coppers. Ouch! I called Carr for a mea culpa and he was generous: "It was my fault. You were just doing your job."

Now, 12 years after I left the roads portfolio, the road toll is lower than when I had the job, but the level of complacency is not. Maybe one day, the community, shock jocks on talkback radio and the tabloid press will be as outraged about the road toll as I think they should be. But that may unfortunately, be a long time coming.

CHAPTER 10

Connecting communities – anecdotes along the way

Perhaps the most rewarding part of my long stint in the roads portfolio was the interaction with rural, regional and remote communities across New South Wales.

In fact, dealing with the Sydney media during my concurrent five-year period as minister responsible for the City Rail Network, as well as the major urban road issues of the time, was a constant energy draining exercise. It was always a very pleasant break to regularly get good old-fashioned country hospitality. Even interacting with the country media was a pleasant event as none of them seemed to be infected with the snarling city desire to attack and denigrate at every opportunity.

There is no doubt that roads are the lifeblood of country communities and my portfolio was of critical significance to them. In the more remote municipalities, the maintenance funds allocated to councils to administer some roads on behalf of the RTA, could in some cases, be as high as 80% of their total revenue.

Railways or 'iron roads' as they used to call them, combined with the advent of the steam engine, had from the 1850s to the early few decades of the 20th Century, taken country and remote transportation from the horse and buggy era into the modern age of connectivity with major urban centres and significant mobility within and between country centres. The age of isolation had ended.

The age of the railway as the lifeblood of country communities gradually declined from the 1940s with the slowly, but ever-increasing spread of trucking transportation and of course, the motor vehicle. The 1970s through to the early 1990s saw the mass closure of unproductive rail lines, as the hardly efficient publicly-owned freight rail services could not compete with the flexibility and efficiencies of trucking fleets. The golden era of country passenger rail services had long gone by the time I was elevated to the Cabinet and had been replaced by the car or the long-haul coach.

All this meant that when the Roads Minister came to town, what he or she had to say, mattered very much to these communities. If rail was nostalgic to them as a relic of a bygone era, then roads were an essential part of their fabric. As an infrastructure history buff, I clearly understood the tremendous role that public infrastructure played as the 'heart and soul' of those communities.

Even now across New South Wales, there are many well-preserved sandstone government structures such as court houses, police stations, and bridges over local rivers, which were all installed in the 1800s. Such installations demonstrated the reach of government administrative presence, power and commitment to those remote communities. Such structures were usually complimented by a large sandstone church and then in time, the railway.

Whenever I was considering the allocation of funds to a rural or remote community, I would sometimes visualise the Colonial Secretary in London or after 1856, the self-governing colony in New South Wales, consciously allocating public funds to build these structures as a way to ensure that government had arrived and was there to stay. It must have been reassuring for the locals who would have been living in quite isolated circumstances.

In the 1990s and to this day, country communities needed to know that government all the way back in Sydney cared and worried about their plight. They asked and expected to see government express this care and concern, not in stone, not in iron or steam, but in bitumen. And the more bitumen the better.

There are a many stories and anecdotes during this time in my favourite portfolio and a few are listed below.

The Shires Conference

The Local Government Conference for Urban and Regional Councils was held annually and I was always invited. It tended to be a little testy, as there were always enough councils with some card-carrying Tories who wanted to use the event to score a political point with an ALP Minister for Roads. Attending was part of what I was required to do. Some were productive and some were not.

But what I particularly loved doing, was attending the Annual Shires Conference held in Sydney's Sheraton on the Park Hotel for all the rural and country councils. It was the signature event of the year for the Mayors, Councillors and General Managers of the State's remote municipalities.

Chapter 10: Connecting communities

When I turned up at my first conference to start one of the day's proceedings at 8.30 am, I was expecting a small show and not a great deal of interest. Wow! There must have been 500 in the hall already seated with every rural council in the State well represented.

I gave the usual routine kind of speech which ministers give at those types of events and let it be known that I was happy to take questions. I couldn't believe what I was seeing and hearing – genuine, heartfelt concern for their communities and how just a little additional road funding would help was both moving and convincing.

But the real surprise was not the productive and mature way in which the questions were canvassed, it was the sheer number lining up behind every microphone queuing up to put their case. I undertook to do what I could to get around to as many of those communities as I could, to learn for myself about their situation which would enable me to better prioritise expenditure rather than just rely on an RTA brief.

After three or four years of doing just that, I felt confident enough to dispense with the speech at the annual conference and just open it for questions for over an hour. The shires loved it and so did I. At one conference, I informed the delegates that a condition of asking me a question was that they had to first let the conference know what I had done for their community, to thank me for it and then to ask their question. It was good fun, great sportsmanship and everyone got to hear what a Labor Government was doing for the country.

I worked the country hard, engaged with as many stakeholders as I could and regularly visited with commitments, which were then delivered in full. I wanted the conference to reflect on the work we had done and not just on what more we needed to do. It was a good arrangement.

The Mayor of Cobar, Lillian Brady, who I got on very well with, was an outstanding mayor and significant local farmer. Lillian came up to me at one conference just before I was about to start and suggested some mischief for the both of us with a pre-arranged routine to lighten things up a little. She was a legend at these conferences and had been around for some time. When her time came to ask me a question on behalf of the good folks of Cobar Shire, I quickly piped in as agreed with: "Lillian, aren't you looking terrific" and as agreed she quick as a flash responded with: "Minister, I don't want your romance. I want your finance." It brought the house down. Every single delegate and country media outlet loved it too and it got a fantastic run around the conference and in country media. I was seen as good natured in copping a whack from the maestro herself, and she was seen as sticking up for local shires. Good stuff all round. I don't think either of us fessed up about orchestrating the exchange until now.

One of the many Urban and Regional Council Annual Conferences I attended one year was held at Coffs Harbour. My Campaign Director and head of my local ALP 'Praetorian Guard', Anwar Khoshaba, was in attendance in his capacity as a Councillor of Fairfield City Council. After I had concluded an exhaustive Question and Answer session I finished off with: "If anyone of you still has things you would like brought to my attention, my Campaign Director, Anwar Khoshaba is here. Please talk to him about any issues you would like him to pass on to me." This worked a treat and gave me a good chuckle, as before I had even left the stage, I could see a large swarm of Mayors, Councillors and GMs already milling around my man. Anwar told me later that he loved every minute of it.

Chapter 10: Connecting communities

The demise of Ray Chappell

Ray Chappell was the serving National Party MP for the seat of New England which centred on the regional city of Armidale. He had dudded me big time when he had left me to bear the full brunt of a large irate crowd of local businessmen angry about the loosening up of shop trading hours for large supermarkets. Chappell excused himself from the meeting as he was leaving on an overseas trip the next day, and said he needed the time to pack his bags. Given the unbridled anger I had to absorb from his local constituents, I thought it was poor form from a local MP towards a visiting minister.

Unexpectedly, a few years later when I had moved onto the roads portfolio, an important road issue in his electorate provided an irresistible opportunity to return the favour leading up to the 1999 election.

Richard Torbay was the Independent Mayor of Armidale and Chairman of the Country Mayor's Association. He had a terrific profile, but a Labor brand in wall to wall National Party territory would simply fail politically. In a fantastic stunt in front of his local media, he had found some excuse to express disgust with the Carr Government and tore up his party ticket and threw it in the bin. It worked a treat in convincing the good folk of Armidale that they had a genuine Independent candidate for the next State Election. It was pure theatre!

Torbay had a huge following in Armidale, but was not well known around the Glen Innis area where he needed to take a swag of votes off the National Party if he had any hope of winning a seat in Parliament. Enter stage right – the roads portfolio.

Setting the Record Straight | Carl Scully

John Anderson, the Federal Minister for Transport and Deputy Prime Minister had announced a cutback in maintenance funds for the New England Highway. The RTA advised that as a result, we would need to lay off a number of employees at the Glen Innis depot as there would now be little work for them. I duly announced this and roundly blamed the Federal Government for forcing my hand.

The reaction around Glen Innis was swift. The community was very angry about the impact of losing these jobs on their local economy. There was a lot of local coverage about it.

Torbay and I then discussed a course of action, where he would get heavily involved in his capacity as Chair of the Country Mayors Association and I gave him a green light to rip in to me as much as possible and demand the overturning of the decision to lay off the workers. At the same time, I gave Chappell a whack in Parliament and his local paper ran with it on its front page: "Chappell a Bozo says Minister." Torbay and I thought it was terrific although I am sure Mr Chappell did not enjoy it.

Torbay then publicly demanded that he lead a delegation of the two local mayors, to put the case that I should reverse my decision. The three of them came down to my Parliament office and I told the mayors that owing to the very strong campaign which Mr Torbay had run and notwithstanding the Federal Government's disinterest, I would keep the workers on and direct the RTA to find them other work. They were ecstatic and I could see the glint in Torbay's eye saying: "Minister, we have done well."

They all flew back to Armidale that evening and when the plane landed they could see a throng of local media present to record the event. Torbay switched to showman and had all three of them stop at the top of the steps of the plane with a thumbs up sign in the air for a 'peace in our time' sort of moment. The only problem was that there were six fists, but only five thumbs. Torbay said to the offending Mayor: "Where's your thumb?" and got a wonderful response: "I lost it years ago in a sawing accident."

In a great irony of politics, an issue initiated by the Federal National Party Minister for Transport, John Anderson, had unwittingly given us both a great narrative to undermine the local State National Party MP. Chappell never recovered from that blow and only made matters worse by saying: "I wasn't invited to the meeting." It had been a superbly orchestrated pincer movement on the local MP and the National Party's hold on the seat. The local MP had been left looking isolated and ineffective.

Torbay came out looking strong, effective and dogged for his community and most importantly had come across as an independent who could work with the Labor Government in getting results for his community. The whole drawn-out story on the future of the Glen Innis RTA jobs had been on reflection a long campaign launch. At the end, Torbay was on top and the local MP never really recovered.

Torbay was duly elected as the Independent MP for Armidale and Ray Chappell quickly disappeared into obscurity. Torbay credited the campaign on the Glen Innis RTA jobs as a critical component of his win.

The road with no cars

Torbay was always on campaign mode and in my view, probably the best country MP to work his electorate. One of the many road issues we worked on together was the sealing of the Guyra to Ebor Road. It was a local road and therefore the full responsibility of Guyra Council to fund and maintain, but the $3M cost was always going to be beyond its financial capacity.

The RTA always resisted my many 'special grants' but I insisted and went all the way to the local Guyra Council chambers with Torbay to inform the Council of my decision. Torbay and I with the Mayor and the General Manager, went out on to the road to do the announcement for the local media, which included the local TVs. What worried me was that we had spent just over an hour before, during and after the event and not one single vehicle had passed us going in either direction. After the media had left, I said to Torbay: "Where are the cars? Does anyone use this road?" I was unconvinced by the response and began to wonder if I was overreaching in making this guy look good.

Tony McGrane

Tony McGrane was a physically huge, popular and larger-than-life figure in the wider Dubbo region. It had been assumed that the ageing local National Party MP, Gerry Peacocke, would retire at the 1999 election providing a great opportunity to test the Dubbo electorate's interest in a change of the type of local member it would like to have.

McGrane had seen the stunt which Torbay had delivered in tearing-up his ALP ticket as he announced his candidacy as an Independent at the upcoming election. The only problem was that McGrane wanted to run as an ALP candidate and become part of the Labor Government team.

He sought my advice and I was typically blunt: "Tony, there is no way the Dubbo community will ever vote for an ALP candidate even if their lives depended on it. They just won't. If you

Chapter 10: Connecting communities

want to be an MP, then you have to do what Torbay did. Tear up your ALP membership ticket and run as an Independent."

He was unconvinced so for effect I added: "I am absolutely convinced that if you run for the ALP you will not win and if you continue in that vein, then I will not lift a finger to help you as it would just be a waste of my time. But if you do get elected as an Independent, then I will do all I can to ensure your re-election in 2003."

McGrane took advice from others and then duly ran as an Independent, but not before doing the Torbay stunt with his ALP membership ticket. He won the seat at the 1999 election by a mere 14 votes. I think I got that one right. To be part of taking two safe National Party seats from right under their noses and see them vested successfully in Labor 'independents' gave me great pleasure.

As promised, I became a regular visitor and did my very best to make the new MP look effective for his local community and connected as an Independent to a 'broad church' Labor Government in Sydney. Three stories are worth telling.

The Geurie level crossing

Tony had asked me to come out to one of the small towns in his electorate called Geurie, to talk to a number of constituents about the need for a safe crossing over the railway line which regularly had trains running through the main part of town.

I met at the crossing with about 30 local residents, including the local school principal, some school kids, and a few small businessmen. I listened as they put their case for the funds needed to make a much safer place to cross the rail line. As was often the case, I wanted to mull over it, get the local MP to get as indignant as he could about the need for this, and then I would relent under the pressure and approve the funding. I did this a thousand times as a minister, enabling both the community to get what they needed and the local MP getting plenty of publicity in facilitating it.

An angry MP was always much better copy for the local media than a once only visit from a minister to hand over funds. At the end of their exchange, I said: "Thank you for the opportunity of meeting you today. I can clearly see this is an issue which needs addressing. As you would expect, I get many demands on my budget, so I will need to get advice, give it consideration against the many other priorities in my portfolio and come back to you with a decision."

I was used to folks at these sorts of town meetings accepting that this was a reasonable process and happy that they had met with a minister who was sympathetic to their situation. But on this occasion, I got an unexpected response and drew on some advice my driver had given me when I first became a minister.

Joel Donaghy, had driven Paul Keating when he was Federal Treasurer as well as numerous heavyweights like National Party icon, Ian Sinclair, before moving to the State ministerial driver's pool. He had also driven Wendy Machin leading up to the 1995 election. He was Irish, profane, assertive and fiercely loyal. I enjoyed very much our 10 years together before he retired due to ill health.

Joel had learnt a lot indeed at the feet of some of this nation's master politicians. I saw him as much more than a driver and someone I sometimes ran things past. On occasion, he would share his thoughts on certain issues. Most of the time though, he left me alone to work on the phone or buried in briefing papers.

Early on, he proffered three pieces of very good advice:

> *"You are a minister today and tomorrow you are not.*
> *Make sure you enjoy the journey on the way through,*
> *as one day it will all be gone."*

This was certainly true enough, although it was hard at times to 'enjoy' the job and after eight or nine years in it, I did feel like it would go on and on. The end was sudden and unexpected.

> *"When you run out of budget, just get more budget"*

I certainly tried to live by this one as much as possible and drove both the Treasurer and Treasury nuts in assuming I could always drive the Government out of trouble by just spending more money. Joel loved hearing about all my combat stories with Treasury.

> *"If anyone ever asks you for an immediate response to*
> *a request, you should always say "no" on the spot."*

This last one was one I had never really explored with Joel and for several years as a minister, I had never been put in the position of being asked for an instantaneous response. That is, until the town meeting at Geurie railway crossing.

As soon as I announced that I would take on board what they had said and give it consideration back in Sydney, a local standing at the front of the pack pronounced: "Minister that is not good enough." I asked: "What? You don't want me to get advice on this, to think it over and then come back to you with a considered decision?"

He fired back quick as a flash: "No, we want a decision now!" I then remembered the advice Joel had given me all those years before, and I thought now was the time to apply it: "Well, in that case my decision is 'no', you will get no allocation of funds and no upgraded crossing."

It was amazing then to see this demanding local enveloped by the crowd and pushed to the rear and told to shut up. I loved it. A number of locals then asked that I do as I had originally intended, and in due course the local MP did in fact announce the funds to upgrade the crossing. Both Tony Kelly, who was there as Chairman of Country Labor and Tony McGrane himself, spent many a parliamentary night, retelling the story to the great amusement of all who would listen.

The Renshaw – McGirr Way

Of perhaps even greater amusement to many of us, was that with the arrival of a Labor Government in Sydney, the very politically conservative community of the Central West of New South Wales, had taken it on themselves, to rename the road from Parkes to Wellington from a boring and non-descript main road number to "The Renshaw-McGirr Way".

They had picked two former Labor Premiers who had had long associations with country New South Wales and knew enough about internal Labor Party history and politics, to fully realise that we honoured, valued and celebrated our icons of the past. Whoever came up with the idea needs to be acknowledged. It was a masterstroke. Neither the local community nor the local MP realised just how much I had to resist the desire to give immediate funding to seal the entire length of this new 'Labor road'.

Chapter 10: Connecting communities

The road was in poor shape and during my time, we were able to fully seal and upgrade this link. I did feel a bit positioned, but I did not mind too much as it was a good thing we were doing for the locals. I was very pleased a few years later at the opening of the completed upgrade when a local farmer came up to me and said: "Minister, I am embarrassed to say this. I have been a member of the Liberal Party for many years and for a time, I was on its State Executive. I have lived out here for 30 years now and what I have witnessed in these last few years is that a Labor Government has done more for us than both the National Party and Liberal Party combined in the last 30 years." This made me feel very proud that someone from within the heart and soul of our political enemies could say such a thing. I loved using the roads portfolio as a platform for continuous campaigning in both the city and the country. This guy's very nice comment made me realise that there were great rewards in this challenging job.

Tony McGrane was almost as good as Torbay in using his connection with the Labor Government in delivering for his community. I often wondered how both the Government and these Independents got away with the arrangement for so long.

If local folks were in on the joke, nobody said anything and I like to think that if they did realise what we were up to politically, then they probably would not mind, as long as Government largesse kept coming their way. I saw it as providing two very conservative communities the means by which they could be represented in a Labor Government without actually be asked to do the unthinkable – vote for the ALP.

Main Road 354

Main Road 354 runs from Dubbo out to the town of Narromine and early in my term as Minister for Roads, was substantially a dirt road. I liked McGrane and his rural community and over the years, I would regularly visit and either open new sections of sealed road or make funding commitments for more.

On one occasion, I was unable to make the trip, but two of my staffers including Gary Sargent did so on my behalf. I still have the photo of McGrane with my two staffers next to one of my MR 354 plaques, holding a cloth and can of cleaning fluid, with the caption written by McGrane himself: 'Giving Carl a polish'. Priceless.

The Copmanhurst Approach

Bob Carr like a lot of heads of government, liked to hold community Cabinet meetings to demonstrate the Government's interest and commitment to regional and rural New South Wales. At one point, after I had been Minister for a while, he decided to hold a Cabinet meeting in the Grafton Council Chambers in the heart of the electorate of Clarence, about an hour's drive from Coffs Harbour on the State's North Coast.

It was not often that I would get the flu, but on this particular week I had a fairly bad bout of it and I called the Premier the afternoon prior to the Cabinet meeting to seek his permission to miss the meeting. He insisted I attend: "I'm sorry Carl, but I have six ministers already away and I need you to attend. There are just too many who will be away."

As was usually the case when a country Cabinet meeting had concluded its business, there was a long line of petitioners who wished to meet with the Minister for Roads. On this occasion, I was joined by Les Wielinga, who was then based at Grafton and Head of the massive Pacific Highway Programme.

Chapter 10: Connecting communities

After about four or five drawn-out meetings with Mayors and General Managers putting up all kinds of road related requests, I had had enough and wanted to finish up and go home to bed and try to recover as quickly as possible. Then another petitioner plopped down on the seat at the table in front of me, and announced that he was the Mayor of Copmanhurst Council and was accompanied by his General Manager and his Head of Engineering.

As I was somewhat short of my normal levels of patience and charm and not feeling too good, I blurted out: "Where the hell is Copmanhurst?" The Mayor without seeming offended, politely responded by explaining that it was near to another place which I had never heard of in the far north east of the State.

I responded: "Look I have no idea where that is either, but how can I help. I see you have a submission." The Mayor talked at length about some detailed work the council staff had done on their road needs, which was well beyond the capacity of council to afford and needed a special grant of $1M to assist them in implementing their upgrade programme.

The meeting and the request were typical of countless others I had already done as minister and typical of countless more I would do in the future. But on this day, I was not in a mood for reading submissions so I said to the Mayor: "I'm not feeling very well Mr Mayor, so I will do you a deal. You keep your report and never ask me again to read it and I will give you an extra $500,000 over the next two financial years or you can ask me to take your report and read it, which I will do, but I will then give you nothing. Which one would you like to take?" I couldn't believe what happened next. Quicker than an Olympic 100 metre sprint final, he reached across the table, grabbed the report sitting in front of me and exclaimed firmly: "Minister, there is no need for you to ever read this report. We will be delighted to take the funds you have now offered and very much appreciate your generosity and wish you a speedy recovery." I leaned over to Les Wielinga and said loud enough for the Mayor to hear: "Les, make sure in our next budget that we have a figure of $250,000 as per my commitment" and that was it. An unusual way in which to treat a delegation, but they all went away very happy.

The Moree to Mungindi Road

Wal Murray was the Deputy Premier and Leader of the National Party in the Greiner administration, as well as Minister for Roads. A huge man and a dominant character both in the bush and in Parliament. He was well respected on our side of politics and seen as effective on bush politics.

He had allegedly promised his local electorate if he didn't seal the Moree to Mungindi Road up towards a remote part of the border with Queensland, he would run through the main town of Moree naked. It would have been a safe bet for him given that he was Minister for Roads and Local MP when he made the alleged commitment. Except as is often the case, events took the better of that lofty promise.

The Nyngan Flood of 1990 had caused havoc to local road infrastructure across the State's North West, requiring a significant diversion of country and city road maintenance funds just to get all these roads back into a reasonable condition. It meant that the sealing of the road from Moree to Mungindi was put off and soon enough Wal was out of the portfolio and out of Parliament.

Whilst I did concentrate on visits in the country to Labor or Independent-held seats, I did try to also regularly visit National Party 'Tiger' country areas. It was important to demonstrate to these communities that their voice would also be heard across the political aisle. I loved the sound of the alleged Wal commitment and it intrigued me enough to take a drive along the road. I found a gravel road in mediocre condition, but not terrible either. However, the road would become almost impassable with a solid rainfall. I decided to see if we could fit the additional cost of sealing it into our forward budgets. I also asked around about Wal's promise and I got enough positive feedback to suggest that there were legs to the story. That alone, was almost enough to justify a bit of fun at the expense of the National Party whilst still delivering for their community.

I returned a few months later to a gathering of about 400 local residents in a large town hall in Moree, who had all been enticed to attend with an open invitation to come and discuss the issue with me in a public forum. I was delighted with both the community and media turnout. I told the crowd that I had seen the road for myself, agreed that it was an awful stretch of mud in the wet and that they had made a convincing case for sealing it.

I then announced that I had personally approved the necessary funds to enable the sealing to be put in place. Like any minister of any time addressing a town hall of petitioners, it was great to hear the cheers and handclapping which immediately followed. And it gave me great pleasure in then reminding them that their local MP, Wal Murray, had been the Minister for Roads and had not delivered it, but that I would. And I enjoyed it even more when I reminded everyone of his promise to run through the town naked: "Wal, we know it may not be pretty, but I want to see it. Are you here today?" I think the local folks enjoyed it all as much as I did.

Calling the bluff

Local councils never have enough money to pay for major upgrades of their local road network and many became what would in other circumstances be called 'bait and pull' experts.

Council engineering staff were always able to produce a report demonstrating that only a modest commitment of State Government funds over a few years would enable their dream road to become a reality. On more than a few occasions with the funding and work under way, the budget would be found to be way too little and surprise, the council would in due course plead: "please sir, can I have some more" to get the job finished.

After a few years of this, I became a little wary of any council report alleging works could be done for any particular amount. I started to treat them as their way to what they regarded as 'the magic pudding' of the RTA road budget.

By the time the Mayor of the Great Lakes Shire Council, covering the wider Forster area on the mid north New South Wales coast, asked for a meeting to request funding for a new realigned Lakes Way running from the Pacific Highway to the coast, I had the RTA first do a confidential detailed study on the likely real cost of the project. They came up with a figure of $14M.

I wish we had taken a video clip of the subsequent meeting. When the mayor ceremoniously presented the official report of his engineering department claiming a cost of $6M only, I saw an opportunity to have a bit of fun by calling his bluff and offering the mayor what he had come all the way to Sydney seeking.

I said to the mayor: "This is a good project and one I fully support and I am prepared to make a special grant of the full cost of $6M to get the job done, but on two very important conditions. First, council will need to sign under your hand a Deed of Agreement with the RTA that if the $6M is not enough then council will be fully responsible for the cost of completing the project. And second, the council is to agree that when the road is built, it will be classified as a local road under the full responsibility of council to maintain."

The mayor looked more than a little sheepish, a bit like a kid caught with his hand in the lolly jar and meekly responded: "Thank you Minister. I will need to discuss this with my council colleagues and come back to you".

I never heard from him again! In late November 2016, I again had the opportunity of driving the still un-realigned Lakes Way and had some fun recalling this classic 'take the bait' pitch from local government of many years before

Stymying Clover Moore

Clover Moore as Independent Mayor of the Council of the City of Sydney had received many protests from residents in Paddington complaining about excessive traffic on their local streets from motorists attempting to avoid the congestion on Oxford Street.

Oxford Street was my responsibility as a State road and the local streets and council voters were clearly the responsibility and worry of the Lord Mayor. Instead of requesting a discussion on achieving a good balance between neighbourhood quiet enjoyment and the needs of through traffic, the Lord Mayor announced unilaterally that speed and traffic restrictions would soon be installed on local streets.

This was great for local residents, but a poor outcome for scores of motorists who would be forced back onto an already congested Oxford Street. I then decided on what I still regard as a beautiful pincer movement which both protected the needs of motorists and reminded the mayor of just who was in charge of the road network. I signed a decree withdrawing the local road delegations to every single council across the State and then re-issued them providing that no alteration to a local street could be made without the written consent of the RTA. On cue, the Lord Mayor let rip. Marvellous! RTA 1 Lord Mayor 0.

The Tugun Bypass

In early 1998, I was invited to speak at a conference on the Gold Coast and the Queensland National Party Minister for Roads asked to meet up with me about a proposal to divert congested traffic on the border into New South Wales and around the edge of Coolangatta Airport.

Tugun is an urban centre in South East Queensland which runs right up to the border. It was a marginal seat in Queensland and of interest to both sides of politics as local folks were getting agitated about the levels of traffic congestion in their community.

On the New South Wales side of the border, there was mainly open space, farms and a small part of the Coolangatta Airport. Compared to Tugun across the border, it was undeveloped and had no traffic needs whatsoever. The far north of New South Wales in the Tweed Heads area on the coast just below the Queensland border, had seen most development.

Road infrastructure on our side of the border along the coast was very good and further upgrades and extensions of the Pacific Highway were well addressing the traffic expectations of the

Chapter 10: Connecting communities

wider regional community. We did not need a Tugun bypass, but Queensland did. The only way they could manage the traffic congestion problem, which was going to get worse, was to divert it through our land towards Tweeds Heads.

Vaughan Johnson was the Queensland Minister, a wily, tough ex-shearer, who had for some years been the local MP for the State seat of Gregory in the Longreach area that included the famous ALP's 'Tree of Knowledge' at Barcaldine. Even though he was National Party, he looked and spoke like a worker straight from a local meeting of the Queensland Australian Workers Union. He was liked by the ALP north of the border and I could immediately see why. In fact, some years later, just after an election which Labor won, the Labor Queensland Minister, Rob Schwarten, went on Brisbane radio to congratulate and name all the country Labor candidates who had won their seats and added: "including the member for Gregory."

I had been briefed by the RTA that there could be significant environmental issues if the Tugun Bypass was built. A big concern was that as this was likely to be eligible for federal funding, that New South Wales federal funds earmarked for New South Wales might be diverted to this project. I could and would handle the former, but the latter was a showstopper. We did a joint press conference for the Queensland TVs and as Vaughan stood next to me, I explained that we had had a good discussion, but I was concerned about the possible environmental impact and that "unlike Queensland, New South Wales has environmental laws".

Vaughan would often remind me of how cheeky I had been that day, but as I was agreeing to cooperate with him, he said he was hardly in a position to complain. We became good friends and in due course, when Iemma 'threw me out of the building', he was one of the first to call. At his invitation, I joined him in December

2006 on a three-day road trip through his electorate, which took me to Barcaldine, Charleville and Birdsville. It was a great trip and he knew it was the tonic I needed at that time. Whenever our paths cross, we always have a good laugh about that press conference.

As the 1998 Queensland election approached, Peter Beattie, the then Leader of the Opposition and his Deputy, Jim Elder, met with me in my Sydney office and asked for help in being able to say that only they could find a solution with a New South Wales Labor Government and that we had agreed to work together in solving Tugun traffic congestion. Helping Labor win anywhere was always a good task, as far as I was concerned.

The ALP won the 1998 Queensland election and its new Roads Minister, Steve Bredhauer, commenced what would be a long-drawn-out process to get my commitment to support a Queensland road that was actually in New South Wales. I was convinced that Queensland would leave me holding the running costs of maintaining the road and that New South Wales commonwealth road funds would be diverted to the project.

To put pressure on Queensland, I asked the RTA to engage consultants to search high and low for any possible environmental reason why the project should not proceed. They soon found that the Wallum Sedge Frog and some rare orchards would be threatened if the road proceeded. I announced my decision in Parliament based on those findings, and advised that the project could not proceed unless Queensland could satisfy our concerns. I met with the new Queensland minister, Paul Lucas, and told him on the quiet, that I could dispense with the environmental issues, if not one dollar of our forecast Commonwealth road allocations was used on the road and if they committed $90M over 10 years for its upkeep.

Chapter 10: Connecting communities

The Federal Minister gave me the commitment I needed and so did the Queensland Minister. A couple of years later, the $300M bypass was opened at zero cost to the New South Wales budget and at no cost to the RTA for maintenance for the next 10 years. It was the single best deal I would ever do in delivering a major new road for our State. New South Wales residents in the far north of the State were free to use it and it had cost nothing to them or to their Government. I was more than chuffed by what I had been able to negotiate. I am still in contact with Paul Lucas and I do remind him from time to time of the great deal he gave me on the Tugun Bypass.

Michael Caton gives it to the RTA

The Pacific Highway upgrade was a huge long term multi-billion Federal State initiative which even in 2017, is still not yet complete.

I was involved in many Pacific Highway projects during my eight years as Minister for Roads and many created stakeholder challenges and environmental concerns. On one of these projects on the far north of the State, the Green MPs in the Upper House had called on me to step-in and change a proposed alignment which they claimed, if implemented, would be ruinous to the local environment. I went up to have a look and got fully briefed on the options and alternatives by Les Wielinga. The RTA had six alternative alignment options ranging from A to F and had built a huge model of them to enable community consultation. The preferred option for the RTA and the one causing the most community angst was option F.

A famous Australian actor, by the name of Michael Caton, well known for his role in the 1997 Australian movie 'The Castle' must have lived up that way, as he popped in one day to see the model of all the possible options for himself. He had a good look and with a devastating one liner quipped to Les: "I can see why you've called it option F." Les advised me that never again would any of his projects go past the letter E.

Gate crashing a press conference

The proposed bypass of the town of Urunga was one of many Pacific Highway projects. The RTA Pacific Highway team had developed a number of possible new alignments and then worked the issues through with the local council to come up with a preferred option for the bypass.

I was always fascinated that some communities wanted a complete bypass of their town to be built as they hated cars, trucks and buses trundling through their local town centre, while others lamented the end of their local economy if even a dollar of passing trade and business was lost to a bypass. I never did get a good handle on why some communities supported a bypass whereas others profoundly hated the idea. It just emphasised the diversity of country communities.

In the case of Urunga, the RTA advised that the local mayor loved the idea of a bypass and would welcome joining with me in announcing it. I had assumed that there had been at least some semblance of consultation with the local community. The two regional TVs turned up, as did the local paper and radio station. It was always great copy in the bush to be in town to announce another milestone towards delivering a long sheet of new bitumen for a local community.

I was accompanied at the press conference by the RTA CEO, Paul Forward, the local MP, Harry Woods and the local Mayor, which turned out to be an event of extremes. As I met the Mayor,

Chapter 10: Connecting communities

he quietly said he was so pleased with the results that he could kiss me. That was the one and only time I had a mayor or councillor ever expressing their delight in such a way about work that the RTA had been doing.

It looked to me like the announcement was going to be good copy for the cameras with the Mayor, face to camera, saying great things about the RTA and the Government at the right moment. We had a large map of the preferred alignment as a prop set up behind us for good effect. I had only spoken a few words when the doors burst open and an irate mother and daughter combination gate-crashed the party. The older woman opened up with: "It is disgraceful what you are trying to do to our dairy farms. This is going to go straight through our two properties and will ruin our farms. We are very angry and want to know what you are going to do about it."

My instant thought was: "Holy shit, what do I do or say now? The cameras are rolling and this could make national news if I don't immediately defuse the situation." I quickly responded: "Isn't this a great country?" to which came the reply: "What do you mean?" and I replied to the somewhat perplexed local resident: "Where in the world can you interrupt a press conference of a Minister of State to put your case and be heard? That is one of the things I love about this country. It sounds like you have not been properly consulted on this which is not good enough. As far as I am concerned the proposed alignment is now on hold until your concerns have been properly considered and addressed."

I closed up the press conference and met privately with the two of them along with Paul Forward and Les Wielinga. I kept an eye on it from a distance and was satisfied that with some fine-tuning and some cattle underpasses they were appropriately protected from any adverse impact.

As far as I was concerned, I got out of the situation with my shirt still on and my expression of delight at what a great country we all lived in, got a good run on the regional TVs. It could have been much worse.

We all know that the media is easily distracted whenever any form of negativity presents itself near a camera recording something positive. It never matters how important the announcement or how well it is delivered or how important the person delivering it is. If a lone person throws a piece of fruit or shouts a slogan in opposition, then that gets equal or better billing. Thankfully, I had very few invasions of my media events or press conferences over a long period of office and this one would have to be the most memorable.

Profanities over a cup of tea

The MP for Wollongong and its former Lord Mayor, David Campbell was and remains a good friend and I tried as often as I could to visit his electorate and fund solutions to his community's road and transport problems.

On one occasion, after concluding a mid-morning visit to his electorate, we stopped for a cup of tea at a local café and talked as we sat at one of the outside tables. Before long, I heard a loud female voice directed at the back of my head: "You fucken ...." and quick as a flash I swivelled round to face the offender and said: "I would like to thank you" and when she replied: "What for", I responded with: "Did that make you feel better" and when she said: "as a matter fact it did", I added: "Well, I would like to thank you then for allowing me to be of service to you this morning" she responded rather politely with: "you're welcome" and wandered off.

Campbell was left speechless and often recounted the tale with: "How did you manage to do that" to which I always replied: "What was I supposed to do? Abuse her. It seemed to me that the only possible way out was to be polite to her. I did not know if it would work, but thankfully it did."

Luxury cars and the Hunter Valley

A trip to the Hunter Valley wine country about two hours north of Sydney is always a good tonic from the busy urban life of the metropolis.

On one of my trips to this great part of New South Wales, I met with the local mayor together with local winemaking legend, Murray Tyrell. Both of them complained that the good wine-buying folks of well-heeled Eastern and Northern Sydney were complaining that the gravel roads around the wine area were throwing up stones and damaging the paint on their Mercedes Benzs and BMWs.

They asked that I seal these roads to prevent these luxury cars from being damaged in the future. I almost fell off my chair. I wondered if I or they were on another planet. Once I realised that they were not kidding but were genuinely putting the case that a Labor Minister for Roads representing a working-class electorate in Western Sydney, should earmark funds from his portfolio budget to protect some high Tories and their designer cars I let it rip: "You want me to pour money in to the local roads of this wine district just so the residents of the Eastern Suburbs and the North Shore of Sydney won't get a few scratches on their Mercs and BMWs. You can get fucked. It's not happening."

Murray Tyrell must have also seen the humorous side to it, as several years later I got a phone call from Tony Burke, then a minister in the Gillard Government, telling me that both he and Tyrell had just had a very funny moment as Tyrell recounted in full my somewhat profane reaction to their road funding request.

The 'Carl' Expressway

The eyesore in front of the wharves at Circular Quay, known as the Cahill Expressway, provided a wonderful vantage point for me to construct $9M worth of lifts and lookout platform for visitors and locals to enjoy a world-famous view of both the Sydney Harbour Bridge and the Opera House. I told both my rail and road CEOs to work together and come up with a joint internally funded project which the people of Sydney still enjoy to this day. This was not a project I put before either Egan or Carr, or bothered submitting to Budget Committee, as I knew that it would have hit the 'cutting room floor' the moment I put it forward. Despite that, I still remain very proud of this great legacy to one of the iconic harbour areas of our city.

The name of the expressway may sound like my first name but honours the Labor premier, Joe Cahill, who was the intellectual architect of the Opera House. Somewhat ironically and probably more of a consequence of abusive media directed my way, my then Chief of Staff, Chris Bowen, whilst sipping a coffee one weekend with his wife up on the Central Coast, overheard a local opine to another old local: 'You know that Carl Scully has even named an expressway after himself'. I know folks assume we have egos but that one took the cake.

Shining shoes

Bob Carr was well known as a stickler for spotlessly cleaned shoes on both himself and others. On one occasion, I had led a delegation of Gwenn Hanns and family to see the new Premier early in our term, about our desire to keep the killer of her child, John Lewthwaite, in jail for as long as possible.

We had a good meeting and the family seemed content with the discussion. As we all approached the door to leave, the Premier called out: "Carl" and as we all stopped and turned around in unison he added: "You need to polish your shoes." As we departed, Howard Brown from the Homicide Victims Support Group summed it up best: "He's a funny bloke isn't he."

Cyclists leak too

Whenever I asked as Roads Minister, to be briefed on anything in the portfolio, up would come a serious, experienced and not very young, senior bureaucrat. But, when I asked to be briefed on RTA plans for cycleways, up came a kid in jeans with a beard and healthy dose of inexperience. It was one of the few areas where I needed to remind the RTA to be serious about something.

Ironically, the RTA would then at my request, do more for cycling and cycleway construction than anything which had been done in the previous 30 years. I was very excited about Bike Plan 2010 which dovetailed with Action for Transport 2010 and set out a bold $250M, 10-year plan for off road cycleway construction.

I had spent over a year working with the RTA and my own office, in developing the Plan to what we were sure would be a very good announcement. That was until one of my own policy officers thought it prudent to consult with the cycling lobby organisation, Bicycle New South Wales, on the details of what we proposed to announce.

And what would have been predictable to me, but not so to my young staffer, was that within 10 minutes of this consultation, the Sydney Morning Herald called to check the accuracy of every morsel we had briefed them on. Unfortunately, we had to give the Sydney Morning Herald an exclusive for the next day and run with a terrific story at a time not of our choosing.

Of all the stakeholder groups, I had to deal with as an MP and then a minister, easily the most difficult and the most irrational would have to been the cycling community. Otherwise well educated, professional, articulate and successful men, who would no doubt conduct themselves in the workplace with all the decorum and professionalism you would expect, go through some kind of metamorphous once a pair of skin hugging Lycra is pulled on, or when they hear the slightest suggestion of what they interpret, as even just a whiff of a negative cycling policy position.

I still find the Jekyll and Hyde approach of male cyclists to their professional work and to their cycling as psychologically fascinating. Long after I had left politics, I was asked by Darren Goodsir of the Sydney Morning Herald, to write a short piece on my own record and views on cycling for the Sydney Morning Herald online blog. I should have run (or at least cycled) away, but instead, I took up the offer and set out all I had done, including the $141M off-road, grade separated M7 Motorway Cycleway. I thought it was a well-argued piece which outlined what I regarded as an impressive delivery of cycling infrastructure and policy development.

But, cyclists took a dim view of my claim that they were not, as they claimed, non-motorised vehicular transport with equal rights to the road as all other vehicles. They also did not welcome my call for them to be encouraged to off road cycleways when built, and possibly banned from using major roads in dangerously busy peak traffic times. The response was swift. About 500 mostly male and very angry professional and articulate cyclists vented their fury. One even emailed my workplace and called for my sacking. I think there was one or maybe two responses acknowledging that I had made some good points and agreed that I had done more for cycling than any other Roads Minister.

After that experience, I extended my retirement from politics to retirement from commenting on cycling policy as well. I have not regretted it. However, I still believe that the split personalities of many male cyclists are worthy of closer psychological study.

Traffic lights at Edensor Park

On one rare occasion when our son James had to walk home from school, I strongly reminded him not to cross any road on his way home until the green walk sign had appeared at each set of traffic lights.

But, when I came home that evening, he was concerned that he had had to break his promise to me at the intersection of Edensor Road and Smithfield Road not far from our Edensor Park home, as the lights failed on several cycles to light up the green walk sign. I called the RTA traffic light guru, Chris Ford, who expressed surprise, but quickly phoned back to say he had just found out from the traffic light engineers, that this intersection was one of only three that operated independently of the nearly 2,000 sets of traffic lights controlled by the Transport Management Centre. They were very soon brought within the system.

Vegetarian in the Louvre

Being a non-drinking vegetarian atheist from the very Catholic political hard men of the New South Wales ALP right, certainly did give me some unusual maverick credentials. When in opposition, I was even advised by one of my Terrigal sub-faction compatriots, that if I wanted a successful political career, I would need to eat meat and drink alcohol. I ignored the request.

One very amusing vegetarian encounter did occur whilst enjoying a lavish banquet in the dining hall of the great Louvre museum in the heart of Paris. Paul Forward and I were attending the World Roads Congress and I had presented a paper on what we had done to deliver transport for the Sydney 2000 Olympics.

When my meal came with a huge steak and a paltry side of overcooked vegetables, I asked for the vegetarian option. The French waiter must have come straight off the set of Fawlty Towers. When I made the request, he snorted, grabbed my plate, went straight to a nearby rubbish bin, flicked the steak into the bin and then just about dropped my plate back in front of me with a second, but even louder snort. Paul Forward almost fell off his chair laughing.

UTS Railway Station

I occasionally get asked why I never built a railway station for the University of Technology campus at Lindfield on Sydney's leafy North Shore as part of the Epping to Parramatta railway project.

It is true that the station would have been expensive and almost as deep as the one constructed in the 1930s as part of the incredible Moscow metro. But that is not why I declined the request. I had heard from a few informal sources that the University planned to vacate its valuable site for a major residential property development and house all its students at its main Sydney CBD campus at Ultimo near Central Railway station.

Chapter 10: Connecting communities

I asked the Department of Transport to put out feelers to the university hierarchy that I was inclined to not build such a costly and deep station near or on their campus if they were not intending to stay. And the response from the university was such a light touch, it convinced me that in time they did in fact intend to leave.

All I got from the UTS Vice-Chancellor was a letter assuring me of their long-term commitment to staying at their Lindfield campus. That was it. No phone call. No request for a meeting. No student, teacher or community protest and not a whimper from the local MP. I was so used to having to manage or mitigate community angst at how I proposed to manage project impacts I was somewhat underwhelmed by the university's sheer lack of agitation or anger. Where was the passion?

Perhaps they were poorly advised, or were so used to the polite society of university life, that they were simply unaware that to get heard during planning of a major project, you needed to be louder than the D9 bulldozers coming down the road to deliver it.

In this environment, I regarded the letter being the only vehicle to convey a view on the issue, as proof enough that the university, either could not care less about whether a station got built, or that it did in fact intend at some future date to close its north side campus and could not comfortably eyeball me and say something to the contrary.

I directed my agencies to remove a railway station at the UTS campus from our design for the new railway. The Epping to Parramatta railway opened to passengers in 2008. In November 2015 UTS finally, as I predicted, closed its Lindfield campus and all students are now located at Ultimo in the heart of CBD Sydney.

Tunnelling under Lane Cove River

I also get asked from time to time why I directed the Epping to Chatswood rail project to pass under the Lane Cove River rather than bridge over it as originally planned.

The easiest and most cost-effective way to cross the Lane Cove River was by bridge, but when this was first mooted, it brought some local and environmental reaction protesting at the aesthetic impact this would have on Lane Cove Park.

The protests were modest and probably manageable, but I decided for nostalgic reasons to request my agencies to find a way to tunnel under the river, so on completion, no one would know that a rail line had been built. The proposed bridge was an eye-popping structure, spanning right across the very spot I had once kayaked as a young teenager. Whilst I had long ago left this part of Sydney to pursue professional and political opportunities in Western Sydney, I did have many positive memories which I did not wish erased by a project under my control.

As it turned out, the construction of the tunnel made the project about one kilometre longer and made the line itself much steeper than would have been otherwise necessary. It was certainly more expensive to build than the bridge option.

Had the project been a road construction project, the RTA would have probably given some pushback and if I resisted, then a robust discussion with both CEO, Paul Forward and Head of Network Infrastructure, Mike Hannon would have ensued. I welcomed these discussions in the roads portfolio, as I pushed the boundaries on a project and they pushed back due to possible impacts. Sometimes I withdrew but more often than not, after considering their views I pushed on and they accepted my decisions.

The RTA and its Major Road Project Division had decades of experience advising Government on building game-changing infrastructure, which I could rely on. Such was not the case with the building of railways.

The Wran Government had built the Eastern Suburbs rail line in the 1970s and apart from the airport rail line built in the late 1990s, no new rail line had been constructed for a very long time.

Treasury and governments willingly supported and funded road construction to keep up with the growing economy and expanding population, but they did not do so for rail construction. As a result, rail expansion had languished both in terms of new projects and the development of any sort of experienced major rail project advisory personnel.

So, whilst I pushed the nostalgic button in response to some mild community pressure, there was no rail equivalent of either Paul Forward or Mike Hannon to question and test me, push back and then and only then, acquiesce in my decisions.

Thankfully, given the sheer magnitude of the Liberal state Government initiatives on major rail projects, that is very likely to change in the future.

Since retiring from politics, I have on a few occasions visited this part of the Lane Cove River and allowed myself a quiet smile as I recall my own time as a kid, messing about in boats as well as a time many years later, when I could prevent an eyesore from being built right across that very same spot.

The weighted average cost of capital

The quarterly meeting of senior rail personnel and union leaders was held on the same morning that I was newly sworn in as Transport Minister (end of 1997), so I went straight from Government House to the meeting and was given a very warm welcome by all attending.

Little did I know then how tough the portfolio would be, or just how much Carr and Egan had already structured and staffed the New South Wales railways as a Treasury economic rationalist outpost. But at the morning tea break, I did get a quick introduction of things to come, when I advised Judi Stack, the CEO of the rail track owner, Rail Access Corporation, that I needed $2M to fund a spur line into the Port Kembla area.

"It depends on the weighted average cost capital" she immediately responded and not surprisingly I replied: "What on earth is that?" After a quick lesson from her about only being able to invest in rail track capital works which would provide a viable commercial return, I advised her: "We will get along fine if you just find the money." To her credit, she did find the money from a 'hollow log' and the work was done, but it was a very early introduction to the huge shift which had occurred early in the life of a Labor Government, on how the railways were now going to be economically managed.

Railway investment decisions had for nearly 150 years been assessed and put forward by very experienced railway personnel, which were then considered by Treasury bean counters against all the other priorities of Government. That was now turned completely around, so that financially-skilled personnel were put in charge of railway tracks and were already putting up their own commercial obstacles before any funding proposals went anywhere near Treasury.

Thwarting FOIs on crime statistics

When Barry O'Farrell was Opposition Spokesman on Transport, he drove me nuts with his non-stop Freedom of Information applications to my rail agencies seeking every possible detail on crime levels on our trains and railway stations. If crime was down, he said nothing; but if any crime category showed the slightest blimp of an increase, he was faster out of the blocks than Usain Bolt, to bemoan the disgraceful state of public transport security. And the press just lapped it up.

When two security guards on every night train and CCTV security cameras on all our stations, increased detection and therefore, showed up as an increase in recorded rather than actual crime, O'Farrell had a field day arguing that my $100M rail security initiative had actually increased crime. And the press reported that nonsense as a reasonable possibility. 'Fake news' is what it might be called now.

From then on, any FOI application was reported to me in detail, especially any from an opposition MP. I never once told my agencies what they should or should not release under an FOI application, but I did insist that I be told at least a few days before it went out to the applicant. That way, I was able to develop an effective process where I would release the details of any negative figures in the broader context and as a much as possible, in a positive light. The $30 application fee would then be returned to the applicant.

O'Farrell was also driven nuts by my approach. He in turn complained to the New South Wales Ombudsman that I was flouting the spirit if not the letter of our FOI laws. Ron Christie as Coordinator General of Rail, provided a vigorous response to the Ombudsman, pointing out that not only was all the requested information being released to the public at the earliest possible time, but that it was also released with a proper explanation from the affected government agency.

I heard no more about the issue.

Reviving Country Rail services

The Sydney rail scene was one long five-year stint with little joy except, of course, for the delivery of transport for the Sydney 2000 Olympic Games. What a contrast when I was able to carry out initiatives in regional and rural areas. The level of appreciation from these communities was both astounding and uplifting.

Three initiatives stand out in my memory.

The Broken Hill Explorer

The SRA had withdrawn the train service to Broken Hill about 1,200 km west of Sydney as the train carriages were old, run down, unreliable and potentially unsafe. The privately-run Sydney to Perth Indian Pacific continued to provide rail options for the local community, but they clamoured for a return of their publicly subsidised service.

I authorised the construction of two new carriages which took about two years to be built and then arranged for the 'return of the Broken Hill Explorer'. It was a great event. I flew into Ivanhoe airport about 300 km east of Broken Hill and took the train from there into Broken Hill. This is a town where BHP began in 1885 as Broken Hill Proprietary Limited, long before it became the global

Chapter 10: Connecting communities

firm it is today. With a population of about 18,000 residents, it is certainly an isolated outpost of New South Wales.

However, they certainly came out in force the day their new train arrived. Hundreds of townsfolk and school children lined the platform and as we pulled in, the local band played the Australian unofficial anthem, Waltzing Matilda. Just wonderful stuff and the Opposition who resented the ALP domination in a country seat they believed was rightfully theirs, hated it when I recounted the whole story during the next parliamentary question time.

The Electrification of Dapto to Kiama Railway

For decades, the electrified passenger rail network had ended south of Sydney at Dapto near Wollongong. Passengers wanting to journey further south to the coastal community of Kiama had to alight and change to a diesel motor service.

Matt Brown, the local MP for Kiama, was a big fan of extending electrification all the way to Kiama, so that his local community would then be able to travel with ease to Sydney without changing trains. I approved the works and when it was completed, he with the MP for Dapto, Marianne Saliba, put on such a euphoric community event, I thought I had travelled through and arrived at a Billy Graham Evangelical gathering. Every road/rail crossing, every road overpass, all along the route at every possible vantage point and then at Kiama station itself, were literally thousands and thousands of people, all waving and cheering.

It was just overwhelming and still gives me pleasure now recalling it all these years later. For reasons completely lost on me, many MPs do not enjoy campaigning and delight when the essential requirements of an election are concluded. But I always loved it and events like this reminded me how good campaigning amongst the community can be.

The Kandos to Gulgong Railway

The Greiner years had been ones of unbridled economic rationalism, where the starting point was usually if it was costing money, increase the charge or close the service. Whilst unprofitable freight rail lines in country New South Wales had begun being closed during the Askin Liberal Government and then the Wran Labor Government, the Greiner Government had brought it to a new level.

I was determined not to close any rail line during my period as Transport minister and if possible, re-open some. A project put forward was the Kandos to Gulgong line, about 300 km north west of Sydney, which had been closed due to a rail bridge falling into significant disrepair. Rail stakeholders assured me that if I spent the $15M necessary to repair the bridge, freight and tourist rail would return to the line. So, I did as I was asked.

The opening was grand with over a thousand Mudgee residents crowding around their station as our train pulled in. But apart from one further tourist run there would be no freight and no tourist trains running on the line. I had wasted $15M of public money because I believed the assurances I was given. After that, any requests by rail enthusiasts for me to open closed rail lines was met with an account of my experience on re-opening the Kandos to Gulgong Rail line.

Not his son's father

Bruce Baird was the Minister for Transport for the entire seven-year period of the Greiner/Fahey Liberal New South Wales

Chapter 10: Connecting communities

government from 1988 until we were elected in March 1995. One of the few project promises he actually delivered upon, was the Airport Rail line extension from Central Railway station out to the domestic and international terminals. However, it was a poor financial deal cobbled together in a rush literally days before the caretaker period commenced for the March 1995 state election. Despite Bruce promising the project as a PPP at no net cost to government, taxpayers would have to fork out over $700M to build just the tracks. This left the stations to be built, funded and operated by a private sector consortium. The sting in the tail was that the operator was permitted to charge a premium fare for anyone entering or exiting them.

As a relatively new Minister for Transport, when it came time to open the new line, I asked that an invitation be extended to Bruce as a courtesy to recognise his role in delivering it. I should not have bothered. After Carr and I had done the opening, Bruce, reliving past glories, held his own press conference to denounce the lack of luggage racks on trains using the line. This disingenuous lament from the former minister got a solid run in the media and provided a smudge across what should have been a time to celebrate a new piece of infrastructure for the people of Sydney.

I was astonished that Bruce had behaved in that way. As the original architect of the project, he had never taken any steps to ensure that city rail trains contained luggage racks nor expressed a prior view on it. If he genuinely felt that the crowded Sydney trains of the morning and evening peaks should have made way for mostly absent suit cases, then he was the very person to have done something about it. He did not. I am inclined to think that Bruce was looking for an excuse to poop on the parade. He succeeded.

If Labor wins the next state election there will be a raft of huge rail and road projects coming on line beyond 2019. I am confident a courtesy would be extended by the new Labor government at the opening of those projects, to a now retired Mike Baird who played a significant role in their planning, funding and delivery. I am also very confident that Mike would not do a Bruce in accepting such a courtesy.

Why Malcolm Turnbull joined the Liberal Party

Prime Minister Malcolm Turnbull surprised many when he originally opted to join the Liberal Party rather than the ALP. Turnbull had for some years shone as the public face and advocate of moving Australia to a republic. This and he, were certainly seen as arguing a core Labor Party value. Despite being the high-profile lawyer to business titan Kerry Packer, a successful New York banker and having made millions selling his share in Ozemail, many of us in the ALP assumed he would join our cause and seek office supporting our natural base of working class families, industrial constituents, protection of the environment and social equality.

When he did make a move, and join the Liberal Party, many of us were taken by surprise. Not surprisingly, many still wonder on both sides of politics, despite being elected Prime Minister, if Turnbull has had to spend his time in public life suppressing a natural bent for the Labor cause.

Just after Turnbull had made his choice to shun that cause and opt for the 'big end of town' party, I ran into him unexpectedly at a Sydney harbourside function. I then had an incredible conversation which I will never forget. My recollection of the substance of that conversation is as follows:

Chapter 10: Connecting communities

Me: "Malcolm, why on earth did you join the Libs and not the ALP?"

I was expecting to hear a philosophical commitment to Liberal Party values and some kind of intellectual rejection of what the Labor Party stood for but instead all I got was:

Malcolm: "I could never succeed in the Labor Party as it would be unforgiving towards someone who had been a successful businessman."

Me: "Is that it. That's why you chose to join the Libs?"

Malcolm: "Yes, it is. The ALP would just not tolerate someone who had succeeded in business."

I then asked him if he was going into New South Wales politics, attain the leadership of the Opposition and have a tilt at the premiership:

Malcolm: "I couldn't do that to Bob."

Me: "What do you mean?"

Malcolm: "Bob Carr and I are friends. I couldn't do it to him."

I was left feeling that Malcolm Turnbull had a very optimistic view of his political abilities in the face of Bob Carr at the height of his popularity. I was also simply astonished that with no stated philosophical commitment to the Liberal Party, he was quite prepared to leave its political opponents in power, rather than take the reins of government away from a personal friend. Bob Carr, of course, found the latter part of the conversation, as simply hilarious.

Banning jet skis on Sydney Harbour

Carr was certainly the opposite of what I would imagine a hands-on micro managing Premier would be like. Just as well he behaved more like a Chairman than a CEO, as the latter would have driven me nuts. Certainly, when media negativity was causing grief, he and his staff would step-in and assist, if not sometimes steer the story to calmer waters. But if the journalists had other 'bird seed' to chew, then a minister was substantially left alone to plan and develop what was needed for projects, policies and programmes in his or her portfolio.

So apart from times of media grief and the funding battles with Egan, Carr mostly left me alone. However, there was one exception – he directed me to ban jet skis on Sydney Harbour.

Carr called me up to his office one day to complain that at a lunch he had had over the previous weekend with friends at a Sydney Harbour residence, the event was spoilt by the constant noise of passing jet skis. So, he decided to ban them from Sydney Harbour.

I was astonished to say the least. Looking after Sydney Harbour property owners so they could more conveniently enjoy quiet lunches with friends in their mega million dollar mansions, hardly seemed to me the priority of a Labor Government. If anything, I was rather pleased to hear that the battlers of the Sydney Harbour foreshore were being rudely interrupted by the occasional young hoon on a jet ski. I articulated none of this to Carr of course, and undertook to take the issue under my wing.

But I was never a fan and I told my maritime agencies that we were to undertake all the necessary consideration that such a 10th order policy issue required, but that I had no intention of implementing it. I even had a map prepared which showed that a large majority of jet ski owners actually lived in western Sydney ALP seats – a long way from the Sydney Harbour foreshore.

However, this filibuster of mine came to an abrupt end one day when I was summoned to Carr's office for a memorable exchange:

Carr: "I am the Premier and you are one of my Ministers."

Me: "Yes, that's right."

Carr: "I asked you to ban jet skis on Sydney Harbour and you have delayed it for two years. I know what you have been up to and I am now directing you to proceed immediately to implement the ban."

Me: "Yes Premier. But, subject to one condition."

Carr: "What's that?"

Me: "I want you to announce it."

Carr: "OK."

With that I directed the Maritime agency to prepare the necessary regulation, Carr announced it and jet skis were banned from Sydney Harbour. They have not returned.

So, I like to boast that whilst Carr never directed me to build a motorway or the bus-only transitways or the Epping to Chatswood railway or anything at all on road or rail safety, he did direct me to ban jet skis on Sydney Harbour. And it was one Carr initiative I intended to reverse if I was ever appointed Premier.

Protecting Sydney Harbour Bridge after 9/11

Following the New York attacks of September 2001, Paul Forward as CEO of the Roads and Traffic Authority and his senior leadership team were straight onto any risks which global terror, might present for our own Sydney Harbour Bridge.

He quickly had the RTA engineers do a detailed bomb exposure risk to the structural fabric of one of Australia's most recognised infrastructure icons. The analysis showed that the famous arch and almost all of the bridge could withstand either a truck bomb or an impact from an aeroplane. But, the analysis also showed that there was a particular point or two, where with detailed knowledge and the right amount of explosive, the integrity of the bridge could be challenged with the possibility of catastrophic collapse of all or part of the road deck into the sea below.

Chris Ford of the RTA, who was at the time in charge of ensuring bridge security, recently let me know, that at the time, he had brought to his attention, similar detailed analysis undertaken in 1942. This had been conducted for General Douglas Macarthur, on how to bring the bridge down if the Brisbane Line failed and the Japanese army came marching south. The plan was incredible but not surprising, given the threat to our national survival in the early 1940s.

In late 2001, early 2002 following the recent destruction of the World Trade Centre Towers and the murder of over 3,000 people, we did not know what to expect. We were assuming the worst. The Sydney Harbour Bridge was and still is an icon of national significance. We were determined to do all we could to protect it from attack. Substantial works were quietly undertaken with my approval to strengthen the integrity of the bridge. I also approved the installation of CCTV cameras, thermal imaging and movement detection equipment and for good measure 24/7 private security guards, who are still to this day, walking the bridge deck. Chris Ford then installed literally kilometres of razor barbed wire over large sections of the bridge to prevent unauthorised access.

The other very important but quiet initiative, was Paul Forward ascertaining from the State Librarian, what holdings they had in the State Library collection of the plans and designs of the Sydney Harbour Bridge. The advice came back that they had all the original plans and drawings in their possession which were publicly available for anyone coming in off the street and requesting to view them. This was not good. At Forward's request, these documents were locked away and have been archived that way ever since.

Wran waits for Klugman too

In early 1986, I had arranged a fundraising dinner in Fairfield and had been able to secure through our local MP, Janice Crosio, the attendance of no less than the then Premier, Neville Wran.

As the Smithfield ALP State Electorate council-elected organiser, I was the MC for the evening. Unbeknownst to me or anyone else, Wran was just six months away from announcing his retirement from politics at the July 1986 ALP Annual Conference. Furthermore, just a few years earlier, he had seriously contemplated appointing Federal ALP MP for Prospect, Dr Dick Klugman, to the post of Director General of New South Wales Health to enable the Premier to pursue a role in national politics.

So, the short conversation Wran had late that evening with Crosio is both ironic and amusing:

Wran: "What is Carl waiting for?"

Crosio: "He is waiting for Dick Klugman to retire."

Wran: "No. I meant, why hasn't he started the speeches."

Clearly, whilst Crosio was focussing on my political future, Wran was focussing on getting home early!

Fairfield City

It is a rare local MP indeed who can spend years asking for public infrastructure for his or her electorate and then be able to do something about it. When I was elected in 1990, it soon became very apparent that South West Sydney had been ignored by successive governments for over 30 years.

The Greiner/Fahey Government saw Western and South Western Sydney as rock solid ALP territory and unworthy of their care and attention. Before them, the Wran Government had so many marginal seats to take care of and retain, that there was often little left for the 'safe' West. The result of this was an unfortunate twenty plus years of neglect by governments of both political complexions with respect to western Sydney road and rail infrastructure. I intended to do something about it.

Fairfield City is in the heart of South West Sydney and covered all the area of my electorate of Smithfield. By the time my local political mentor, Anwar Khoshaba, had been elected as a local Councillor to Fairfield City Council, I was already Minister for Roads. He came in with one of the senior staff responsible for strategic planning and preparing the wish lists for State Government funding. They put to me that Elizabeth Road, Cowpasture Road and Horsley Drive were not only important

Chapter 10: Connecting communities

State roads in their council area, but were essential links with Liverpool, the huge Wetherill Park Industrial Estate and the Fairfield CBD. They claimed that the roads had been basically ignored for years and would need substantial investment to bring them up to four-lane standard.

I did not need convincing that Fairfield had missed out on its fair share for a very long time and I was very sympathetic as one of its local members. I could not see how I could accuse the former government of neglect and disinterest in my capacity as an MP, and then not take steps to rectify it when I could do so as a minister.

I surprised both by committing to the complete rebuilding and upgrading of these three important links. Over the next few years, all the roads were brought up to four lane status. I like to think that I left my electorate in 2007 in much better shape than I found it as its new MP in 1990.

One of the things I was committed to building through the heart of my Smithfield electorate was a dedicated bus only road running over 20 kilometres from Liverpool Railway Station to Parramatta Railway Station. Thousands of commuters now use this wonderful public transport option every day. However, it ended up costing $300M not $200M as estimated, and took longer to build than anticipated. This of course, all provided great copy for the negaholic journalists of the daily newspapers.

But there was an ironic angle to this great public transport outcome for south west Sydney. When I was just a backbench MP in 1994, Anwar Khoshaba led a delegation from the Niniveh Assyrian Club complaining that the Department of Planning and Fairfield Council, had designated public land behind the club as a future transport corridor. I was unaware of the issue until the Club officials complained that this could jeopardise their plans to expand their soccer field and stadium. We were all assured by both the Council and the Department that nothing would be built for at least 20 years and could not see any problem with the club expanding in the meantime across public land.

Three years later, I was Minister for Transport and had to spend a lot of time, effort and negotiation, to make sure we could squeeze both the new Bus Transitway and the proposed extended Club facilities, into the same available space. It was not a challenge I had anticipated in 1994 when getting the go ahead for the club.

The demise of the king and queen maker

On the 15th of December 2016, former New South Wales Minister and MP, Eddie Obeid was sentenced to 5 years in gaol with a minimum non-parole period of 3 years after having been convicted of Misconduct in Public Office.

The misconduct related to Obeid making representations to a senior maritime public servant regarding lease conditions at various business premises at Circular Quay on Sydney Harbour without disclosing that he had commercial interests in some of those premises.

Obeid had entered parliament in 1991 after a long and successful business career and many of us simply assumed that he was motivated only by a desire to put something back into the community. The Terrigal sub-faction in the New South Wales ALP parliamentary right was formed in 1992 by a small group of disgruntled, disempowered but ambitious younger MPs with its fulcrum around a more senior Eddie Obeid. By 1995, Michael Knight, Faye Lo Po and I were Terrigal ministers in the Cabinet.

Chapter 10: Connecting communities

After the 1999 election, Morris Iemma (the future premier) and Eddie Obeid himself, would be propelled into the Cabinet room.

The then MP for Fairfield, Joe Tripodi, elected in 1995, became Obeid's main Terrigal spear carrier, helping herd MPs to vote in meetings of the parliamentary Labor Party caucus and at meetings of the ALP right faction, and crucially, organising the numbers for future MPs to win local ALP branch pre-selections. One of those pre-selections was for the safe Labor seat of Heffron, when Tripodi put forward his long-time friend from his university days, Ben Keneally, as a suitable Labor candidate to remove the sitting ALP MP Deidre Grusovin. However, as women were given a 20% bonus vote in pre-selections, a woman was needed to ensure a fellow member of the ALP NSW right was removed from the parliament. Ben Keneally's wife, Kristina, was then put forward and successfully became the MP for Heffron at the 2003 election. Tripodi would become a Minister in 2005, and in 2007 Kristina Keneally would become a Minister and then Premier in 2009. The advancement of all depended on support from Eddie Obeid, Joe Tripodi and the Terrigal group they controlled.

Very few knew what Obeid had been up to as he gathered and garnered MPs around him, ostensibly for what we naively believed was a desire to control the party and its government for public good. However, many of us including former premiers, Morris Iemma, Nathan Rees and finally Kristina Keneally, were all huge beneficiaries of Eddie Obeid's political patronage. Iemma's appointment to the top job was secured once Ian McDonald as leader of the ALP parliamentary hard-left and Obeid and Tripodi as leaders of the Terrigal sub faction of the ALP right strongly backed him. I had thought I had been a friend of Obeid's and a close colleague, until he and Tripodi unexpectedly and aggressively supported Iemma for the premiership over my candidacy. Nathan Rees brought an early end to his own premiership when he sacked Tripodi and McDonald from Cabinet only to have his replacement, Keneally, reinstate McDonald and appoint him as Minister for Mines.

Iemma, Rees and Keneally all became Labor Premiers with the full backing of Eddie Obeid, Joe Tripodi and Ian McDonald. It is inconceivable that they could have done so without that pivotally important support. Iemma and Keneally, like many of us, were members of the Terrigal group, socialised with its MPs and regarded Obeid as a friend and colleague. With the conviction and gaoling of Obeid, I do not intend to now pretend otherwise. Like the former premiers, who were quick out of the blocks to express delight at his demise, I neither knew nor now condone what he did. However, I will resist the temptation to ignore or gloss over the significant role he played in our political advancement.

I do not share the glee of the three former premiers but instead I feel a sense of despondency and sadness at Obeid's betrayal of trust to the community, to his colleagues, to the ALP and to me. We all thought he was better than that.

Photo album

My Parents

My parents Patrick Christian Scully and Carmen Catherine Howard on their wedding day, 15th December, 1951

Our home at 112 Beaconsfield Road in West Chatswood, Sydney

Childhood Memories

With my Dad, 1958

With my Mum at 2 years, 3 months, June 1959

Family portrait of the Scully siblings, Maryanne, Kathy, Marie, Carl and baby Martin, August 1960

Four of the Scully siblings exploring the edges of Lane Cove River, early 1960s

Christmas (Age 6), 1963

First school formal (Age 9), 1966

Mum with her five children outside our
West Chatswood home, 1964

Photo album

At Centennial Park with my brother Martin, late 1960s

Garden duty at our home in West Chatswood, 1971

We had just three family holidays during my childhood and teenage years. This is the start of the final one; a road trip to Central West New South Wales and Southern Queensland, 1974

Photo album

The early 1970s – High school days

Chatswood High School (age 13), 1970

First press photo in Sydney Morning Herald (age 15), 1972

University days

Sister Marie, brother Martin, Mum, me and sister Maryanne, late 1970s

Working the phone, organising the numbers for Young Labor

Photo album

Ann and I at the Copper Canyon Restaurant, Parramatta, just after we started dating in early 1980

Celebrating the end of law school, November 1981

Graduating BA, LLB (Hons), Macquarie University, May 1982

Family and political career

Ann and I on our wedding day, 17th December 1983

Talking NSW State Election results with Janice Crosio, and her daughter and son-in-law, Linda and Jim Crestani, 1984

At the Castle Hill home of Ann's parents about 2 years after we married, mid 1980s

My parents, late 1980s

With my Mum, 1989

Photo album

The day I won pre-selection as the candidate for the ALP for the State electorate of Smithfield on 2nd December, 1989

Ann would lament:
"Huh! You look happier here
than you were on our wedding day."

Official campaign photo, 1990-1999

By-election campaign admobile, Smithfield, 1990

Doorknock campaigning with Bob Carr, shown here arriving at home of Sam and Rose Mittiga, Smithfield, 1990

By-election campaign outing with Bob Carr and Campaign Director, Anwar Khoshaba, 1990

By-election victory night with Mum and Aunt Gay,
June 1990

By-election victory
night with my wife
Ann, June 1990

In my new role as MP for Smithfield, July 1990

Ann and I in a campaign photo with our two children
James and Sarah, 1991

James, Ann and Sarah on the day we leave for our holiday in Port Douglas, 1993

Mum's jail battle not over yet

By KATE DWYER

GWEN Hanns has just won her battle to keep convicted murderer John Lewthwaite behind bars.

However, the fight is not over for Mrs Hanns, who must be prepared to contest Lewthwaite's parole again next year.

Mrs Hanns's struggle to keep her daughter's killer imprisoned highlighted two important issues about victims' versus offenders' rights, according to Member for Smithfield Carl Scully.

"There is an urgent need to change the law because at the moment an offender can come before the parole board annually, which only adds to the heartache of the victim and their family," he said.

"I think the annual review for serious offenders should be changed to at least every three years, possibly as much as every five years and, on top of this, there needs to be a Victim's Rights Authority which looks after victims' needs."

He said the authority could provide bereavement counselling, free legal aid so the victim can be represented at the parole board and it could also keep victims up-to-date as to where the offender is.

John Lewthwaite was jailed for life for the murder of five-year-old Nicole Hanns at her home in Greystanes in 1974.

The sentence was later reduced to a minimum of 20 years.

Gwen Hanns, with the help of Carl Scully, stepped up her fight for justice when Lewthwaite asked for day release in April this year after the Serious Offenders Review Council reduced his classification, thus making him eligible for the program.

The battle was divided in two, first, to get Lewthwaite's parole rejected, and second, to make sure he did not receive day release.

Both these contests were won about two weeks ago when Lewthwaite was deemed not suitable for parole or day leave.

Mrs Hanns said she felt relieved but realised the

● Continued Page 2

DRAWING breath after a four-month battle to keep a convicted murderer behind bars, Member for Smithfield Carl Scully and Gwen Hanns. Photo by Armen Deushian

Campaigning with Gwen Hanns vs John Lewthwaite, 1994

Photo album

Christmas with Ann's parents, Rose and Alf Leaf, 1990s

Swearing in ceremony with NSW Governor, April 1995

My first swearing in as a minister on my 38th birthday,
April 1995

Photo album

Celebrating the day I was appointed minister with Dad and Anwar Khoshaba, April 1995

James and Sarah joining me at a weekend function in Blacktown, circa 1995

Opening the Far West Electrification project near Broken Hill with Ann, Sarah and James, 1995

Minister for Roads inspecting a job site, late 1990s

Photo album

Connecting with the Sydney Harbour Bridge maintenance team

Making a point by the roadside at a road construction site, late 1990s

James, Ann and Sarah joining me at the opening of the Woronora Bridge

Guest of Honour of Fairfield City Mayor, Anwar Khoshaba with his wife Athour at the Mayoral Ball, 1998

James and Sarah attend a road opening with me, 1997

At a road tunnel event with Ann, James and Sarah

Launching $3B Action for Transport 2010 Blueprint with Bob Carr, November 1998

Inspecting progress Eastern Distributor, late 1990s

Photo album

Ann, James and Sarah joined me for the official opening of the M5 East Motorway

My favourite plaque unveiled by Bob Carr for the opening of the Eastern Distributor Landbridge in front of the Art Gallery, with John Caldon of Macquarie Bank and Ron Christie, CEO of RTA, January 1999

Preparing for ABC TV 730 Report Interview, 2000

The Geurie Level Crossing Press Conference near Dubbo with local MP, Tony McGrane, 2000

Photo album

Ann, James and Sarah join me with police officers at Paralympic Games Sydney, 2000

With Paul Forward, CEO RTA, prior to completion of M5 East Motorway, 2000

Announcing plans for the Cross City Tunnel, 2002

Speaking as Roads Minister at a country event
with Lew Laing, 2003

Updated campaign photo, 2003

Visiting Arnhem Land as Minister for Aboriginal Housing with Ann and Chief of Staff, Gary Sargent (with hat), 2003

At a birthday function for Ann, 2008

A final visit to my home in Chatswood with Sarah and James
after settling my parents' estate, 2010

Photo album

International career – post politics

Angolan Police rescue the WorleyParsons team
(including colleague Jonathan Horn) after running out of fuel
about 50 kms out of Luanda, Angola, 2011

With Henry Mukisa in Kampala, Uganda, 2014

Retirement from full-time employment

Ann's speech at my retirement party in St Ives, with our daughter Sarah and our son James next to her, November 2015

Photo by Vincent Lai Photography

Photo album

Chairman Mine Safety Advisory Council NSW

150m underground at Ulan West Coal Mine, Mudgee,
with Jim Middleton of Glencore, September 2016

CHAPTER 11

Running the railways – managing unbridled economic rationalism

The morning of the 2nd of December 1999 was the end of my relatively long honeymoon as Transport Minister. This was the morning of the Glenbrook train accident in the Blue Mountains west of Sydney. Seven people were killed when a passenger train collided into the rear of a stationary Pacific National freight train.

I was still a relatively new minister and neither the media nor the public held me responsible for what had occurred. This would be in sharp contrast to the Waterfall train accident of January 2003. Seven people were also killed in that accident when the train driver had a heart attack just after pulling out of Waterfall station. The train came off the tracks and crashed as it was going around a bend way over the allowable speed limit. By then, I had been minister for just over five years and the media and shock jocks were unforgiving in blaming me.

Whilst the media impact on my career after Glenbrook was relatively fair and measured, this soon made way for a much harsher assessment of my performance as train 'on-time' running began to decline as we approached the Sydney 2000 Olympics. This caused commuters to be late for work, which was an issue for which both they and the media needed a defendant in the dock. I

Chapter 11: Running the railways

very soon became that defendant. I had had a relatively calm, peaceful and enjoyable five years as a minister of the crown. That was now at an abrupt end!

As it turned out, my least pleasant period as a minister would easily be my five tough years in the challenging Transport portfolio. There were great highs such as successfully delivering the transport task for the Sydney 2000 Olympics, as well as delivering the $2.3B Epping to Chatswood railway. But even these only happened after years of tough haggling with Treasury and a long period of media and stakeholder cynicism and substantial criticism.

When I see the enormous budget allocations now made to roads and transport every year, I do wonder if the ministers of the day realise just how much easier the job is with a large allocated budget for the portfolio. When in 2016 I ran into the former Minister for Transport for New South Wales (and now Premier), Gladys Berejiklian, I lamented at how tough it had been under Carr and Egan and said: 'I don't know how I lasted as long as I did'. She responded: 'I had Barry (the then premier, Barry O'Farrell) fully on side. It makes a big difference having the Premier on side'.

I started in the rail portfolio at the end of 1997 with Mike Egan as Treasurer, disinterested in doing anything which might vaguely assist me politically, a Government which had just broken up the State Rail Authority into four separate entities and then put bean counters in charge, and a Premier and a Treasurer who were not overly focussed, nor all that interested, in improving public transport.

The combination of Egan and Carr pruning the funding of the railways, the decline in performance and the merciless media attacks which duly followed, and the deaths of both passengers and maintenance workers, made for a very tough few years. But I stuck it out despite wondering more than a few times why I did.

As a Cabinet minister, if one ever inherits a flawed administrative structure, unsuitable board appointments, CEOs with no direct experience of the industry and remorseless budget cuts year on year, one is expected to play the loyal game by absorbing and tolerating the situation, defend the Premier and the Treasurer, and blindly pretend that all the problems which in due course do occur, were caused by some other factors. This was the sometimes thankless game I had to play as a member of Carr and Egan's team, as the loyal Transport Minister for over 5 years.

When Carr called me in at the end of 1997 to tell me he was adding Transport to my Roads and Ports portfolios, I was a little overwhelmed at first. For the next five and a half years, I would be responsible for 10 separate government entities, 30,000 public servants and an annual expenditure of $6B with an enormous responsibility to the wider community. Some ministers are given this sort of humbling responsibility, but not many. It was a huge task and interestingly, after the 2003 election, Carr split the job between three ministers saying to me: "The job is too much for one person." I was inclined to agree.

Carr and Egan had already allowed the economic rationalists in the Treasury and the Cabinet office to convince them to split the State Rail Authority into four new entities: the owner of all rail assets; Rail Access Corporation, the maintainer of all rail tracks; Rail Services Corporation, the operator of the Government-owned freight rail business; Freight Corp and finally, the passenger rail operator which kept the name; State Rail Authority.

Chapter 11: Running the railways

The former Minister for Transport, Brian Langton, was right to almost resign over the issue. Treasury and Cabinet Office bean counters and policy theoreticians had won the day over an unsuspecting brand-new Treasurer and Premier, which with the passage of years would not have been possible. The only reform which made sense, was to hive-off the freight business, which did well on its own and in time became a worthy asset for private sale.

However, splitting rail track ownership, track maintenance and passenger rail services into three separate entities, was a very poor decision indeed, and one I had to live with for most of my time as Minister. In time, the track ownership and maintenance functions were joined into one entity, but were still kept separate from the passenger rail entity. This all might have looked good for a transport economics textbook, but made for an awful way to manage a railway or the media scrutiny and politics which followed. To make matters worse, the track owner and maintainer were independent State-owned corporations (SOCs) with the main shareholder being the Treasurer. Unlike in Queensland, the Minister for Transport in New South Wales, was not even a shareholder of these rail SOCs and not surprisingly, when I held that position, I was rarely consulted on decisions made by the rail entity shareholder ministers. More recent Transport Ministers would regard this as both bizarre and untenable, and for the many years it was in place from the mid-1990s onwards, it certainly was.

This meant that Michael Egan as Treasurer and main rail SOC shareholder, was in everything but name, the Minister for Rail Tracks, leaving me as the Minister for Transport, as a mere rail SOC interested stakeholder. And as Egan was a devoted political opponent of mine, he was more than content for me to be presented publicly as in charge of rail track condition whilst leaving me with no power to direct the two agencies responsible for it, Rail Access Corporation and Rail Services Corporation, and critically, no power over their funds. I never came across a more absurd way to organise a section of government than this one. It was virtually custom built for failure.

From the end of 1997 until the March 1999 election, my close colleague in the Cabinet room, Michael Knight, was the second shareholder minister after Egan, for my three transport State-owned enterprises. During this period, if Knight thought either Treasury or Egan were up to something not in my interest, he would refuse to sign off on it until he had briefed me in person, usually with the offending Treasury brief in hand with a flourishing signature of the Treasurer already secured. Not surprisingly, that all ended abruptly after the 1999 election when Egan acolyte, John Della Bosca, replaced Knight as the second shareholding minister and both Knight and I were removed at Egan's insistence, from the Budget Committee of Cabinet. Needless to say, the regular Knight briefings on what Treasury was up to in my portfolio immediately went to zero under Della Bosca.

Whilst the State Rail Authority was subject to my direction and control as Minister, the three State-Owned Corporations covering track, maintenance and freight were not. Michael Egan in his capacity as Treasurer was the major shareholder of each and could issue directions as he pleased. The railways had been subject to ministerial direction and control, since a special amendment had gone through Parliament in the early 1960s, but this had now been dispensed with.

This was a major flaw that Carr and Egan had implemented for the Government Railways and not one removed until well after all three of us had left politics. For decades prior to our election in 1995 the Minister for Transport had full power of direction and control over the whole rail network. What a novel approach to have continued that and one I would have very much welcomed. Egan had never had ministerial experience before being appointed Treasurer and would not have been aware of the intended or unintended pitfalls of Treasury and Cabinet Office inspired experiments with restructuring government for economic or policy testing reasons alone. Carr could draw on his time in the Wran and Unsworth Governments when he served as a Minister for Consumer Affairs, Heritage, and Planning and Environment, but had not had any time in the heavy hitting major spending portfolios. Had either of them had such experience, I am inclined to think, that the rail restructure plan presented to them, would have been quickly consigned to the office shredding machine where it belonged.

As it was, Carr was so impressed early on with separating State Owned Corporations from ministerial influence, that he said to me during a private audience: 'I actually think a Minister for Energy should be required to seek the permission of the Chairman before visiting a power station'. Thankfully, that never saw the light of day.

However, plenty of structural damage was done to the administrative organisation of the railways and it would take years before being fully reversed. This is a clear-cut example of accountants and economists in Treasury and policy wonks in the Cabinet office, getting way too much unbridled influence with the leaders of a new government, in implementing textbook experiments of economic rationalism with the railways. When this all literally fell off the rails, none of these interfering bureaucrats with no railway experience emerged from the shadows, to either take some responsibility, or admit it was all a big mistake. Whilst under this experiment I was the Minister for Passenger Train

Operations, my authority on rail track and its condition would have been more accurately described, as only being the Minister for Adverse Rail Track News. Egan was effectively the Shareholder Minister for Rail Track and Maintenance. As control over where and how funds were expended was the single most important part of ministerial authority in terms of these critically important agencies, the Treasurer remained in the box seat for all my long time in the Transport portfolio. However, as the Minister for Transport and despite the reality of who yielded real financial authority and ultimate control on the rail tracks organisations, I had to take all public responsibility for all and any adverse events and media, with enthusiasm and without demur. I am inclined to think that Egan probably enjoyed my predicament very much.

About two and half years into the job, rail on time running began to decline significantly, upsetting thousands of commuters and placing rail performance, as a serious threat to the September 2000 Sydney Olympics and therefore, the standing of not just the Minister for Transport, but the whole government. Not surprisingly, this attracted the attention of both the premier and the treasurer, as potential Olympic transport chaos and the consequent erosion of our political standing loomed as strong possibilities.

In this troubling political environment, I was able just a few weeks before the start of the Olympics, to secure Cabinet agreement to the appointment of a Rail Coordinator General, who had the power of direction and control over all rail agencies and their boards. This worked a treat for securing a successful Olympic Games, but afterwards, with the structure still in place, left me with a large section of my portfolio financially and managerially independent. I cannot think of another time when a Minister for

Chapter 11: Running the railways

Transport has had to manage the portfolio in such difficult circumstances.

Despite the heavy organisational ballast which was weighing down the portfolio, I tried to do the best I could with what I had inherited.

Once I was appointed as Minister for Transport, it seemed to me I had two very important tasks ahead of me, one immediate and one longer term. The first was to cancel the Rail Access Corporation plan to outsource hundreds of rail maintenance jobs to the private sector, and the second, to prepare a detailed transport plan for the City and the State ahead of the 1999 election.

Alarmingly, Treasury had managed to ensure that an economist and an accountant were now running the two rail track owner, and rail track maintenance organisations. This had been a conscious decision of Treasury to ensure that there was a very strong focus on cutting costs and lowering the need for financial support from the budget, rather than on what was needed to run a reliable, safe and well-maintained railway. This would directly cause a major slide in performance and untold media grief for me as Minister. It is hard to imagine government now making a rational decision to put accountants and economists in charge of a huge chunk of the railways, but that is precisely what had happened just before my arrival in the portfolio. An analogy would be the Transport minister convincing the premier and cabinet to put railway engineers in charge of the Treasury! Imagine how Egan might have reacted to that scenario.

Treasury always resented spending anything on the railways and could never see that subsidising a large rail network was as important to a functioning modern city, as were government-funded schools, roads, hospitals and police stations. In my five years as Minister, I don't recall them ever acknowledging what an important community service the railways provided. The senior officials in Treasury were convinced that the railways were overweight, over funded and inefficient and in much need of a solid dose of rationalisation, cost cutting, staff reductions and private sector efficiency. Carr and Egan did not seem to be overly interested in challenging this view.

And the man to achieve much of this for them was the Treasury-appointed Chairman of Rail Access Corporation, Rod Sims. It was not enough for Treasury to appoint CEOs with absolutely no rail experience, but they had to also appoint an economist and one of their own long-standing consultants, to the critical role of chairing the new rail asset entity. Sims never realised that he had been appointed as Chairman of a section of the New South Wales Government Railways, which for want of a better term, should have been called the Department of Railway Tracks but instead, was given the far more fancy and ominous title of the Rail Access Corporation.

The naming of the new entity as Rail Access reflected an almost miniscule part of its responsibilities, but one Treasury fancied as critical in the new railway economic order. Over 90% of the movement of trains in the massively important Sydney metropolitan area involved city rail passenger trains. There were a few Pacific National private freight trains and a few publicly owned Freight Corp trains, but these were just incidental to making sure that the track was always in a fit and good condition for running passenger trains in the morning and evening peaks. This was not achieved for several months leading up to the Sydney 2000 Olympics and it was not the board or its chairman who had to answer for it. I had to do that!

Chapter 11: Running the railways

A bizarre system of payments was then set in place by Treasury to give the appearance of corporate and commercial Australia having arrived at Platform 1. The State Rail Authority was given a budget by Treasury to pay the Rail Access Corporation for using the tracks which would then pay Rail Services Corporation an amount for maintaining them. The aim was clear: keep a close watch on the accounts and rail performance can take care of itself. It didn't!

This experiment with rail structure and operations was along the lines of a not yet discredited UK model. When I recently lamented with Arthur Smith, who I had appointed as Deputy CEO of the SRA, on what a disaster this experiment had been, he gave me some chilling accounts of just how much worse it actually was on the ground for people like him trying to run a reliable passenger train network.

As minister, I regarded Arthur Smith as one of the best railwaymen in the country and in New South Wales, second only to Ron Christie. Arthur had been a long serving employee of the State Rail Authority, had enormous on the track experience and impact, and unsurprisingly, over the years had risen through the ranks. I often sought his counsel, away from the more formal strictures of the rail organisational model I had inherited. And it was Arthur Smith who convinced me, that I needed someone else other than him, to take over the strategic cross-rail agency solution I eventually found in Ron Chrisite when he lamented: "Who will do my job if I am doing that for you".

His two examples are worth recounting as a reminder of the structural madness the government had knowingly inflicted upon itself prior to my arrival in the portfolio:

> "We were getting significant timetable performance issues on the City South Western line because a set of rail crossovers near Cabramatta Station were in such poor condition, I had to put a speed restriction on that part of the line to keep train movements safe. When SRA was a single organisation, there would have been no difficulty in getting the necessary work done to remove speed restrictions. But with the break-up of SRA, I had to put my case for the work to RAC, but they refused to fund it and argued that 'the track was fit for purpose'. When I again requested the work be done I was asked to 'prove you need it'. I then went to RSA and they told me: "We're the contractor. You need to get RAC to direct us on that or it won't get done". I decided I was going to get nowhere with senior management on this, so I made contact with some lower management guys in RSA who I had known for years at SRA, and they located a spare crossover in a warehouse which was apparently under the radar. I immediately took possession of it and had it installed in the track the following weekend. The timetable improved immediately on that part of the track."

But it gets worse. Arthur also gave me an even more bizarre account of the consequences of letting accountants and economists run the railways:

> "Track grinders are a very important part of the equipment required to keep rail track in good working order. Rail track across the network needs to be grinded at regular intervals to make sure that the metal surface profile of the track matches that of each wheel of a train. There had been a derailment a couple

Chapter 11: Running the railways

of years before the Olympics on the Olympic rail loop, which we attributed to insufficient match between the tracks and train wheels. I requested RSA to grind the track and fix the problem. I was then told by senior RSA management, that as RAC had told them to look for maintenance work outside the New South Wales rail network, they had recently won a maintenance job for WA Rail and that the grinder was in Perth working on WA rail tracks. They even had the nerve to suggest an alternative; "why don't you run a one kilometre fully laden coal train around the track which should make a difference". I made such a song and dance on this one that RSA carried out works to fix the problem."

I recall vividly, an exasperating conversation I had one day with the State Rail CEO, Simon Lane, when I complained vigorously about some recent whole of rail performance issues. His response summed up succinctly the situation: "I am only responsible for trains. I am not responsible for the tracks they run on."

So, in a nutshell: The passenger rail CEO tells me the track condition is not his problem. The track maintenance company then tells me that they are just the contractor and to go talk to the track owner. But the track owner then protests that the track is gold plated, too expensive to maintain and funding needs to be cut. How we got through to deliver it all for the Sydney 2000 Olympics still amazes me, but I am not amazed that rail did political damage to me.

The new model was set up and designed to save money by lowering the amount allocated for running the railways. Looking back to the period from when we were elected in 1995 through to the Sydney Olympics in September 2000, it is quite apparent, that there had been a deliberate and substantial reduction in most of the essential work needed to run a well-maintained railway. Track, sleepers, overhead wires, crossovers, switching gear, ballast renewal and more were not being replaced or renewed at anywhere near the amount which had taken place for years before our election. Treasury had no idea what the actual amount was, that was needed to run a safe, reliable and well-maintained railway, but they firmly believed, that whatever it was, it would always be a lot less than the year before. No wonder performance declined ahead of the Sydney 2000 Olympics.

Treasury now had a great structure and process in place for running down the funding of the rail track network and when the obvious happened, I had to take the heat as Minister. That is how our system works even though I had inherited the people, structure and the underlying agenda, which had caused a good deal of the performance issues in rail that inevitably followed. Egan, as quasi Minister for Rail Tracks, never took any of the media heat and nor did Carr except when absolutely necessary, such as the Waterfall rail accident.

The rail track owner, Rail Access Corporation (RAC) was responsible for determining when, where and to some extent how, maintenance would be carried out by Rail Services Corporation (RSC). It seemed very clear to me, very early on, that both Rail Access and New South Wales Treasury, had a clear agenda to reduce rail maintenance costs by taking work off the public-sector rail workforce and tendering it out to private sector bidders. The Rail, Tram and Bus Union (RTBU) was not impressed.

RAC had broken Sydney and the rest of the New South Wales rail network into separate sectors that they intended to run on a rolling tender process for rail maintenance contracts over the

Chapter 11: Running the railways

following two years. One had been completed and unsurprisingly, the public-sector rail maintenance company, RSC, had been unsuccessful and the contract had been awarded to a private company.

Initially RAC tried to convince me that the tender process did not have a pre-determined outcome, but when pushed, its senior managers conceded that a desirable outcome at the end of all the tender processes, would be four separate rail maintenance companies, including RSC, each having 25% of the cake. I was appalled. So far as I was aware, there had never been a Cabinet decision to privatise the New South Wales railway network and kill off 150 years of publicly-owned railways.

I had a nostalgic and affectionate soft spot for the railways. I had worked at the Darling Harbour Rail Goods Yard every summer holiday during my six years at university. I was also very proud of the fact that my grandfather, Patrick Charles Scully and later ALP MP for Namoi, had been a big supporter of the Australian Railway Union in the 1917 strike. He was one of many who were granted a medal by the Railway Union for supporting the union during a very difficult time. A publicly-owned railway was a big deal to me and it was obvious to me that Treasury was driving a massive change to our railways in which the Cabinet, the caucus and the wider community would have no say. I quickly came to the view that RAC and Treasury had no right to proceed with this sort of change and that I intended to stop it.

Early in my tenure as Transport Minister, I informed both Rod Sims as RAC Chairman and Judi Stack as its CEO, that I had decided to terminate the outsourcing programme and to commit to continued public ownership of our rail track maintenance workforce. I requested that the tender programme be discontinued. This sort of decision making authority over the railways had resided with the Minister for Transport for decades but had now been considerably eroded.

Both Sims and Stack rejected my decision to take charge of the track maintenance agenda, and appeared all but horrified, that I would want to interfere, in what they perceived to be the independent business of their semi-sovereign organisation. It was almost the reaction I would have expected from a private sector company board Chairman and its CEO, if I had tried to tell them both, how to run their company business. Except in this case, it was a government entity charged with operating an important part of the New South Wales Government Railway. The public rightly expects the relevant minister, as trustee of a public asset, to be in charge, and not subordinate personnel.

Sims then embarked on a process, which I am sure few ministers have had to experience from a government entity within their own portfolio. He and Stack took RAC into the bunker and commenced an all-out campaign to win the day on this issue.

Rod Sims was blunt:

> *"Treasury has made it clear that these reforms need to go ahead; we have started the process and we need to continue it. We are an independent SOC and it is the Treasurer as shareholder who directs us and not the Minister".*

The initial difficulty I had with RAC was solely about my wish to protect public sector rail jobs, but based on the strength of opposition from Sims and Stack, it quickly became an issue about who was running the railways. Was it Rod Sims supported by Judi Stack, or was it the Minister for Transport? I then decided to commit fully all my capability and all my influence within the

Chapter 11: Running the railways

Government to bring RAC to heal, to ensure that the Chairman and the CEO were in no doubt that they served not Treasury and its accountants, but the commissioned Minister for Transport. It was an absolutely fundamental position which had to be settled urgently, but unfortunately, the RAC leadership strongly resisted, both my demand and expectation of their complying role. As a result, a real bunker versus bunker battle unfolded between my office and the RAC command headquarters. I intended to win.

I knew that with less than a year to go to the next election, Carr as always, would be impressionable to a well-argued political survival case against the RAC/Treasury agenda. I was confident that he would not care a hoot about the need for the minister to win the day, or that we should be philosophically committed to public sector rail jobs. I prepared a detailed list of the job reductions which would occur in each region proposed to be tendered out, and then superimposed this on to the electoral map of New South Wales. It did not make for a pleasant sight and I think it weighed on Carr's mind.

Carr could often be easily distracted. During a meeting with him on this issue, which included senior rail public servants and some of his own personal staff, I lamented at just how many rail maintenance jobs would be lost in region after region, but then made an inexcusable Carr grammatical faux pas: "and in Newcastle alone, there will be 1,000 less jobs", and quick as a flash, Carr chimed in with, "you mean fewer jobs." I quietly thought to myself: 'is he kidding' but I did respond with: "Premier, are you correcting my grammar", to which he replied, "Yes, you need to work on that." It was very hard sometimes to get him to properly focus on the matter in question. He often got quickly bored on even the most important and pressing issues.

A short while after my pitch to Carr on 'fewer jobs', I was called-in to a private meeting with him and he said he was going to give me a win on the issue. "After your performance in creating the three port corporations, you have credibility in dealing with SOCs and it is defendable that you be supported on this."

I had taken a big gamble in taking the RAC Chairman, CEO and senior executives to the brink and neither side took a step back throughout. For me, it was a stunning victory that had put the RAC organisation and its leadership in the box they deserved. Or so I thought. As it turned out, the outsourcing agenda had merely been deferred and not defeated. At least not yet.

As soon as the 1999 election was out of the way and I was re-appointed as minister, the RAC was at it again, as if nothing had happened. I had won the day on the first round because an election was looming and I knew that the Treasurer would not be so accommodating this time around.

However, the new attempt by RAC to re-start the killing-off of Government railway jobs also failed.

Egan was very keen to sell the publicly-owned Freight Corp and I saw an unexpected opportunity. The Rail, Tram and Bus Union, with a little encouragement from me, made it plain to Egan that if he wanted their support on the sale, then he would have to commit to ending for good the outsourcing of rail maintenance work. When I brought up a Cabinet Minute to formalise this decision, all Egan had to say was: "Normally I would never agree to something like this, but in the special circumstances it has my support". I was delighted that a long drawn-out, knock them down fight in the sun had finally gone my way. What is extraordinary is that I had to expend so much energy and time in

Chapter 11: Running the railways

battling not all the usual suspects of political life and office, but one of my own agencies.

But despite the loss of the outsourcing programme, RAC would continue the Treasury agenda under another guise, by simply cutting the annual maintenance budget of the Rail Services Corporation (RSC), and claimed that they would, or even could, keep on doing more with less. This caused considerable harm to the performance of the track and the train schedules over a sustained period, and undermined public confidence in the railways in the critical period leading up to the Sydney 2000 Olympics and beyond. And I was the one held to account for it.

However, whilst battling with RAC and Treasury over the future of our railways, I also started to plan for a long-term Transport Blueprint for Sydney and New South Wales. In December 1998, Carr and I released 'Action for Transport 2010', which was a comprehensive plan for delivering new motorways, freeways, rail lines, bus ways and light rail across the state for the next 12 years. It was a great process which for the first time, brought all the road and transport agencies together to consider how people wanted to move, where they wanted to live and work, and the challenges in achieving those objectives.

It was an exciting document which had taken 12 months to steer through my own agencies and those of the broader Government with a $3B commitment over a 10-year period. The big winner was Western Sydney with the 40 km M7 Motorway, a huge upgrade of Windsor Road and Old Windsor Road to four lanes, an extensive Bus-only Transitways network, as well as the new Parramatta to Chatswood railway. But there would also be new ferries, trains, light rail and finally, the completion of the Sydney Orbitol Motorway network, around and through urban and Sydney CBD. It was stimulating stuff and I felt I was on a magnificent journey of improving the quality of life and mobility of millions of people. But as always, it would be a lot easier to plan and announce than to fund and deliver.

It often amused me that journalists, who had never delivered a project in their lives, just loved to proclaim my own and my agencies' alleged incompetence in not be able to deliver a project to the original estimated cost. In time, I would add more and more contingency to the original estimated cost to deal with the many costly unknowns which would usually surface as a project was being planned and delivered over time.

But during 1998, as we put pen to paper for the Budget Committee on what we thought would be the cost of delivering such a massive Transport Blueprint for Sydney and New South Wales, I was yet to be burnt by the media, talkback radio or Treasury for this sort of cost estimating 'incompetence'. I always believed and still believe, that the most important thing is for government to commit to the projects it believes are needed, build a consensus for them across the community, the political aisle and the broader media, and then just find the money to deliver them. This is the fundamental way in which government should approach the delivery of major projects during its term in office. I was able to do this successfully in creating major new road infrastructure for Sydney, only because most of these were PPP-funded private tollways. This meant that Carr, Egan and Treasury did not have to spend one cent more on the roads portfolio than what they had intended to already spend without any Transport Blueprint.

The $1.4B estimate for the Parramatta to Chatswood railway was already in the forward estimates by the time I came to the Transport portfolio and would sadly, be the first major rail project in Sydney since the Wran Labor Government had completed the

Chapter 11: Running the railways

Eastern Suburbs Railway in the 1970s. As I would soon learn, this amount was woefully inadequate and would only fund half of the original project. This did not concern the Premier, the Treasurer or Treasury, who insisted that only the original estimated amount of $1.4B be allocated and consequently, only half the project proceeded.

Unlike roads, there were only very limited Public Private Partnership (PPP) opportunities to pursue private finance alternatives for new rail projects. Motorists will complain a bit about paying tolls yet pay them every working day of the year and some. But, rail commuters start from the premise that rail tickets should be so cheap as to be closer to zero than anywhere near the true cost of providing a rail service for a big city. It is the same across the developed world. The difference during the Carr/Egan administration, was that most governments in the developed world recognised both this resistance to paying and the vital contribution a modern railway contributes to a large city and would fund them accordingly. The period of Liberal rule from 2011, has now adopted this approach, with literally billions of dollars of extra public funds for both heavy and light rail. I can only look on in awe and wonder how different would have been the legacies of our long years in office, if Carr and Egan had shown the same level of interest.

However, it was only going to be the $1.4B for the original estimate of the whole Parramatta to Chatswood and not a cent more. But even this amount soon appeared to be insufficient to fund even half the project, and most of the other rail projects in Action for Transport 2010 were stranded as unfunded and unwanted projects. The Rail Blueprint set out a plan to build a new rail line from Epping to Castle Hill and onto Rouse Hill. This was long before former New South Wales Liberal Leader Barry

O'Farrell had 'discovered' this as a project and even the Liberal Shadow Minister for Transport at the time complimented me with: "I give you credit for the line to Rouse Hill, we didn't even think of that one." Unfortunately, it took a new Liberal Government to start building it.

There was no good reason why the last 12 years of Labor Government including six without Carr and Egan, was unable to plan, fund and deliver, not only all of the Parramatta to Chatswood rail link, but also all of the Epping to Rouse Hill rail link. It still grieves me to see the justified stature of a hundred years of Labor Governments as the big builders of Sydney, being handed over, by the last Labor government in power, to our political opponents, simply because of that Labor Government's lack of will, lack of talent and lack of interest. It will be a long time before we get the title back!

But with some decent funding, so much more could have been achieved over a sustained period of time. Carr and Egan had little interest in transport projects or policy, or in their funding and delivery, although Carr would always get excited about any media event arising after the long hard yards had been done in delivering the project.

This is the real story behind the successes and failures of Action for Transport 2010. It was an ambitious plan which naively committed to cost, time and scope. In time, over many years in both the roads and Transport portfolios, I would learn the hard way that major projects are always without fail, far more expensive, far more time-consuming and far more difficult to deliver than ever envisaged at the first stages of planning. No transport plan since has so aggressively committed to cost, time and scope as Action for Transport did. Unfortunately, these sorts of plans normally now contain so much waffle in this regard, that

Chapter 11: Running the railways

it is almost impossible sometimes to glean from Government just when, where and how they intend to build new infrastructure.

I think my experience on Action for Transport was an unfortunate contributing factor in the timidity of the last six years of Labor Government in the delivery of major transport projects. Iemma, Rees and Keneally basically set up the 'closed for business' sign and waited for the inevitable defeat in March 2011 election. I never was one for the 'under-promise and over-deliver' mantra of the typical modern day timorous holder of executive office. If I had my time over again, I would still think that over-promising and under-delivering gets a lot more done as you and your agencies strive to deliver a difficult and challenging task.

If only journalists and their editors cared just a little about this sort of approach being better for the community rather than being on a constant roaming 'attack mode' looking for the 'over-promiser' and running damning articles on what was still left to be delivered. The usual media approach only compounds ministerial timidity when 'under-promisers' are lauded by them for having achieved more than they set out to do.

Despite the serious lack of funding which Action for Transport needed, a lot was done and not just on roads. The biggest rail upgrade in 30 years was achieved with the building of the Epping to Chatswood passenger rail tunnel. But even at a final cost of $2.3B, it was still only half the promised project which was supposed to go all the way from Parramatta to Chatswood rather than from just Epping.

During its planning stages, I found that I could not get the State Rail executives to focus on it, as they were almost completely distracted by ensuring folks got to work and home on time. So, I set up a new entity called the Parramatta Rail Link Company as a corporate subsidiary of the Department of Transport which reported directly to me. It was a much better way to deliver major rail projects and this approach, under a different guise and different name, has continued to this day.

Following the Waterfall train disaster of January 2003, and the aggressive way in which I was pursued by the media, my life as Minister for Transport soon came to an end at the March 2003 election. It had been a very tough five and half years and I can't deny how relieved I was to be rid of the portfolio. Despite the experience, I can look back with fond regard on more than a few things which I think have made a difference. This among others includes upgrading the very run down shopping precinct along Argyle Street in Parramatta and greatly improving security and crime prevention on our trains and stations.

I was also able to use the upgrade of Parramatta Rail Station combined with building a bus rail interchange for the new Liverpool to Parramatta Bus Transitway, as an excuse to compulsorily acquire all the ugly strip of shops along Argyle Street, Parramatta, which ran up the hill away from the Westfield shopping mall towards the rail station. This is now a pleasant, busy and popular restaurant precinct connected to the shopping mall. The tattoo parlours and an awful rundown part of CBD Parramatta are now gone. That still gives me a lot of pleasure.

One of the recurring issues throughout my time as Transport Minister was personal security on our trains and stations. I found it almost unreasonable that the media and the public could be so relaxed about crime figures for the general community, but still hold the view that our railways should be 'zero crime zones'. Whilst it was an irrational position to take from the media and an unfair one from the travelling public, I understood what motivated it.

Chapter 11: Running the railways

Most folks have no real choice about travelling on the railways and clearly empathise with a crime victim when assaulted on our public transport network, as something which could have happened to them. When the same crime occurs elsewhere in the community, there is not anywhere near the same empathy or heightened sense of personal threat. This made for a compelling case to implement some major initiatives to deal with both the actual and perceived risk of assault, as well as providing police with a greater capacity to apprehend offenders when an incident did occur.

In July 1998, I introduced two security guards on every night train after 7.00 pm. This immediately made people feel safer on our trains especially women. This security measure was in place for five years until the next minister, Michael Costa, removed it as a cost cutting exercise. In addition to the security guards, I created a small army of some 600 transit officers to patrol trains across the network. Their job was to look out for fare evaders, hooligans and criminals. Whilst neither the security guards nor the transit officers could provide the level of comfort that police would have been able to, I believe they filled a valuable role as 'human security cameras'. The new Liberal Government elected in March 2011, abolished the transit officers and replaced them with an expanded Police Transport Command. It will be interesting to see if over time, rail passengers get anywhere near the same level of presence and attention.

To complement the night security guards and the full-time transit officers, I decided to introduce a network of modern digital CCTV cameras and help points on every platform of every one of our 307 stations across the entire City Rail Network. It was an expensive exercise, but an effective one in both deterring crime and later detecting it. Unexpectedly, the 5,000 cameras provided new and vitally useful evidence in general policing work. All the security initiatives cost over $100M to implement, but in my view, were well worth the public expense.

Whenever I see footage from rail security cameras on the TV news when a crime has been committed, I do feel very pleased that this initiative of over 15 years ago, is still, all these years later, working so effectively. Many criminals have been successfully pursued by police for serious crimes, because of the availability of irrefutable rail camera evidence.

When we were developing the proposal to install security cameras across the rail network, Simon Lane, the SRA CEO, put the case that a few outlying rail stations which serviced only a small number of commuters, ought not to have funds allocated for cameras, help points and cabling back to a monitoring station. I was mortified; "Simon, I want to give a simple message. Every station, everywhere, across the entire network. No exceptions".

It never crossed my mind that he may have a point. However, many years later, long after leaving the portfolio, I was walking the Great North Walk which extends 250 km from Sydney Harbour all the way to Newcastle. It took myself and my walking companion, my brother-in-law David Honer, eight years to complete in roughly 20 km chunks. On one of those many pleasant occasions, the day's walk ended at Wondabyne Rail Station on the Central Coast Line. It was rather isolated being surrounded by the national park on one side and water on the other. I noted one home and one access road and apart from the occasional bushwalker, that was it. The station had a sign up on both sides advising that you would need to signal the driver to stop. That's when I looked up and noticed a help point on both platforms and no fewer than eight digital cameras taking direct feed of mostly nothing most days of the week. Perhaps the CEO had actually made a sound point.

One of my most enduringly amusing memories from these security initiatives is the one-off spike in the quarterly crime figures which followed the introduction of night security guards and then the thousands of CCTV cameras. I explained this on the basis that previously undetected crime was now being thankfully detected and was making our railways safer, not the opposite. In both cases after the one-off dramatic spike, as I expected, crime began to fall and continued to fall over time. But at the time, the media and Barry O'Farrell, the Opposition Transport spokesman, were not having a bar of it. Crime had gone up because I was incompetent and had wasted taxpayers' money in causing it. I still can't believe that either actually believed what they were saying, but it got a great run nonetheless, at my expense. That the installation of cameras and the provision of hundreds of security guards led to increased crime were probably the most ridiculous media and political attacks I had to answer for in my 17 years as an MP. Today it would be labelled as 'fake news'.

If implementing security measures on our trains and stations gave me great pleasure, then trying to implement station staff number reforms had the opposite effect.

If I thought dealing with Treasury on project funding for new railway projects was tough, then trying to implement a Carr/Egan initiative to implement a much-needed reform on railway station staffing was a whole lot tougher. And on this occasion, I was gladly carrying out one of their cost cutting plans for the State Rail Authority.

When I inherited the Transport portfolio, Treasury was in full swing in pulling as much funding out of the railways as it could.

The operations of the Sydney passenger service known as City Rail was far from immune. The approach of Treasury was to ask for as much cost cutting initiatives as the agency could think of, and then reduce annual funding allocations as if all the selected initiatives would be successfully implemented. One of these included the rationalising of staff on our City Rail stations.

The number of staff allocated to particular stations had not been reviewed in years and it was proposed to reduce some, increase others and where appropriate offer redundancies to interested employees who wished to take a package. Unlike the RAC outsourcing agenda, this one was not forced on employees and no one needed to leave the railways if they chose not to do so.

When surveyed, many station employees indicated that they were interested in taking a package and were willing to depart the employment of the New South Wales Government railways. This seemed a win-win to me. The State Rail Authority (SRA) convinced me that the total number of station staff was excessive for the modern demands of managing railway stations, and that we should also move employees to where they were most needed. No one was going to be forced out, which supported an assumption made by both me and the SRA leadership, that the rail unions should not have a problem with the reform. How wrong we were!

The Australian Services Union (ASU) and the Rail Tram and Bus Union (RTBU) went berserk as if this was Armageddon itself. Their anger took me by surprise, particularly the RTBU, as it did not cover many of the station staff, but was protesting in sympathy. The ASU leadership argued that they were not going to allow a reduction in their number of members, and that voluntary redundancy was beside the point. A number of station staff employees began to complain about the delay this was causing to

Chapter 11: Running the railways

their exit and referring them back to their union only exacerbated the reaction of officials.

I was between a rock and a hard place. The Premier, Bob Carr and the Treasurer, Mike Egan, had both presided over a Budget Committee of Cabinet which approved both the reductions in funding for the SRA and the station staff initiative which underpinned it. Neither they nor Treasury were going to approve an increase in funding to offset rolling over to union pressure on this reform. Likewise, the unions made it clear that if I proceeded, I would be in for one hell of a fight. Either I rolled over and conceded that the unions were running the railways, or I stood my ground and let them know who was in charge. To me, this was even more fundamental than the issue of whether I was in charge of determining policy on track maintenance.

I had worked on the railways every university summer for six years. I had been a member of the Australian Railways Union. I was sympathetic to what I regarded as the union cause and where appropriate, industrial action. But on this occasion, I could see that union opposition was not solely motivated by their members' interests, but was instead about trying to prevent a reduction of their membership. Hardly a justifiable position for them to take.

I decided to stand my ground. In private, the leadership of both unions had threatened to shut down commuter trains for 48 hours if I announced that I was proceeding with the station reform initiative. It was mid-year 1999 and just three months earlier, we had been given a stunning electoral victory at the polls with a substantially increased majority. We were riding high in the post-election polls and with no election in sight for nearly four years, I could not think of a better time to stare down the rail unions even it meant strike action, so we could take control of the railways off the union leadership to achieve a good reform and save $20M every year for the budget … and so did Bob Carr; for precisely five hours!

To cover myself, I asked for a private meeting with the Premier to explain again why the union was threatening strike action if I did not roll over to their demands. His reaction to me was one of the most memorable ones I had with our Leader; "fuck'em, fuck'em" he said. "You tell them that this is being implemented and we don't care what their threats are. We are not backing down on this one bit." I sought reassurance; "Bob, are you sure. Once I announce to them that this is proceeding, they will shut down the railways and cause all manner of grief to the public." and he responded; "Yes, I am. We need to do this and threatening a strike is not going to change what we need to do here."

I told the unions what our decision was and they abruptly announced a full 48-hour strike. I briefed Col Allan, the Editor of the Daily Telegraph, who was very supportive and ran a very strong position in the following day's paper in favour of what I was trying to do.

And then I got a call from Bob Carr around 8.00 pm that same night prior to the strike. His opening line left me speechless, feeling isolated, like a branch chopped off a tree, and still to this day completely astonished; "Carl, I have got Michael Costa (then Secretary of the Labor Council) and Nick Lewocki (then Secretary of the RTBU) on the line. They think that this can be settled without industrial action" to which I said; "Bob, are you kidding? The only way to avoid that is if we do not proceed with these reforms." Carr then said; "I want you to meet them tomorrow and see if you can sort it out".

Chapter 11: Running the railways

I knew immediately the moment I put the phone down that the dispute was over and that I would have to eat humble pie the next day in front of Lewocki and Costa. I knew also that it meant union influence over the management decisions on what was best for the railways would continue unabated, and that any budget savings earmarked as a result of the initiative were now illusory. It was about as awful a phone call you can get from a boss and still keep your job. I had naively assumed that an emphatic sign off from the head of government meant that I could proceed with him at my back. I learnt the hard way that when Carr said something, he did not necessarily mean it and that "fuck'em, fuck'em" was just tough talk inside the privacy of his office.

It was too late to call off the first day of the strike which proceeded. The following day with Lewocki and Costa, I rolled over as requested and the reform bit the dust.

In the 1980s, the Labor Premier, Neville Wran, had supported his Transport Minister in reducing the crew of publicly-owned freight trains from three to two, and when the rail unions went on strike for three weeks the Premier held firm. The reform was implemented. Carr would have been fully aware of this as he was a minister in Wran's Cabinet at the time. Wran lasted 21 days to see the reform through, but Carr didn't even last the night. I knew it was going to be a tough public brawl, but if Carr had remained firm, I would have let the strike go on for as long as it took to win the dispute. My hunch at the time was that the initial 48-hour strike was probably all they had in them. It was a tall order to ask train drivers and guards to lose two days' pay for station staff in a different union for whom there was no great love. I am convinced I would have won the day. However, that would have needed resolve and patience. I had the blood for it, but Carr clearly did not.

I met with Carr shortly afterwards and he said he was very concerned that public support could have quickly evaporated for the government in that kind of dispute and that was why he wanted it wound up quickly. I just wish he had told me that in our private conversation before I walked the plank on the issue and not afterwards! I learnt the hard way that interpreting what the leader really meant by unequivocally strong language was sometimes as hard as reading tea leaves.

Many years after this event when both Carr and I had left politics and happened to be at the same function, I gave some advice to two of the Labor ministers in attendance in front of Carr;

> *"Always remember, that when you are out on a limb and you hear the sound of a saw cutting the limb you are on, and you see that the guy who sent you out on that limb, is now the guy cutting it, then you better very quickly get a hold of the trunk of the tree he has also grabbed a good hold of".*

Quick as a tack and unprompted, Carr chimed in;

> *"You are referring to the station reform initiative. I was not satisfied that you had argued your case sufficiently in the community".*

Really? Somewhat 'he protesteth too much' I thought. Now at least I know what the Secretary of Treasury had meant way back in 1999 after I told him it was no fault of mine that the budget savings would not be met; he had said: "That is not the story I was told".

Once I received this searing experience, I informed my personal staff that all aggressive reforms in the portfolio were now off the table. Once I had implemented the station reform initiative,

Chapter 11: Running the railways

I had decided to put an axe into the School Transport Subsidy Scheme which even back in the late 1990s at about $400M per year, was the most expensive in the western world. I had spent a lot of time in devising a long transition period so that over a 15-year period, parents would slowly but eventually be weaned back to a more affordable level of public support. I was confident I could sell this to the community and the media to steer it through. But if Carr was going to back down on a two-day rail strike, then he would have little appetite for this kind of long drawn-out battle. I withdrew it and it never saw the light of day. On reform, I realised I needed to watch my back rather than step out on the front foot.

But there would be soon enough a much tougher assignment in rail than trying to reform station staff in the face of a timid premier.

On the 2nd of December 1999 at 8.22 am, the Glenbrook Rail accident took place. Seven people sitting in the front compartment of the passenger train were killed and 51 passengers were taken to hospital with injuries.

Justice Peter McInerney of the New South Wales Supreme Court was appointed to conduct a full open judicial inquiry into the causes of the accident and give recommendations on what needed to be done to ensure it did not happen again. He found that a series of signalling and communication failures of either equipment or procedure had caused the accident and made a number of strong recommendations in this regard.

The whole process from the morning of the accident on the 2nd of December 1999 right through to its final report on the 11th of April 2001 was confronting and distressing at a personal level, and gruelling and exhausting at a political level.

In the months leading up to the Glenbrook train accident, there had been signs that things were not heading in the right direction. There had been some derailments and safety issues for track maintenance workers including a couple of fatalities. But, on-time running continued to perform well for passenger rail services until late 1999.

The only real measure of customer satisfaction for an urban passenger rail service is on-time running for the morning and evening weekday peaks. There is no need to ask commuters what they think of the service if on-time running starts to dip much below 90%. They get angry and certainly do not hold back in letting the media and the government know about it.

For most of my five and a half years as Transport Minister, the on-time figure hovered around 92%, which was a good figure, and one the travelling public were comfortable with.

In December 1999, the on-time running started to slightly decline and a little more in January 2000, followed by a wholesale decline to well below 90% in March-April and beyond. There was a whole raft of reasons for this decline, but the underlying cause was track condition. When Treasury and RAC started on a programme of reducing the funding of 'fat' in the railways, no one could accurately say where the fat ended and the thin began. As a result, the annual allocations for maintaining the railway track in a fit for purpose condition kept being reduced from our election in 1995, until rail performance began to be impaired from early 2000 onwards.

The Granville train disaster of January 1977, which killed 81 people, was blamed primarily on inadequate maintenance funding. For the next 20 years, the approach of rail management and Treasury, was to ensure, not to fix after the track failed, but to always fix it before it failed. Under a new Labor Government, this had now changed back to the pre-Granville days of running a railway based on always playing catch up with too little funds for maintenance and operations. Once again, I had to do the explaining when on-time running and safety came to a crashing thud.

At the same time as Treasury and RAC were thinning the fat in rail maintenance funding, the same government from which they sprang, was gold plating our electricity assets to ensure availability of supply, and as much as possible, eliminate the possibility of blackouts. Treasury, The Independent Pricing and Regulatory Tribunal, the electricity authorities and the Government, all supported the approach that the power we supplied to business and households had to have gold plated reliability. However, when it came to the railways, it was acceptable to search for the efficient cost of maintaining the rail network, instead of the guaranteed reliable supply cost, which was the funding and investment approach applied each and every year to the electricity network. The only difference between maintaining rail assets and electricity assets is that electricity assets provide a welcome cash cow of revenue and profit, whereas the world over, rail assets make a loss. But then, so do schools, hospitals and police stations.

Treasury had no idea what the right amount of annual spend ought to be on track maintenance. It just knew that each year, it had to be less than the previous year.

I was concerned right from the start about the diminishing annual allocations for track maintenance and I regularly questioned the track owner, RAC, and the track maintainer, RSA, on the subject and asked how the railways could be kept in a well-maintained position with falling funds. Judi Stack and Rod Sims would constantly assure me that sufficient funds were being paid to RSA to maintain an appropriate track condition and that RSA was expected to achieve this by continually attaining improvements in its efficiency and productivity. In other words, keep achieving more each year, with fewer resources.

I regularly grilled Terry Ogg, a former accountant who was then CEO of RSA. He equally assured me that he was maintaining the track in an adequate condition despite RAC reducing funding each and every year. I was troubled that at the same time as the CEO was asserting this fact, he was also seeking and winning rail maintenance work for his workforce in Western Australia and even in Hong Kong. This alarmed me all the more so, as the private sector dominated RSA board seemed rather pleased with this sort of diversification. This looked like an unwanted distraction from the main game. I thought they had lost their way.

The RSA CEO assured me that the reduced funding was being met by improved efficiency, but as this would leave a number of rail track workers without employment, he needed to find work for them interstate or overseas. Protecting the jobs of public sector rail workers was a noble thing to do. However, it was motivated by a desire of one part of the New South Wales Government railway (the track maintainer RSA) to thwart the impact of the cost cutting agenda of another part of the same railway (the track owner RAC). It was that perverse! A system which compelled a part of senior rail management to seek rail maintenance jobs in WA and Hong Kong sounds bizarre today, but it is actually what was happening during my time as Minister for Transport for New South Wales.

The structure I had inherited was so absurd, that simply strange public management outcomes like this, were the order of the day. It now looks and sounds ridiculous, but it was the rail structure I had to work with as best I could.

Treasury and RAC had set an aggressive funding reduction programme for the fiscal years of 1996/97, 1997/98 and 1998/99 and beyond, on the assumption that the RAC programme for outsourcing 75% of track maintenance would have been implemented and delivered considerable reductions in staff numbers, employee costs and track maintenance costs. When the outsourcing programme was cancelled in 1999 and the station staff reforms were discontinued after the rail unions went on strike, Treasury and RAC just continued on with the same path of reduced maintenance funding as if nothing had changed. This directly led to the performance disaster period leading up to the September 2000 Olympics. It was not pretty! And I was the only one who had to front the media about it.

I had appointed a well-known construction industry CEO, Tony Shepard, to the Board of the SRA and sought out his advice on what had occurred. He advised that a well-maintained asset can continue to perform for up to three years without adequate levels of maintenance, but relatively quickly and unexpectedly after that, the performance falls off a cliff which is exactly what had happened here. He used the term "sweating the asset" to describe the Treasury/RAC approach to rail maintenance funding and I passed this on to Carr who noted it in his diary at the time.

In due course and long after the dust had settled and acceptable performance levels had returned to on-time running, it transpired that the RAC assurances of RSA achieving more with less was just wishful thinking and that RSA assurances to me were inaccurate. The RSA was doing just the thing I worried most about. It was not achieving a more efficient way to carry out rail track maintenance to offset funding reductions, but was just reducing the level of maintenance to match those reductions. The CEO was a Treasury appointed accountant to run the track maintenance organisation. He may not have had been equipped to know what was really going on in his organisation. That is why an experienced railway person is needed to run a railway!

Managing the whole Transport portfolio during this time was a very tough environment for a minister to get any oxygen or clear air. The media attacks were constant, derailments were on the increase, track workers were being killed, commuters were late for work and the Glenbrook train accident had killed seven passengers.

In a crisis of this proportion, a minister is expected to take charge, assess the problems, find effective solutions and then implement corrective actions. However, I had a dysfunctional rail structure with two independent State-owned corporations which reported, not to me, but to the Treasury and the Treasurer.

Despite those shortcomings, I did find a way through which I was compelled to take, as by then, the Sydney 2000 Olympics were looming. I appointed a Rail Czar to take charge and steer us through and beyond the Sydney 2000 Olympics. He reported directly to me. It worked! Rail gave a stellar performance for the Sydney 2000 Olympics under the gaze of the global media.

The critical need after the Sydney 2000 Olympics was to avoid a repeat of the decline in rail performance from late 1999 through to just before the September 2000 Olympics. This was done by positioning Egan to grant sufficient funds for rail track maintenance. We were able to do this by submitting a report to him on the 'State of the New South Wales Rail System'. I decided to split the wish list between 'urgent and essential' and 'important and desirable'. It worked a treat and I got an extra $270M to carry

Chapter 11: Running the railways

out all of the 'urgent and essential' work needed for the rail system. Predictably, neither Egan nor Carr saw any need to fund projects that were considered to be 'important and desirable'.

After the Sydney 2000 Olympics, I did manage to push through the amalgamation of RAC (rail track owner) and RSA (rail track maintainer) so that the one organisation was now responsible for both track ownership and maintenance. It helped, but Sims was still at the helm. The new organisation was called the Rail Infrastructure Corporation (RIC).

I decided to appoint David Richmond as Chairman of the State Rail Authority (SRA) and bring to bear the huge skills he had so ably used in running the Olympic Coordination Authority. I told Richmond that I wanted to appoint him also as Chairman of RIC to bring much better synergy between the RIC and the SRA which was still operating passenger trains. He agreed provided 'Egan was happy with it'.

Getting Egan to agree to anything that would facilitate making my ministerial program and agenda any easier to achieve, would usually be next to impossible, so I decided to tackle Carr directly. He was supportive of the joint appointment, but I knew that for the appointment to be approved, it needed Egan's blessing and I well knew that hell would freeze over before that happened. I made a rash decision to appeal to Sims directly: "Rod, I want to make a change in the position of Chairman and I need you to step down, so I can appoint David Richmond to Chair both RIC and SRA. You have been in the job for four years and it's time for a change". He was not for 'turning' unless "the Treasurer requests me to do so".

Sims knew that under our bizarre railway structure, that as the shareholder Minister of Rail Infrastructure Corporation, Egan was effectively, in all but name, the actual Minister for Rail Infrastructure, leaving me as Transport Minister, as a very publicly accountable bystander. Sims also knew very well, that there was no way that Egan would allow me, as minister, to determine who ought to be the chairman of an agency for which I was publicly responsible, and he didn't. Sims must have hot footed it over to Egan, as only a few days later, Carr called me in and berated me for not first clearing it with Egan: "You needed to have worked this past Egan first. You've got to consult your colleagues on these sorts of things". I assumed Carr must have had tongue firmly in cheek, as he would have been well aware that for me, trying to convince Egan on anything, was never going to happen. So, I am inclined to think Carr chided me for amusement, rather than anything resembling what might have passed in other circumstances, as advice on how to deal with a colleague. I then had to tolerate Sims as Chairman of RIC, all the way to the March 2003 election. No other Minister for Transport, before or since, has had to continue working with a Rail Authority Chairman in whom he no longer had confidence and wished to remove.

After the election, Carr appointed me to the Roads and Housing portfolio. It was a welcome relief from five hard grinding years in Transport. I had by then, been in roads for over six years which had been both rewarding and challenging. I had enjoyed the experience, and the prospect of a few more years in the portfolio was welcome. Housing gave me the opportunity to live out my Labor values and get deeply involved in welfare housing issues and communities as well as remote aboriginal housing issues.

Chapter 11: Running the railways

CHAPTER 12

Delivering transport for a successful Sydney Olympics

One of the most rewarding moments in my long period as a Cabinet Minister, was the realisation at the end of the Sydney 2000 Olympics, that a long and herculean effort by many, had delivered a successful transport logistics task for this huge global sporting event.

I had spent three years of my ministerial life to get to this point and countless public servants, officials, workers and volunteers had risen to the occasion to provide the platform for the "best ever Olympic games". To have been directly involved in this enormous team effort across both the Olympic and Transport portfolios was an incredible privilege. Like the rest of the community, I was both delighted and pleasantly surprised as the critical employees across the Transport agencies rose to the occasion. This was their finest hour and I was proud of them, and I still am today.

Whilst it was mostly tough hard work to get to this point, there were some lighter moments. The Olympics Minister, Michael Knight, had determined that he needed a high level strategic transport body to oversee the delivery of transport by the operating agencies in rail, roads and maritime.

Chapter 12: Delivering transport for the Sydney Olympics

Brian Langton was still the Transport Minister at the time, and I was the relatively new Roads Minister. I am confident that if I had then had Transport as well, Knight would have seen much less of a need for an Olympic Transport Agency. We were friends well before we became Cabinet colleagues. We trusted each other, looked out for one another and had a high regard for each other's abilities. I have always believed that this was a critical factor in ensuring the level of cooperation between the Olympic and Transport agencies needed to deliver a great Olympic Games event in Sydney.

As it was, Michael was my mate and I was happy to support him in whatever he needed to successfully deliver the games. He drafted a Cabinet Minute seeking approval for the establishment of the Olympic Roads and Transport Authority (ORTA) and the Treasurer unsurprisingly expressed opposition with one of his more ridiculous lines of argument: "Why don't you instead have the Olympic Coordination Authority (OCA) purchase transport services for the games from the Department of Transport".

This was the sort of economic rationalist claptrap which Treasury used to throw up from time to time, straight out of one of their manuals on how to save cost by not governing at all. As with rail, an awful administrative structure which ruined transport for the Olympics, would have been for Knight and me to manage as best we could, as the policy architects of it quickly disappeared into the unaccountable bureaucratic woodwork. Whilst sounding like it carried a tinge of administrative sensibility to it, the idea would have been disastrously impractical if implemented. The Department of Transport at that time, was a small agency completely ill-equipped to take on such a huge task and if it had, both Knight and I undoubtedly knew how bad the result would have been. Egan would have known this. I was just dumb enough to say so!

There was a room full of relevant public sector CEOs, several relevant ministers and advisors. Perhaps 30 or so huddled in a small room just next door to the larger Cabinet Room. Premier Bob Carr was in the chair. I said to the Treasurer: "Treasurer, that is a whole lot of Treasury, purchaser provider, gobbledegook" and his response was priceless; "You are a fuckwit". I then retorted: "I always know when you have lost an argument, as you play the man and not the ball" and his response was even better: "That just proves you are a fuckwit". Carr stepped in and asked Egan to calm down before the Treasurer chimed in again with: "OK, but he's a fucken prick". Nothing like a good intellectual discussion in the New South Wales Cabinet!

The proposal to establish ORTA was approved and Ron Christie, who was my CEO at the Roads and Traffic Authority (RTA) transferred across to the new entity. It was a useful body for Knight, but it was not an operating transport delivery agency. That would have to be done by my fractured rail agencies, by the RTA and the Government bus and ferry agency then known as the State Transit Authority (STA). We all worked very hard to make sure it all worked. ORTA did a fantastic job in ensuring the public was kept informed with an effective communication plan in place before and during the games. ORTA also did a great job in running 'test' events at Olympic Park, so that my delivery agencies could iron out any operating issues and it did a good job overseeing the transport management plans of each agency. But, it was never designed to deliver transport to the games. That was front and centre my responsibility and the 30,000 public servants who worked in the many agencies in my portfolio.

Chapter 12: Delivering transport for the Sydney Olympics

When the games were over and Knight was rightly basking in the glory of delivering a fantastic event, I said to him; "Michael, you know that if Transport had not been an outstanding success, I would have copped the blame for a disastrous Olympics. But, with it succeeding, you have got all the credit" and his wry and sharp sense of humour immediately came into play: "And your point is?" What more could I say?

The three critical agencies I had to oversee in delivering transport for the games were the SRA (passenger rail), STA (buses) and the RTA (traffic management). The RSA (track maintenance) and the Department of Transport also played important roles.

These agencies and all of their means of transport had to be planned, tested and delivered in a way and to a demand level that had never been required before. It still gives me enormous pride that despite the huge challenges, despite the performance setbacks beforehand, the agencies and their workforces stepped up to the occasion.

But it was no easy task.

Rail was always going to be the heavy lifting means of getting tens of thousands of spectators to and from Olympic venues. The Glenbrook train accident in December 1999, combined with the collapse in on-time running performance from January 2000 onwards worried me very much indeed as it did Michael Knight, ORTA, the SRA and the Premier. By May 2000, it got so bad that I began to worry that Carr may make a sacrifice of me and bring in a new Minister for the Transport.

Splitting up the old New South Wales Government Railways into a Treasury-run rail track owner (RAC), an indirectly Treasury-run track maintenance organisation (RSA) and leaving only the

Minister for Transport to have direction and control over the passenger rail services (SRA) had been an unmitigated disaster.

Passenger train services remained with a strangulated SRA, but responsibility for track and its maintenance was placed in the hands of two separate independent State-owned organisations, subject to the direction and control of the Treasurer, Michael Egan and not the Minister. Treasury ensured that cost cutting and staff reductions rather than rail performance and customer satisfaction were to be the main priorities for the Labor Government in respect of its rail network.

The track maintainer, Rail Services Corporation, was headed by an accountant, Terry Ogg, who was under the RAC's 'thumb', as he needed their sign-off on any funds for track maintenance. RAC was headed by an economist CEO and its Chairman was also an economist. Not much rail experience in sight there. There was no science to this. Just a solid cut to the rail budget each and every year until things went 'off the rails' literally.

By late May 2000, the likelihood of the railways performing well for the September 2000 Olympics was looking grim. Drastic action was needed. The boards and CEOs of both RAC and RSA were not just a Treasury-run nuisance for a minister, but had become a serious hindrance to delivering the transport logistics for the games. I decided to act!

I knew that Egan as Treasurer would resist any attempt on my part to put the railways back into one organisation under my direction and control. That is what should have happened, but I knew it was unachievable at that point despite the urgency of the hour. However, I was confident that Carr would allow me to appoint a Rail Czar to cut through all the problems as we led up to and beyond the Sydney 2000 Olympics.

Chapter 12: Delivering transport for the Sydney Olympics

I talked it over with Knight and he suggested Ron Christie, who was then running ORTA. I liked the idea. Christie was a public servant through and through and one of the best and most experienced railwaymen in the country. He had led the railway team in the aftermath of the Granville train disaster in 1977, had been number two at SRA under David Hill, and had been the Director General of the Department of Public Works and CEO of the Roads and Traffic Authority. I could not think of a better candidate.

Now that I had my man to take over the railways and dislodge the accountants and economists, I needed to find a way to do it quickly and in a way, that would not overly alarm my friends at Treasury who would voice serious opposition if I tried to go too far.

I knew that under the relevant transport legislation, as Minister, I could delegate certain roles and functions to a specified person. Much to my astonishment, the way the Act had been drafted by Parliamentary Counsel and passed into law, enabled me to not only delegate my powers and functions, but also to delegate more powers and functions than I could personally hold as Minister. This seemed a little unusual and I had it checked out by the lawyers. The advice was what I had thought. I could delegate to Ron Christie power and control over the entire rail network, which I was not able to exercise myself as the relevant Minister. As the Director General of the Cabinet Office, Roger Wilkins, said at the time: "We did not see that one coming. It was not something we would have expected."

The appointment of Christie was that important, that I rang the Premier one evening and asked for a special urgent Cabinet meeting, which he unexpectedly appointed on the spot for 9.00 am the following morning. It was 6.00 pm and all my public servants had gone home. Of the more than 200 Cabinet Minutes I would submit in my nearly 12 years as a Minister, this was the only one I would wholly write myself word for word. As I scribbled out page after page, my Chief of Staff, Lisa Hunt, and my Senior Policy Advisor, Liz McNamara, busily typed it into Cabinet Minute format. Knight paid me a compliment the next morning: "This is the best Cabinet Minute I have seen you put up".

I sought Cabinet approval for the appointment of Ron Christie as the Coordinator General of Rail with power and responsibility over all rail entities, all boards, CEOs and senior management. He was to take charge under my direction and control, as a special measure, to get rail performing for the Sydney 2000 Olympics. There was expected resistance from Treasury, from the Treasurer and of course, from John Della Bosca.

Carr insisted I work such a momentous decision carefully through the Cabinet. It would take four special Cabinet meetings over several days before I got the decision I had been seeking. When it finally went through, I felt so elated I wanted to jump 10 feet in the air and cheer, but that would not do in the Cabinet Room.

Christie and I then held a press conference and the decision got a great run. I was seen as taking charge and appointing a 'Mr fix it' to get trains ready for the Sydney 2000 Olympics. I had also secured approval for Christie to set up a Coordinator General's Office with adequate funding and he quickly began to fill critical positions with very capable people, who would all make their mark in delivering trains for the Olympics; they included: John Lee, Fran McPherson, Helen Vickers and Jane McAloon to name a few.

Chapter 12: Delivering transport for the Sydney Olympics

To their credit, both Egan as Treasurer and John Pierce as Secretary of the Treasury, fully supported the Cabinet decision once it was made. Pierce even offered to meet with me and the Chairman of RAC, Rod Sims, to make sure that Sims knew that the whole Government was behind this initiative. I took up the offer, Sims accepted the decision and also to his credit, got out of the way and let us get on with doing what was needed to be done for the Olympics.

It was June 2000 when I was able to announce Christie's appointment. Even though there was not much time left, this would be the single most important thing I would do to support a great transport outcome for the Sydney 2000 Olympics.

The 1999/2000 financial year was about to close and I told Christie that I wanted him to spend as much of the 2000/2001 budget as he possibly could in the next three months: "Let me worry about the budget. If we run out before the end of the financial year, I'll just say to the Premier 'sorry, but we needed to spend quickly for the Olympic Games and I now need additional funds'. Just spend all you need and we will worry about it after the Games". And that is pretty much what happened.

Christie was a workaholic, details man and led by example. He and his team were soon over all that needed to be done and used their powers and funds effectively and efficiently. In quick time, the system performance returned to acceptable levels just in time for the start of the Games. I shudder to think what would have happened if this initiative had not been put in place. The dismembered rail structure I had inherited was much like the US political system: lots of chiefs, but no one person responsible and accountable for performance and results across the whole. In appointing Ron Christie as Coordinator General of Rail, I was able to vest all authority and all accountability into one person. And it worked!

It is important to point out that all the senior and mid-management personnel of all the rail entities swung in behind Christie to get the job done for the Olympics. They greatly respected his acumen as a railwayman, and accepted that the Government had vested all the authority in him, bypassing all and any structural restraints to achieve a great rail outcome for the Games. Had there been even a whiff of resistance, then it would have been a lot more difficult to achieve what we did in the timeframe that we had. Christie showed leadership and skill in drawing all this together in a very short time.

Several important new works were put in place ahead of the Olympics. This included the expanded train stabling yard facilities at Blacktown and Hornsby, and new rail junctions near Olympic Park at Flemington and Lidcombe. These certainly made a difference, but the most important new works were the building of the Olympic Park Rail Loop and the Lidcombe Shuttle Line. These two projects enabled the rail network to move thousands of passengers per hour into and out of the main Olympic precinct. They made a massive difference to the transport logistics task.

The Transport Management Centre (TMC) had been the brain child of Christie whilst he was CEO of the RTA. It proved to be the best way to manage road and bus transport for the Games and is still a great legacy of the Games. I approved Simon Lane as CEO of SRA, setting up a mini Rail Management Centre for the Games and it was a great success. After the Games, a huge and modern replacement was installed at Central Railway doing for rail, what the TMC does for the road network.

Chapter 12: Delivering transport for the Sydney Olympics

The genius behind the outstanding success of rail performance for the Sydney Olympics was its simplicity. But this was not so easy to discern amongst an incredibly complex Sydney urban rail network.

Owing to the piecemeal way in which the founders of our rail network designed and delivered it over 100 years ago, the City Rail Network had become as complicated and interconnected as a bowl of spaghetti. Whenever anything went wrong in the network, it sent a ripple of non-performance throughout the system because of its interconnectedness. Most modern urban railways work on the concept of independent stand-alone lines, which if out of action for any reason, have no impact at all on any other lines. Not so for the City Rail Network. The only exception is the Eastern Suburbs Line which connects Bondi Junction in the Eastern Suburbs of Sydney with the city of Wollongong just south of Sydney. To have changed this would have cost billions of dollars and years of disruption to commuters. Unfortunately, the system is unlikely to ever be permanently untangled, but we were able to do so temporarily for the 16 days of the Games.

A critical decision was made, which I fully supported, to disconnect the rail network just for the Games period and to configure train movements as if they were two independent Metro lines running from the west: Blacktown-Olympic Park-Blacktown and from the main Central Station in the City: Central-Olympic Park-Central. The beauty of the ORTA test events in the two years leading up to the Games, meant we could demonstrate that this would work well when put under passenger pressure. These events included major sporting fixtures and the massively popular Royal Easter Agricultural Shows which had been moved from Moore Park in the city to Olympic Park.

Another series of critically important test events were the two New Year's Eve occasions at the end of 1998 and 1999, which enabled us to test crowd control and passenger and train movements in and around the city in accordance with what would be our plans for every single day of the 16 days of the Olympic Games. Whenever I am asked what is needed to deliver a successful transport logistics task for an Olympics, high on my list, is to make sure that there is a long lead-in of major test events. This is the best way to make sure that what is planned, is actually going to work – when the rail and bus network is put to the greatest test it will ever be put under.

A lot of effort also went into planning and managing crowd control and the movement in and around railway stations, especially Central and Olympic Park. This was a work of art in itself, and with the help of hundreds of volunteers and thousands of patient and understanding passengers, it all worked well and safely. Passengers coming in from the Central Coast alighted at Concord West Station and cheerily walked the one kilometre to Olympic Park. Folks usually don't want to do that!

In the 1990s, we were delivering one million passengers per weekday. We knew that in the Olympic period, this would double to two million passengers per day. Running a loop metro style conveyor belt was the only way we could have handled such a massive increase on the demands of the network. It meant folks had to get out at Central, Blacktown and Concord West and either change trains or walk. It was the only way. And it worked!

To ensure we could deal with problems during the Games, emergency response teams were established at various points around the network to rapidly deal with any track or train issues which may have arisen. These flying squads of experienced train and track maintenance workers made a difference. At my

Chapter 12: Delivering transport for the Sydney Olympics

insistence and under Christie's management, funding and work on track and train maintenance were increased significantly in the months leading up to the Games. This also included 'Operation Sparkle' to make sure our trains looked the very best for the Games. And long before my own self-inflicted nickname of 'Sparkles'.

Once the Games started in September 2000, I worried incessantly that something would go wrong on our rail network. For 15 of the 16 days of the Games, rail performance rose to the occasion and on day 16, I happily attended the Closing Ceremony with my wife at Olympic Park. I was feeling ecstatic about how far we had come, especially after all the drama and challenges of the previous nine months since the Glenbrook train accident.

As the Closing Ceremony began and just as I sighed with relief at having gotten this far, I got a call on my mobile telling me that there had just been a derailment of a train coming out of the Flemington Yard which was now blocking the main line. This meant that trains could not get into Olympic Park Station and in a couple of hours there would be tens of thousands of passengers making their way to Olympic Park Station expecting to take the train home after the concluding night of a great Olympics. My heart sank.

I could just imagine the headlines. I could see all our hard work over the previous three years fall to dust in a barrage of negative publicity. I knew that a derailment on the last evening of the Olympics would send the media into a tail spin. I asked, if not insisted, that the senior rail guys do all they could to fix the problem immediately. And much to my astonishment they did. The train was only partly off the track and in a flagrant breach of the safety rules which apply in these circumstances, the driver walked to the other end of the train and reversed it out of the way.

The event went unreported and the reputation of transport for the whole Olympics survived and endures to this day. But it was a closely run operation to the last hour of the last day.

This mishap still gives me a shiver all these years later when I think about it. I think I lost one of my nine lives that evening!

Managing the road network is also a critical part of delivering a successful transport logistics task for an Olympic event. In addition to the Transport Management Centre at Redfern, the RTA had installed across Sydney, hundreds of traffic monitoring cameras and several large message signs. This was all connected by modern traffic light software systems so that traffic lights could be altered to allow for both smoother vehicle flow or to facilitate dignitary protection.

ORTA and the OCA worked closely with the RTA in settling and implementing the designated Olympic routes into the Olympic Park, particularly from Sydney Airport. To make this work properly, a number of 24-hour clearways were put in place to keep lanes both clear and secure. The record for transferring athletes from the airport to the Olympic Village was 12 minutes, which for general motoring public is just incredible at any time of the day. It showed just how much effort had been put into making this work.

As with rail, I insisted we do all we could to make sure that we had strategically placed emergency response vehicles to manage and if necessary remove, any broken-down vehicles in the way of getting athletes, the IOC or spectators to and from events.

Eight response vehicles were stationed at key points supported by several tow trucks. If cars were parked in the wrong spot or just inconveniently broken down, they were quickly towed

Chapter 12: Delivering transport for the Sydney Olympics

away. Olympic Park was the main site, but there were many other locations which from time to time required this rapid road clearance facility. This included the Marathon through the streets of Sydney and long road cycle events, as well as stray vehicles which would breach security protocols for the movement of dignitaries.

It is not well known that the almost complete collapse of the performance of buses just a few days before the start of the Olympic Games came close to wrecking what would soon be an internationally recognised, superbly delivered Games. It was a close call and ORTA had very little to do with fixing it.

Whilst about two million passenger journeys per day would be managed by the rail network during every one of the 16 days of the Games, more than 500,000 passenger journeys per day would have to be managed by thousands of buses provided by both the Government and the private bus industry.

In fact, the vast bulk of the thousands of buses to service all the six-strategic cross-Sydney bus routes came from numerous private bus companies from all over the State. The Sydney Organising Committee for the Olympic Games (SOCOG) made a very wise decision to hold the Games in a school holiday period, which was extended from the usual two weeks to three. This ensured fewer traffic demands on the road network and freed up thousands of buses which could be driven in to Sydney for use during the Olympic period.

ORTA, the Department of Transport and the RTA all worked well together in identifying, putting in place and enforcing the six bus routes which served the Olympic Transport task so well throughout the Games. However, for reasons which are still not clear, ORTA effectively outsourced the planning and delivery of actual bus operations of Olympic Transport to the private bus industry. It all sounded convincing, as a dedicated bus company called Bus 2000 was formed, with its own board of directors and management.

The performance of buses came under scrutiny before the Games formally began, when athletes who were in town needed ferrying to training venues, and school children who would be their spectators experienced problems. Just a few days out and on the first day of this pre-Olympic task, 23 buses did not show up, on the second it was 34 buses and on the third it was 76 buses. Clearly, something very wrong was afoot. When this was brought to my attention, I worried very much that if the system was failing even before the day of the Opening Ceremony, then it could not possibly perform on full Olympic mode. Drastic action was needed. Even Graham Richardson rang me in his capacity as Mayor of the Olympic Village, to personally request a bus for some athletes which had not shown up. He was getting in the way: "Richo, I am aware of the problem and I am now onto it. It won't help if you keep ringing me or other public servants to get a resolution."

I called John Stott, CEO of the State Transit Authority (STA), and told him I wanted a detailed and immediate analysis of what was going wrong and why, and most importantly, what we needed to do to fix it as soon as possible. I called Knight's Chief of Staff, Michael Deegan, and arranged to meet him, Stott and a senior representative from ORTA, Stephen McIntyre, at one of the designated Olympic bus depots at 5.00 pm the next day. What was revealed to me was nothing short of horrifying in terms of how we were going to perform in delivering bus services for the rest of the Olympic Games.

Chapter 12: Delivering transport for the Sydney Olympics

A great many of the private bus companies were very small family run outfits with few buses and drivers and even fewer formal management positions. Unlike the government owned and operated STA, there was no real management depth in any but the largest private bus companies, needed to manage, monitor and deliver literally thousands of buses to a unique and one-off task. ORTA should have been aware of this. Stott was able to report that there were too few timetable schedulers and planners on the ground at each of the bus depots. This meant that buses and drivers were not being connected, which in turn meant that not only were buses not where they were supposed to be, but no one really knew where they were at any particular point in time. No wonder it was a disaster unfolding before our very eyes.

It even got as silly as no one knowing where the keys to some of the buses were, no meal or accommodation arrangements being put in place or in some instances, toilet facilities not being provided. Stott also pointed out that even if the STA provided the skilled personnel to fix these issues, there was no official management in place within Bus 2000 to even put these positions into effective use. I then made what I think was a fundamentally critical decision, not only for the delivery of the transport task for the Games, but also for how well the Games would be perceived by all when the closing ceremony was done and dusted. I directed Stott to arrange immediately for the STA senior management to step-in and take over all and every aspect of Bus 2000 and to bring in every scheduler and planner he could get his hands on.

I told him: "John, I want the entire STA to be placed at the disposal of the Olympic Games. I want all those managers and schedulers you have on duty on this tonight, and by tomorrow I want 250 STA busses in addition to what you have already committed, redirected to the Games". At that point, Bus 2000 effectively ceased to exist, or to have any relevance to the Olympic Games. There were still thousands of private buses and their drivers and with effective management in place, they quickly began to do a sterling job for the Olympics. The only query which Stott raised with me, was that the immediate removal of so many buses from their normal routes would impact on non-Olympic services, to which I told him I would take the heat if there were complaints. I do not recall getting a single complaint.

Deegan for Knight and McIntyre for ORTA, expressed full support for what I had directed the STA to accomplish, and within a couple of days and just before the Olympics had started, a miracle had been put in place. I still marvel at how close we came to the edge, how we did not for a moment panic and how we delivered quickly what was needed to pull the Games back from disaster. Guy Thurston, then the CEO of ACTON which was the Australian Capital Territory (ACT) bus service and former STA executive, was brought in to run what was really the new STA Olympic Bus Unit. He was supported by 50 senior STA managers, as well as numerous additional drivers to support the additional bus resources. Even the Army contributed over 40 buses from its Holsworthy Army Barracks in South Western Sydney. It was in my view, the outstanding performance of the Games and probably the least acknowledged or recognised.

Sadly, John Stott passed away in 2010. He is worthy of an appropriate posthumous award from the International Olympic Committee (IOC) for outstanding service to the Olympic movement. I am inclined to think that if there is such an award, that it would probably only go to the Olympic 'family' rather than the 'help'. The IOC deliberately limits its focus and vision when it comes to who gets credit for what in delivering an Olympic event.

Chapter 12: Delivering transport for the Sydney Olympics

There was however, an amusing anecdote in relation to the launch of Bus 2000 at the Olympic Park Stadium about two years before the Games. The private bus industry had asked Knight to do the formal launch against a backdrop of scores of private buses spread out on the competition area below, in the shape of the words 'Bus 2000'. It looked great and all sounded like the private bus industry had its act together well ahead of the Games.

On the way to work a few hours before the scheduled launch, Knight's ministerial vehicle was hit in the rear by an STA government bus. Knight was OK, but the accident had caused an exacerbation of a previous neck injury and he was unable to be present at this major press conference. So, he asked me to stand in for him. We both then workshopped a terrific set of words for me to use for the media: "People often ask me 'what would happen to the Olympic Games if Michael Knight was ever hit by a bus'. Well, that was answered this morning and here I am." I then added for good measure in front of a throng of journalists and cameramen: "That was a joke. Don't tell Michael Knight I said that". As we expected, it got a terrific run. One 2GB political journalist even quipped to me: "We've elevated this from number three on the news to top story".

Juan Antonio Samaranch as President of the International Olympic Committee was the undisputed King of the Olympics wherever and whenever it was held. As an Olympic titan, he was treated like any emperor would expect to be treated. Knight as a good ex left ALP stalwart was unfazed by royalty or pomp and circumstance, but with Samaranch he was cautious and respectful.

When Samaranch announced to Australia and the world that the Sydney 2000 Olympics had been "the best ever Olympics", Knight and I well knew that he would not have done so, if the venues had not been incredibly well delivered and prepared by the OCA. We knew he would not have done so, if the OCA and SOCOG had not put on first class events at multiple Olympic venues for athletes, officials and spectators and we both well knew that he would not have said it, if Olympic transport had been anything short of fantastic.

We were all conscious of how important it was that Samaranch experienced all aspects of the Olympics at their very best. Just prior to the start of the Games when a bus was supposed to pick up some journalists and was a no show, Samaranch let David Richmond, CEO of the OCA, know what he thought of that, who in turn let it be known how unimpressed he was.

Chris Ford, who oversaw the Transport Management Centre (TMC), during the Games, told me years later that he had quickly arranged for a bus to be located behind the hotel where Samaranch was staying, with the driver in radio contact with the TMC. The OCA also had one of its guys in the lobby of the hotel, also with its own bus and radio contact. To ensure all would work without a hitch, Ford had one of our Circular Quay CCTV cameras redirected to point straight at the lobby area of the hotel with a direct feed into the TMC and constantly monitored by staff at the centre.

Its one and only purpose during the Games was to monitor when Samaranch 'left the building'. As Samaranch emerged from the hotel lift into the lobby, the driver was alerted and pulled up just moments after the IOC President had asked the Hotel Concierge for transport. The President thought it was an efficient hotel service and could even be seen nodding appreciation as the bus pulled up so soon. Ford was aware that Samaranch liked to sometimes test services by having some of his staff come a little later than he did and ask to go in a different direction. When that occurred, the second bus ensured a satisfactory and reliable service

Chapter 12: Delivering transport for the Sydney Olympics

to these high-profile visitors to our city. Together they worked wonders in serving the President of the IOC and his retinue, and in helping cement a view in their minds that we were delivering the transport task very well.

The running of all the aspects of transport for the Games could have not run any smoother. It ran like clockwork. Having warned spectators to keep to buses and trains and just how tough and long journeys might be, I delighted on day one, when a couple was on the evening news complaining: "Carl Scully told us to assume it would take three hours to get to Olympic Park, but it only took us one." A great start to a very long 16 days.

I worried all day and night of the entire Olympic period that something would go wrong. I tried to be everywhere to check things were running like clockwork. I was in constant contact with my rail and road senior personnel, getting updates on traffic congestion, passenger and crowd control, train on-time running and any incidents. I was a regular visitor to both the Transport Management Centre and the Rail Management Centre which had eyes and ears on the whole road and rail network. Being amongst the crowds, travelling the trains and even being at Olympic Park station one evening at midnight was all part of making sure our plans were working.

The dust had hardly settled after the conclusion of the Olympic Games, when the Premier called Knight and I in for separate one-on-one meetings, requesting that we refrain from gloating and that we do all we can to make sure the volunteers and public servants got all the credit and not us.

Having spent three years of my professional life on this incredible project, I did think I was allowed just a little indulgence to reflect on a job well done. I was more than a little disappointed with how Carr just seemed to so casually dismiss what the two of us had achieved. Knight was disappointed, having spent nearly six years of his life on the job, which was probably more like double that crammed into the available time. Carr had the politics right, so we both copped it on the chin. As we also did when the rally to thank and celebrate the contribution of the volunteers lifted and carried Carr on their shoulders through the throng, as if he himself had delivered the Games. As is so often the case with a head of government, he was the boss and entitled to take the credit. And so he did. That's how the system works!

I did have one piece of amusement from the press after the conclusion of the Games. Barry O'Farrell, then the Shadow Minister for Transport, had turned his criticism of both my performance and our preparedness for the Games into an art form. He just did not let up at every opportunity to denigrate what both I and my agencies were doing in the lead up to the Games.

To his credit, he did, at my personal request, refrain from adverse public comment during the Games in the presence of thousands of international media. He was clearly a political opponent, but also a patriot and rose, as a result, in my estimation. When the Games were done and the great performance of transport widely acknowledged, O'Farrell was asked by a Channel 7 News reporter: "Will you now apologise to Carl Scully" and he gave a terrific response: "No". Clearly, the time to be an opponent had quickly returned.

I was invited by Knight to attend the IOC awards night on the Monday evening after the conclusion of the Games. Samaranch awarded Knight, in his capacity as President of the Sydney Organising Committee for the Olympic Games (SOCOG) and Olympic Coordination Authority CEO, David Richmond, with gold olive garlands, but the CEO of SOCOG, Sandy Hollway, was

Chapter 12: Delivering transport for the Sydney Olympics

only awarded a silver one, which initiated a furious media response against Knight from the tabloid press.

Apart from a small gold brooch awarded by Samaranch to one of my senior transport officials, there was no official IOC recognition of the herculean effort of my transport agencies in securing the 'best ever Olympics'. They were clearly the 'help' and not the 'main event' which to me, put the IOC in a surreal position of imagining an Olympic Games occurring in isolation of the transport which underpinned it.

In my view the gold to Knight and Richmond was eminently justified but so would at least two and maybe three more to my transport chiefs.

The Sydney 2000 Olympics had been a complete success only because the success of transport underpinned all that occurred in and around the Games. Unlike SOCOG, the OCA and even ORTA, my transport agencies had to ensure rail, road and bus services still functioned for a city of 4 million people, as well as ensuring it also ran smoothly for a massive sporting event. The risk of failure of transport during the Games was far greater than any risk of event failure. That those transport risks were managed, mitigated or avoided was an enormous achievement.

Ron Christie had been CEO of the Roads and Traffic Authority (RTA), then CEO of the Olympic Roads and Transport Authority (ORTA) and finally, Coordinator General of Rail. In my view, Christie's contribution as a public servant to the success of the Sydney Olympics was equal to that of Richmond. I doubt that the IOC will ever rectify the lack of recognition it had shown that evening to a true 'Hero of the Games'.

Paul Forward as CEO of the RTA, John Stott as CEO of STA, Matt Taylor as CEO of the Waterways Authority and Greg Martin as CEO of Sydney Ports Corporation, had all moved mountains to ensure that their respective organisations and the many public servants who worked in them, delivered the road, bus and maritime tasks for the Olympics.

The IOC recognition event and the overwhelmingly successful march and thank you rally to the volunteers gave me an idea on how best to thank the thousands of transport workers who had stepped up and delivered when they were needed most: train drivers, guards, security guards, cleaners, station staff, road workers, maintenance workers on rail and road, emergency response crews, bus drivers, schedulers, planners, IT specialists, Rail and Transport Management Centre personnel, the Coordinator General's office, the policy personnel at the Department of Transport, Sydney Ferries personnel and those at Sydney Ports Corporation and many more. Literally, thousands and thousands of them.

There were 30,000 people in the 10 agencies which reported to me as Roads and Transport Minister. A large majority of them had either directly or indirectly contributed to delivering Olympic transport. I wanted them all to know how much I appreciated what they had done. I had issued a special bronze commemorative coin and delivered one to as many employees as possible. I hope it got to all those who were worthy of receiving one.

When I look back on a public life well led and think of the things I did well and the things that made a difference, I have no hesitation in putting on that list, the delivery of transport for the Sydney 2000 Olympics. The delivery of a successful Olympic Games requires three critically important ingredients. Firstly, sporting venue infrastructure being completed on time. Secondly, a flawlessly organised sporting fixture across multiple disciplines in a range of locations. And thirdly, a smoothly delivered transport task for thousands of spectators, athletes and officials over a 16-day period. I spent three years of my life planning and delivering the third, which underpinned the success of the first and second. It still gives me a lot of pride in reflecting on how well we all did given the sheer enormity of the task and being part of the fantastic team who delivered it.

CHAPTER 13

The premiership denied – what really happened?

The leadership transition from Carr to Iemma happened in the full glare of the media and community's eye over just a few days in late July 2005, but the lead up to it was considerably longer. Between 1995 and 2003, Premier Carr never said or did anything to suggest to us that he was doing anything other than staying put in the job until he was carried out in a box.

But that changed at the March 2003 election with the abrupt and unexpected removal of Eddie Obeid from the Ministry. When Carr insisted that Richard Amery, the leader of the Trog sub-faction of the right also go along with John Aquilina, a number of us assumed that Carr must have decided not to run again, as he had just killed off politically the senior operatives he would need to ensure survival for a new four-year term. There would be other indications as the next two years unfolded towards Carr's 2005 announcement to go.

In late November 2002, I lunched with a senior executive of a major Sydney newspaper as an important prelude to my own lead into the March 2003 election. Transport had long left their pages as an issue, so I was unsurprised but more than a little elated, when he said over a bowl of pasta: "Transport is not an issue for us and

I don't see us doing anything on it for the foreseeable future". I went back to the office feeling very pleased. As Carr's Chief of Staff, Graeme Wedderburn, had said to me earlier in the year: "You have been the architect of your own recovery." It had taken two solid years to get to this point and with only four months to the election I was confident of then breezing into another portfolio. Or so I thought!

Bowen almost swaps with Tripodi

In early 2002, prior to the closure of pre-selections for the 2003 election, Joe Tripodi and Chris Bowen had had a serious discussion about swapping future political careers. Janice Crosio had been the Federal MP for Prospect since 1990 and had made it clear that she would not be running again at the expected 2004 Federal Election. Bowen by then was my Chief of Staff, Secretary of my local ALP branch of Smithfield and a good friend. I had once harboured a long-expired wish to be in federal politics, but with the premiership very much in play and almost staring at me from a distance, I was going nowhere. Anwar Khoshaba and I had made it clear to Bowen and everyone else locally that he was our man and that our machine would deliver for him when Crosio eventually retired. Tripodi started to dabble with the idea of going federal and leaving Bowen to take his seat of Fairfield in the State Parliament.

When Bowen raised it with me, I told him that I loved the idea and that I would do anything he needed to make it happen. He well knew the dangers and pitfalls of trying to get into Parliament and a deal like this was as they say: 'a bird in the hand is worth two in the bush.' Anwar was happy to go with my decision on the idea and I did like it, because whilst Tripodi was then a locked-in supporter of mine, I was much closer to Bowen, who I assumed would be a rock and an unrelenting advocate of mine in the Caucus.

Tripodi in the end made the call to step back and the idea disappeared soon enough as he was preselected for Fairfield and then in turn Bowen for Prospect. I have more than a few times had a chuckle with Bowen about how he might have become Premier in 2008 instead of Nathan Rees, and could have finished a promising political career before his 40th birthday.

The Chiefs of Staff

But Bowen was only one of the five Chiefs of Staff who ably served me during my nearly 12 years as a Minister. They have all gone on to do very well in their own professional lives. John Richardson with his business partner Stephen Coutts, has for many years, run a successful government advisory business. Lisa Hunt went on to become New South Wales General Manager for toll operator Transurban before being appointed CEO of the Workcover Authority. Brent Thomas has had a successful banking and commercial career and is now Head of Public Policy for Airbnb in Australia and New Zealand. Gary Sargent has for many years flourished as a crisis management advisor to major clients in London. My media and policy staff have also gone on to various fulfilling professional positions across Sydney. I like to think that I had a hand in their professional development. They all helped in substantial ways for me to do my job as a Minister as well as I could. It is hard to properly convey the level of appreciation I have for the effort they all put in over a long period of time.

In mid-January 2003, I had a one-on-one meeting with the Premier in his private office overlooking the Domain, the Sydney Botanical Gardens and of course, Sydney Harbour. I said to Carr: "Bob, I have put everything into the Transport portfolio and I have nothing more to give. I have done it for five long years and it now needs someone else with fresh ideas and a fresh approach to take the helm." He said he was thinking of giving me Police after the election which I assumed might end up being a direct swap with Michael Costa.

Waterfall

My plans effectively for the Premiership became a whole lot harder, if not impossible, when in late January 2003, a City Rail train accelerated out of Waterfall station one early workday morning, derailed as it went around a bend and killed seven passengers. The media never need encouragement to put a politician in the dock and charge, try and convict him or her on behalf of what they perceive to be the 'Court of Public Opinion' as they see it. And I was very quickly in their dock.

I had many very lonely and soul-destroying times in politics and this was certainly one of them. The press just loves disasters, tragedy and death, but the part they most love is to pick a person to blame and blame them as hard as they can.

The accident had occurred because a very overweight train driver sustained a heart attack and died just after he had pulled the accelerator lever as he moved out of Waterfall station. It was that plain and simple. It was a one in a trillion chance of ever occurring, but to the media, rail accidents don't just happen: 'they are caused'. The experience of seeing body parts and blood on the tracks and then being excoriated in the press for causing it all, was a very distressing time for me. I can still picture the severed hand lying next to the derailed train, on top of blood splattered notes which looked like they had just been written by someone now deceased. I didn't expect to have to confront that sort of thing

Setting the Record Straight | Carl Scully

when I signed up for a career in politics, but I had to confront it not once, but twice in my time as Transport Minister.

When I challenged the Daily Telegraph on why I was being so savagely attacked day after day, I was given an alarming response: "You had your media advisor go down on the tracks and tell all the journalists that the accident was caused by the driver." Carr and I had been very careful to emphasise that we did not know the facts and that determining them would need to be left to the Judicial Commission of Inquiry. No amount of trying to convince this very senior Telegraph employee of the lead attack paper of Sydney, would deter him from the official News Ltd view, that I had been personally involved in a clumsy attempt to sheet home the blame of the accident to a dead train driver. I tried in vain; all I got was a brick wall and simply: "He works for you and it was obvious he was spruiking your line".

No one from my office had caused this, but Michael Gleeson, then a senior media person working for the State Rail Authority, had gone freestyle with his own version of the facts, whilst the media were taking footage of the train wreckage. The Telegraph alleged to me that whilst pointing in the direction the train had come from he had said: "The driver came around the bend traveling way too fast and came off the tracks right here." I could not believe what I had heard. No one knew what had caused the accident, but here within hours of seven people being killed and wreckage piled by the tracks, we had a senior rail employee, appointing himself as a rail accident expert, and then giving his own uninformed version of the cause of it all. No wonder the press were upset! When Gleeson had sought my approval to allow the media to go down to the track for footage, it simply never occurred to me that this would include his own very damaging narrative.

This unnecessarily contributed directly to quite unpleasant and heightened personal attacks upon me by the Telegraph. Gleeson skated off scot free without apology. However, a tabloid newspaper never needs an excuse to excoriate a minister of the day who they have placed in the dock, so I am inclined to think that the Telegraph would have been no less tough on me whether or not this had occurred. But it is always preferable to not give them a free pass. The then editor of the Telegraph, even wrote me a letter, accusing me of 'welching' on a promise to have the Judicial Commission of Inquiry give preliminary findings prior to the 22nd of March 2003 state election. No amount of assurance that not only had I made no such commitment and even if I had, this was solely within the control of an independently appointed Judge of the Supreme Court, would convince him otherwise. A further torrent of tabloid personal abuse was then hurled my way.

Because the words 'crisis management' have been so overused by crisis management consultants to the point of it having lost its real meaning, I prefer to call it 'catastrophe management'. And for me, my job, my future and potentially the company I worked for, Waterfall was certainly a catastrophe.

I did survive Waterfall and went on for nearly four more years as a Minister before retiring from politics at the 2007 election. But even now, it all gives me a chill just to recount what I had to experience all those years ago. As did being completely shut out of the 2003 election campaign. I am unsure just how well, many self-proclaimed, tough and thick skinned political operatives, would have absorbed this kind of experience.

In 1999, as a relatively new Minister for Transport and Roads, I had travelled all over the State campaigning for our re-election, but in 2003 campaign, my role was best summed up by a supportive phone call I received from Martin Ferguson, then the

Federal Shadow Minister for Transport. He said: "Mate, I have just spoken to Carr's office and offered to help in the campaign and work with you on issues leading up to the election, but I was told: 'Scully is toxic now and we are giving him as wide a berth as possible'".

As if that was not enough, Alan Jones the 2GB radio shock jock and undisputed king of morning talk back radio, spent every weekday for a month leading up to the election excoriating me for anything he could think of because I had dared to deregulate the hire car industry.

Politics certainly is not for the faint-hearted, at least for those who want to stand up above the parapet and make a difference.

One of the things Carr was very good at, was to never take an election result for granted or allow the media or the Opposition to paint him as lazy or indulgent. He knew image was important and cultivated this side of his public presentation with great earnestness and effect.

In an immediate post-election period, Carr would like to present as a man still at work and very much on the job. This could involve a street walk, a visit to an event site, or some orchestrated media occasion to project the image that the Premier was at the helm and the election was just a blip in his busy schedule.

Immediately after the March 2003 election, Carr decided on the following Monday morning to do a train walk at Miranda station on the Cronulla Line with local re-elected MP, Barry Collier. It had the twin effects of the Premier thanking the local voters for returning one of his MPs to Parliament and being seen publicly on a train and ready to deal with whatever it was that was now awful about the state of our railways. With the Waterfall train

Chapter 13: The premiership denied

accident occurring so close to the election, Carr and the campaign had given train visits a wide berth throughout the campaign.

Not surprisingly, I did not get an invitation to this media event from Carr. I had copped a media roasting during the campaign and it was obvious to all, that Carr would be removing me from the portfolio. I thought nothing more of it until I received a strange call from Carr: "Carl, I just wanted to let you know that I have just done a train visit with Collier and I was asked why you were not present and I said a couple of things on the spur of the moment which you should ignore and not worry about".

Despite all that I had been through, I still had the confidence of the Premier to secure another four years in Cabinet, and I decided not to worry about it. But when I was sitting at home watching the evening news, I did feel upset, embarrassed and humiliated by the following exchange on the train between Carr and a TV journalist:

Journalist: "Premier, why isn't Mr Scully here with you today?"

Carr: "I don't want some defensive Transport Minister looking over my shoulder".

At least Carr had apologised for it in a roundabout way in our earlier phone conversation. Heads of government seldom apologise and since Carr vaguely attempted to apologise earlier that day, I took a deep breath and copped it on the chin.

It was ironic that Carr had chosen this part of his domain to disparage his Transport Minister, as it was in this part of Sydney where I had delivered significant rail and road improvements for the local community: The $115M Bangor Bypass which was well underway and opened by Carr in 2005; The $47M Woronora

Bridge which had been opened by Carr in 2001; the $9M rebuilding of the Five Ways intersection, also opened by Carr, which removed Sydney's worst traffic accident spot, and finally, the announcement in April 2002 of the $347M Cronulla Rail Line duplication which was opened by Premier Keneally in 2010. I had worked hard over four years with MPs Barry Collier and Alison Megarrity, and with my own transport agencies, to deliver on these commitments to their local communities. Carr, his staff, and the residents of the Sutherland Shire, all knew my record of substantive delivery, so being traduced as 'some…transport minister', especially in a place and at a time of solid achievement was more than ordinary.

I did not know that very soon after my shift from Transport to Roads and Housing, political life was about to get a whole lot tougher.

Carr shifted me from Transport to Roads and Housing to give me a couple of years to recover from the media onslaught that I had just encountered. He could have removed me from the Cabinet and not a soul would have raised a whimper in my favour, so I appreciated that he had not done that.

I threw myself into roads and started doing all I could to get the M4 East built, planned for the F3 (now M1) to M2 link and tried to do more on improving road safety.

In the Housing portfolio, Carr asked that I bring to bear all that I had learned in delivering PPPs in the Roads portfolio. I endeavoured to do that with the Bonnyrigg Housing PPP. I was also responsible for Aboriginal housing which was a tough, but wonderful introduction to both the challenges and culture of our indigenous Australians. Trips to remote communities across the country were both sad and enlightening and in a small way, I tried to do my bit.

It was challenging dealing with the Howard Government which was determined to scale back its future funding of welfare housing across the country. Early in my stint as Housing Minister, I attended a Labor Housing Minister's caucus meeting the evening before a scheduled ministerial council meeting with the Commonwealth. Rob Schwarten, was the elder amongst us, having been in the Queensland job for over six years. He arrived late, opened the door and said succinctly: "The position of Queensland is that the Commonwealth can get fucked" and then walked out. Priceless, and just the sort of agreed position we had been trying to arrive at.

The Government attacks itself

One of the unwritten and very long-standing conventions of Cabinet Government is that ministers do not attack publicly their Cabinet colleagues or denigrate the same Government's actions in any area of responsibility. This convention was not observed by Michael Costa after his appointment as the new Minister for Transport. The express or implied commentary by Costa on the Transport portfolio during my term of office, put me in an invidious position. Any new minister can find fault with the administration of his predecessor, but it is usually only publicly expressed with a change of government and then is mostly seen by the media and commentators as conventional political point scoring. However, a minister attacking the record of a fellow minister from within the same government was unprecedented. I was tempted on a few occasions to publicly defend both my record and that of the Government, but I felt that with the battering I had received after Waterfall, the media would be deaf to such pleas and would probably stir up all the old headlines for good measure. So

I decided to cop it on the chin again and again and hoped that in time, it would all come to an end.

However, whenever I had just had enough of the attacks, and began to gear up for a launch into an angry public response regarding yet another Costa broadside, my staff, particularly Bowen, would always urge caution: "Carr will sack you if you do that". I met with Carr and complained. He seemed sympathetic, but Costa continued unabated

My gut instinct kept telling me to publicly respond and defend myself against someone who was acting far more like an Opposition spokesman for Transport than a Cabinet colleague. Ann often encouraged me not to suffer the attacks in silence, but Bowen and my senior personal staff, insisted that if I did, my job would be on the line. They were too cautious on this, and I should have dared to test how Carr might have responded. We will never know. What I do know is that when I ignored their advice and angrily spoke out, Carr did step-in and brought the attacks to a quick end. Cautiousness in politics is a worthy tool of managing risk but an overabundance of it can lead to a stifling lack of boldness and lost opportunities. On Costa, I was inclined to be bold and respond in kind after a litany of unprovoked attacks. I regret not calling him out much earlier.

Defending the Transitway

One morning, in the midst of these countless unilateral and unprovoked attacks from my Cabinet colleague, I was in my Parliament House office when it was brought to my attention that Costa had made some quite disparaging remarks the previous day in the Legislative Council about the $800M Bus-only Transitways road network we were in the middle of constructing across Western Sydney. I was as proud as punch about this game-

Chapter 13: The premiership denied

changing public transport project and incensed that it was being denigrated by the new Minister. A subcommittee of Cabinet, on an unrelated area of government, happened to be scheduled that morning and I charged into the meeting with full intention of unleashing on Costa after months and months of unfathomable attacks from him. But, as I flung the doors open, he was a no show. I drew a few slow breaths, calmed the heartbeat down, and concentrated on the meeting at hand.

The Menangle Rail Bridge

Before I could properly move on from the 'Ghosts of Transport Past', I would have to negotiate an unnecessary grilling in ICAC over what became known as the 'Menangle Bridge Affair'.

On the 24th of March 2003, just two days after the election, it was brought to my attention that earlier that same month, a Professor Michael West, had recommended to the Rail Infrastructure Corporation (RIC) that Menangle Rail Bridge be closed for safety reasons. A senior journalist from a current affairs programme claimed that the Professor was alleging that the bridge was left open for political reasons leading up to the election. The claim was nonsense, but that did not stop the media from suggesting or at least implying that I had personally intervened in a Watergate style conspiracy to keep an unsafe rail bridge open for fear of losing votes.

I received a call from Carr a few days after this allegation of political interference on my part got a great airing in the media, to tell me that he had been informed by Costa 'that certain matters had arisen requiring the issue to go to ICAC'. When I asked Carr: 'What matters', he simply replied: 'I don't know, he didn't say'. I was never asked by Costa or his staff about the matter before someone in the Transport portfolio felt the need to have it referred to the Corruption Watchdog. I do not know what motivated either Costa or his Chief of Staff, John Whelan, on the way they handled this issue or why at least neither of them called me about it.

I was then dragged before a corruption inquiry without so much as a whiff of justification. It sounded good. A minister and his railway chiefs plotting and conspiring in the dead of night to keep an unsafe railway bridge open for fear of losing the votes of irate commuters. Journalists just love these sorts of conspiracy theories and spend their careers waiting in vain to be the next Woodward and Bernstein bringing down their own provincial version of a President Richard Nixon. "This is the next Watergate" you could have almost heard them whispering, as I was dragooned off to ICAC. They never need much encouragement to write up a conspiracy story.

Why would I have ever kept an unsafe bridge open? The suggestion was both bizarre and deeply offensive.

The ICAC hearing only went so far as a private hearing. I told the Commissioner and Counsel Assisting that I was unable to get advice on the allegations, as I was no longer minister, but if the usual process had been followed, then senior rail staff would have workshopped with Professor West the appropriate course of action to follow and that a collective consensus would have supported the best way to deal with the situation on the track. Unbeknownst to me, this is exactly what had happened. Professor West had raised his concerns, there had been a huddle with him and then a 20 kph speed restriction was then imposed on the track. And all done without my knowledge.

I also pointed out to the commission that it did not make sense that I would keep an unsafe rail bridge open for votes when at the same time, I had closed a road bridge because it was deemed unsafe, and had done so without any regard for the impact on votes. In February 2003, just a month before the State Election, I had directed the RTA to close Lawrence Hargrave Drive because of the danger of large rocks falling onto the roadway, but apparently just a couple of weeks later I was doing the exact opposite when it came to the railways. It was absurd to suggest I would act appropriately on one matter, but not on the other.

I also told ICAC that I could not think of one MP from either side of politics who would even think for a moment to put votes ahead of safety, let alone to actually do it. I made it clear that I thought the claim was both offensive and completely unsustainable. It would have been nice if Costa had expressed the same view.

The ICAC investigation never went beyond private hearings, as there was nothing in the allegations even if they did provide great copy for the press.

Not surprisingly ICAC found as follows:

- No evidence that any person had engaged in corrupt conduct.

- No evidence that any political considerations affected the way in which either the Rail Infrastructure Corporation (RIC) or the minister had acted.

- The evidence clearly indicated that the minister did not become aware until the 24th of March of Professor West's recommendations that the bridge be closed (i.e., two days after the State Election).

- No evidence that the decisions of RIC were anything other than a professional assessment of the safety risks.

When ICAC gave me what I regard as the most emphatic acquittal of any minister to ever go before them, I sought an apology from John Brogden in the House. He was the Liberal Party Leader of the Opposition who had called for me to be jailed for three years for "what he has done". I wondered about also asking for an apology from Michael Costa, but stepped back from doing so. I should have done so. Had either Costa or his Chief of Staff, John Whelan, bothered to ask me what had happened from my perspective, they would have got a simple response: "Nothing. I did not know about the issue until contacted by a journalist after the election."

The slightest of questioning by Costa or Whelan of any of the senior rail personnel, would have confirmed that I had no knowledge and was not implicated in any way in this bizarre allegation that an unsafe rail bridge was left open for political reasons. If they still felt the need to refer the matter to ICAC, they could have then very easily made it clear that I was not being investigated for any wrongdoing. That is what any other minister or chief of staff would have done. Instead, my reputation was left hanging in the air, leaving the impression that I had deliberately put the lives of rail passengers at risk to lock away a few votes for the 2003 election.

The Millennium Train

One of the things I had been very proud of during my time as Minister for Transport was getting the brand new, state of the art Millennium train finally delivered onto our rail tracks. It had been dearer, more complex and more difficult than any of us imagined it was going to be at the start of the tender process. But, what a

Chapter 13: The premiership denied

great train it was when it did finally come out of the manufacturing plant. Carr and I had done a great launch of the first Millennium train at Central railway before the 2003 election, and it had rightfully got a great run.

Every new train has teething problems which usually require up to two years to iron out between the manufacturer and the rail authority, and the Millennium was no different. This had been the case with the very successful Tangara train fleet, and had I continued as Minister, I would have steered the reputation of the Millennium through to a successful commissioning conclusion.

But after a few failures during this period, Costa announced with some fanfare, that the new trains were being withdrawn from service until the problems were removed. It was a great stunt which I am sure he would have known, would have zero impact on himself, but maximum damage to his predecessor, who just happened to be a member of the same political Party and the same Cabinet.

There were plenty of positives he could have focused on instead. The Millennium had cost over $200M and was the first new train designed in decades. It had advanced electronic information and safety systems which were more advanced than any other train in the country. But, that would have been way too positive. Costa's desired image as a head strong Mr Fixer was achieved, but at the expensive cost of denigrating the Government's record on public transport.

"It's not the previous Minister"

One of Costa's favourite lines of attack was to leave no one in any doubt that he was attacking my record as Transport Minister, but when asked, he would stick to the line: "It's not the previous minister, it's the management and I am fixing that". As Carr would often say to us: "Never use the word 'not' unless you intend to assert the opposite of what you say". In other words, by saying it was "not the previous Minister" Costa was leaving a clear impression in the minds of others that it actually was the previous Minister. But sometimes for Costa, even that level of linguistic gymnastics was not enough. One encounter with Mike Carlton during a radio interview on the 8th of April 2003 went as follows:

Costa: "I certainly believe that not having the regulator independent of the Transport bureaucracy was a fundamental flaw in the old structure. And that's independent of this Menangle issue."

Carlton: "Michael, it seems a hell of a lot was wrong…it seems that …the last Minister, your predecessor, got it very, very wrong, mismanaged it very badly".

Costa: "Well, look, they're really questions for the last Minister"

And this was only three weeks into what would be a 'pretty tough' 12 months.

The Costa approach to denigrating my and the Government's record on rail was best summed up on the 29th August 2003 by Quentin Dempster, an experienced journalist with ABC TV: "Since the dark shadow of Michael Costa fell across the tracks, the new Minister has been repeatedly and energetically pronouncing, that little is well in the rail empire Mr Scully left behind." I could not have articulated it better myself.

And soon enough, the Sydney Morning Herald produced a particularly nasty piece setting out a summary of every negative

Chapter 13: The premiership denied

story I had received over the previous few years. That the journalist who wrote it had never spoken to me before or about the story and never spoke to me during my time in politics, has left me with an enduring suspicion that the whole article had been an Eamonn Fitzpatrick 'special' directly from the desk of Costa's own senior media advisor. I may be wrong, but given other events at the time, I believe the suspicion is a reasonable one.

The attacks come to an end

After enduring the attacks for months, I woke up one morning to see on the front page of the Sydney Morning Herald, the former Premier and Minister for Transport, Barrie Unsworth, saying some unkind things about the Bus-only Transitways which to me, were amongst some of my best achievements as Transport Minister. I was on strong ground. As Roads Minister, I was responsible for building the Transitway roads upon which the buses ran, and Costa as Transport Minister, was responsible for running the buses and the associated stations and information services. The lion's share of the funding was coming from my portfolio. If ever there was a golden opportunity for counter-attacking Costa, then this was it.

I went on Ray Hadley, the mid-morning 2GB Shock Jock, and I let rip on both Unsworth and Costa rejecting out of hand their denigration of such a great public transport initiative. I knew that Carr's media and personal staff would all be listening to Hadley, as he was the dominant player of that section of morning radio. When I arrived in to my ministerial office, Bowen was concerned. Carr was soon on the line to me and letting rip: "I will not have my Ministers stepping out of their portfolios to make public comment. I won't stand for it". I loved it and I knew this would be my moment to let Costa have it.

I said to Carr: "I agree. When you had me commissioned as Minister for Roads, you gave me responsibility for funding and delivering the completion of the Transitway network. I am simply defending and delivering what you asked me to do. I don't know why Costa is on the attack or why he has unleashed the former Premier. I intend to continue defending what is clearly my area of portfolio responsibility". Carr then quietly signed off with: "Leave it with me".

I am told Carr demanded Costa's presence in his office, let rip into him and demanded that the public attacks cease, extracting a promise that this would be done immediately. It must have been one hell of a performance, as all and every attack by Costa on me then ceased immediately. I was pleased, but also left in no doubt that had I commented on my previous portfolio when attacked by Costa rather than my current portfolio of Roads, Carr would not have been so accommodating. If Costa had not over-reached in attacking the bus Transitway programme, I would probably have had to put up with a considerably longer period of his negative public commentary on my period in the Transport portfolio. Ironically, it is the $800M Transitway network across Western Sydney which remains, with the Epping to Chatswood Railway, as outstanding legacies of my period as Transport Minister.

To this day, I do not know why Costa acted as he did and why I and no other ministerial colleague was singled out as I was during his years as a Minister. I do not know if he acted on his own whim, or if anyone else encouraged him to do so. I would certainly like to know, but I am unlikely to ever get an answer. The trio of Michael Costa, John Whelan and Eamonn Fitzpatrick certainly seemed from my perspective, as acting outside the realm of collective Cabinet Government responsibility. A Minister is supposed to defend the decisions of the Government, which

Chapter 13: The premiership denied

includes its record and events over which you may not have been responsible. It is untenable for a Cabinet to have to be on watch and take care for fear that it may at some point in the future attack itself. But this is what Costa did on Rail and what Tripodi would subsequently do in Roads. It still leaves me perplexed that such attacks happened and that Carr and then Iemma allowed it to continue. Costa was always a difficult and cantankerous individual to work with and his only close friends in parliament were Eddie Obeid and Joe Tripodi. After the damage Costa did to the Labor Government's standing in the community, with his and Iemma's disastrous management of selling the publicly owned power industry, I doubt Costa was much missed when he finally left politics.

On one occasion in Cabinet, at the conclusion of the meeting and during this period of Costa attacks, Carr looked down towards my end of the table and said: "By the way, which fuckwit in Rail did not recruit enough drivers." I was astonished and quickly responded: "Bob, someone has obviously sold you a line." Costa at the other end of the table, leant forward, looked at me, opened his mouth to speak, thought the better of it and sat back in his chair. Just as well, as I do not believe our ministerial colleagues would have then witnessed a pleasant profanity free amicable conversation. It confirmed my suspicions that Costa could dish it out, but was thin skinned when on the receiving end. And what really happened behind the scenes regarding the failure to recruit enough drivers?

I had always been deeply cognisant of the disastrous new timetable introduced by a Liberal Government about 18 months before the 1976 election. Neville Wran, as Leader of the Opposition, had a field day as train services descended into a chaotic mess. In 1997, just a few months before my own appointment as Minister for Transport, we had to withdraw a new timetable for similar problems and reinstate the old timetable it had sought to replace. So, when in 2002, with less than a year before the 2003 state election, the State Rail Authority (SRA) advised it was ready to introduce a new timetable with more train services, I was very apprehensive.

The more I challenged the SRA on the 1974 and 1997 timetable experiences, the more I was assured all would be well. However, the unconvincing and almost dismissive assurances from SRA senior management, that all would be well, left me convinced that the timetable would not work, that it would leave thousands of commuters stranded and make our re-election in 2003 that much more difficult. And I worried even more so, when I heard that the CEO had put the decision on the introduction of the new timetable to a vote of senior management, rather than it being backed solely by an exhaustive technical assessment. I felt that comedy hour had arrived at Platform 1.

I quietly asked for the Deputy CEO, Arthur Smith, to find a reason to cancel the proposal. When he came back and advised that there were insufficient drivers to enable the timetable to work, I was ecstatic and responded: "Excellent that is ample justification to not proceed. Well done." But Smith added: "Actually Minister, there really is insufficient drivers. I have calculated there are 60 too few drivers in SRA to make the timetable work." I thought at first that he was kidding and had zealously 'found' a good excuse to justify his minister cancelling a very risky initiative. But he was serious. There really were 60 too few drivers, and if I had implemented the ridiculous vote to approve the new timetable, disaster would have struck. I then directed the CEO to cancel the initiative.

Chapter 13: The premiership denied

Carr had clearly been briefed on only half the story by the new Minister and instead of getting a 'thank you for saving the Government's bacon' from the Premier, all I got was a 'which fuckwit' question. Little wonder that Carr's highly regarded Chief of Staff, Graeme Wedderburn, would years later recount: "The only thing which Carr and I ever argued on, was his failure to rein in Costa especially regarding his attacks on you."

The early retirement of Premier Mike Baird in January 2017, provided an unexpected but impressive example of how government should manage the transition of one senior minister to another. Adrian Piccoli, the Minister for Education had just been 'transferred' to the backbench and his replacement as minister was Rob Stokes. Within only a few days of being appointed, Stokes visited Piccoli's electorate of Griffith in the Riverina nearly 1000 kms from Sydney. The new minister inspected a school with his predecessor and spoke generously of him and his achievements to the media. It reminded me of my own experience with Michael Costa which had been palpably different.

In January 2005, true to his word two years earlier, Carr promoted me to a senior portfolio. Egan had announced his retirement from politics and Carr had decided to move Andrew Refshauge to Treasury, John Watkins from Police to Transport and Michael Costa from Transport to Roads.

Carr believed I had used my time well since the last election and that I was ready for one of the heavy hitting portfolios. Ten days into the new job as Minister for Police, the Macquarie Fields riot broke out and would take days for the police to resolve. Despite being in the job for only a few days, I had to continually question senior police on the resources they were applying until they got the message and brought the riot to a close.

I threw myself into the portfolio and did what I could to enhance police powers, equipment, salaries, stations and compensation for injury. I think the police liked what they saw.

The nuclear codes

One amusing moment is worth retelling. Prior to my appointment, Carr had done a Sunday newspaper stunt showing off the new counter terrorism silver suitcases, which both the Premier and the Minister for Police would have permanently with them whenever they travelled. It looked almost like the nuclear code a US President carries around with him and no doubt backed-up by the Secretary of Defence. When I was appointed, I spoke to Jason Clare about it, who was then working in Carr's office and he advised: "I wouldn't worry about that. It was just a stunt for the Sunday papers and Bob has not given it a moment's thought since".

So, I ignored it too, but my driver dutifully had the very impressive looking suitcase always at the ready in the boot of the ministerial car. After some weeks had passed by, my son James asked me what was inside and was surprised to learn that I had no idea. So, I decided to open it and find out. Inside was what looked like a large satellite phone with a yellow post-it-note attached to it with a rubber band and some thick writing in red text that read: "THIS DOES NOT WORK". My son and I almost fell over laughing. There was also a small mobile phone which had a dead battery and was useless. And finally, a folder with names and phone numbers of senior police officers to contact in the event of a terrorist attack. I knew them all already and never bothered to open the 'nuclear suitcase' again.

Chapter 13: The premiership denied

The contenders

Once the 2003 election was out of the way, it seemed clear enough that Carr was unlikely to run again. There were then a number of possible contenders for the top job. Bowen and I did an analysis of each of those possible contenders taking into account performance in the House and in front of the media, runs on the board, handling challenging circumstances and the sheer drive and determination needed to do the job. After that analysis, the list was soon whittled down to just Craig Knowles, Morris Iemma and myself.

Craig Knowles was capable, a good performer in front of the media, in his portfolio and in the House, but never really seemed to have the passion and drive for politics that was needed for a long-term stint at taking and keeping the leadership. He was, however, almost from the start, the preferred candidate of both Carr and Egan, who had poured huge amounts of money into his health portfolio from 1999 to 2003.

For reasons only known to Knowles, in late 2002, he met alone in his electorate office with nurses from Camden Hospital and Campbelltown Hospital who made serious allegations regarding a number of patient deaths. The nurses claimed he bullied them and did not treat their complaints seriously. This led to inquiries and a little like my Waterfall experience, it did not matter how much Knowles argued he had done what was required and had passed on the allegations for investigation, it did harm him in the public eye. This along with some trivial traffic violations would later cement him as a non-contender.

In March 2003, Morris Iemma had just completed an easy four years as Minister for Sport and Minister for Public Works and as he would boast to me from time to time, a life of working "two and a half days per week". He was more than shocked when Carr elevated him to the Health portfolio. At the time, he was not on anyone's radar as a potential Premier including his own.

Quite late in the Carr Government term of office, Obeid would refer to Iemma as being someone who some had suggested as being a possible candidate, but would then dismiss it as not a serious idea. I naively believed him and never really thought Iemma would actually put his hand up. He had always been considered an expert at backroom Machiavellian operations, as far as possible away from the glare of leadership.

Developing a programme for Government

On any reasonable assessment of likely contenders, it seemed at least on paper, that my prospects of succeeding Carr were very strong. But, I was not going to do this because it was nice to be Head of Government, but because I intended to use the position to make a lasting difference for the people of New South Wales.

Bowen and I discussed at length the need to have a settled policy, programme and project agenda which would be ready to go as soon as I had been appointed. Nothing is for sure in politics and I was far from being presumptuous enough to assume it was in the bag, but what I was not going to do, was be unprepared, if and when the time came to run the Government. And following my Waterfall experience and with Costa in full flight, there were certainly some obstacles ahead of me.

Bowen and I set up a very tight group within my office, which we informally treated as the 'transition to government' committee. This unofficial committee consisted of Bowen as Organiser, as well as my Deputy Chief of Staff, Brent Thomas, one of my Senior

Policy Officers and later Chief of Staff, Gary Sargent and a young Chris Minns on research who is now the State MP for Kogarah.

Bowen and Minns would regularly get me to read thought pieces from a range of policy sources which included the British Labor Party, the Democratic Leadership Council in the US, universities and other think tanks. All sorts of ideas and policy possibilities were canvassed across a large spectrum of governments. I would consume all this at night, on the weekend or whenever I had a spare moment. I would make notes and then share my views with the wider group. I also spent a lot of time thinking and recording what I thought needed to be done across several areas of Government. This included not just investing, but also in changing how the Government would be structured and resourced. My ideas and their ideas were the basis of constant discussion and consideration on how best to formulate an exciting implementable programme, which would leave our opponents gasping for oxygen. Even though ultimately unsuccessful, I very much enjoyed the long period of time we spent on this process. In the end, all the effort was for nought, but had I been appointed, I would have been ready and very busy.

In all the years I had known Morris Iemma, I never once heard him utter anything which might have resembled a serious interest in policy, reform or vision. He was always very much the machine man. If you wanted a branch recruitment strategy or advice on how to win a preselection or how best to develop a marginal seat campaign strategy, he would be the guy. But he was not the guy to talk to you if you wanted to know what to do with power and how to make a difference with it. I assumed that everyone else around me would see that. He would be the man plotting our re-election strategy, but not the one to steer the ship after we won.

I am confident that Iemma would have spent a lot of time applying his well-known machine skills to plotting his campaign to win the premiership, but would have spent little if any time on what he would do when he got there. Not unlike the 1972 film, 'The Candidate', when Robert Redford on learning on election night that he had unexpectedly been elected to the US Senate, saying to his campaign manager: "What do I do now?"

It certainly seemed that Iemma's whole focus was just winning the 2007 election and nothing else and that he really had not given much thought to the long-term direction and soul of his Government. I had determined that if I did win the leadership, I would appoint Iemma as Treasurer and ensure that he took a lead role with me and the Party office on how best to win the next election and the one after that. I still think that we would have been a formidable partnership. If only other things had not been at play. He was ordinary as a Premier, but would have been second to none in organising the strategy and tactics to win elections.

There were many things I had planned to do if the succession went my way:

Infrastructure

I wanted to be seen as the Infrastructure Premier by completing the Parramatta to Epping Rail Tunnel, as well as the Epping to Rouse Hill Rail Line, building the M4 East and F3 to M2 Motorways, and a new dedicated Bus-only Transitway on the corridor set aside for an F6 Freeway. All of this could and should have happened anyway. By 2011, when the Labor Government fell, none of it had been built! They had all gone to sleep at the infrastructure wheel. Most of these proposals and more are now being built by the Liberal Government elected in 2011.

Chapter 13: The premiership denied

Barangaroo

When I was Minister for Ports back in the mid-1990s, I had long planned for the Barangaroo site at Darling Harbour to be set aside as permanent open space with no development on it except for an iconic building on the headland to match the Opera House and the Harbour Bridge. I even had discussions with my Sydney Ports CEO, Greg Martin, to ensure the land continued to be used as a commercial port area until I became Premier. I envisaged at the time that this would still be a few years away.

However, the site was discovered by Carr and his team very late in his premiership. During a special Cabinet meeting on future of the site, I put to Carr that by dedicating the entire site as open space, he would be seen as the Jack Lang of his time. He puffed his chest out, mused for a moment on such a Whitlamesque opportunity to do something grand, and then quickly got back in his box, as Egan moaned about the $140M in cost and a nonsensical claim that "we need this site for office space in Sydney which is rapidly becoming in short supply."

Unfortunately, a lot of the site will be permanently lost to high rise office, hotel and commercial development – a real shame and one which saddens me deeply. The Government lost a unique opportunity to act in the best interest of future generations.

Had I stayed in politics beyond March 2007 and been drafted to replace Iemma in August 2008 instead of the embarrassingly inexperienced Nathan Rees, I would have immediately cancelled the development plans that are now almost fully implemented. A lot of ifs and maybes, but enough to still sadden me, that no one, including Carr, Iemma, Rees and finally Keneally, stepped up and protected this enormously valuable site wholly for permanent open space. The section protected for open space is certainly marvellous, but it could have been so much better.

Western Sydney Regional Park

I planned to do more elsewhere on open space. Having invested $18M of public money creating a fantastic picnic and BBQ area in Abbotsbury in a small section of the huge Western Sydney Parklands as part of the M7 motorway project, I decided that we needed to build a Centennial Park of the west by investing over $100M across the whole length of those parklands. Ten years on and nothing more has happened except Premier Baird did commit $15M during the 2015 election campaign to upgrade a very small part of it.

There were many areas of Government where I intended to quickly act in, which included health, prisons, police equipment, aboriginal affairs and social inclusion.

The Police Air Wing

I intended to dramatically increase the Police Air Wing with several 'eye in the sky' helicopters operating around the clock. The Los Angeles Police Department as well as New York Police Department have long demonstrated just how effective constant aerial monitoring can be for crime detection and pursuit. Nothing of great substance has happened on this in the last 10 years. It is expensive and would require a substantial overhaul of how policing is conducted in the urban environment. But I am hopeful that New South Wales Police will take a leaf out of the modern military use of drones, not for combat per se, but for local crime fighting. Drones can be armed with hand guns as well as cameras enabling the sort of aerial police force I had in mind. And much more cost effective for the bookkeepers who run Treasury.

Prison officials being accountable

On prisons, I was very concerned about just how many criminals left prison and re-offended. I planned to introduce accountability on this for senior prison officials linking their pay and employment longevity to lowering re-offending rates.

Education reform

I particularly wanted to do some good things in education.

1. **Ending nepotism and promotion rorts.**

The first thing I intended to do was to ban schools from promoting teachers from within their own schools. The Greiner Administration had done away with the old seniority system, where a time-based conveyor belt eventually placed a promotion into the lap of a very patient teacher after they had first gone through a very strenuous accreditation process some years before. At least theoretically, this did not allow for our most talented educators to be identified and promoted. So, a merit- based system was introduced in the late 1980s requiring an alleged transparent process of a comprehensive CV application, an interview by a panel and then selection of the most meritorious candidate.

It all sounded good on paper, but in reality, the new and supposedly fairer and meritorious system, allowed school principals to embark on a wholesale preference for internal appointments from within their own school, to the detriment and unfair disadvantage of both excellent external candidates, as well as hindering school renewal.

The problem first came to my attention over 20 years ago when one of my local schools promoted one of its least inspiring head teachers to Deputy Principal at the same school. I was intrigued and made some discrete enquiries to find out that there had been 32 applicants, that the successful candidate was a confidant of the Principal and one of the candidate's faculty members had been the staff representative on the panel. That this was the best candidate amongst so many, to me, just defied belief. The claim of the Principal to school colleagues that she had made sure that all the administrative requirements of the Department for a promotion process had been applied to the letter to ensure no ensuing appeal, only compounded my concern.

I wondered back then if this was happening in other schools and I started to peruse the monthly 'Education Gazette' which lists all promotions across the New South Wales Department. The Gazette listed the name, school, promotion position attained and from what school they had originated. I was astonished at just how many internal appointments were occurring. On average, every month, up to 50% and sometimes more, were being promoted from within their own schools. This seemed to me as nothing more than organisational nepotism wrapped in a merit-based blanket. I suspected that way too many principals were just too reticent to handle some internal school disappointment and look a staff member in the eye to tell them firmly: "You were not the best candidate".

This was enough for me to come to the view that the Department of Education's merit-based promotion system needed to be converted into one that would be genuinely based on merit. Internal applicants would no longer be eligible to apply. Only in this way would schools be forced to consider everyone equally and in turn, end the stultifying effect of nepotism to ensure schools also looked beyond for talent and genuine renewal.

During the Carr/Iemma period of Labor Government, I raised the matter with three separate Education Ministers and two

Chapter 13: The premiership denied

separate Directors General. I got no more than monosyllabic disinterest, but at least one Director General offered: "That would really piss off the Teachers Federation", as if that ought to be the defining guidepost for educational reform!

I had naively assumed that with the passage of time, someone senior within the Department of Education or Government, would have noticed just how rampant this promotional bias was and would have brought it to an end. Disappointingly, some years later, the Education Gazette revealed that for the three-year period of 2011-2013 internal school promotions had never been less than 38%.

I was intrigued to discern what might be the case 10 years on from when I had intended, as Premier in 2005, to bring this inequitable and stultifying practice to an end. Once again, the Department of Education's own document, the Education Gazette, makes for interesting yet dispiriting reading. In 2015, 1,057 teachers applied for promotion and 425 or 40% were internally appointed. From June to November 2015, there were 326 applications for promotion and 167 or 50% went internally.

Just to make sure of the nearly 30-year trend of schools appointing 40% internally year in year out, I also checked the records for the first six months of 2016. Up to June 2016 there were 746 applications for promotion and 303 or 40% went internally. From March to June 2016, it was 140 out of 278 or 50%. Perhaps teachers from outside a school may want to especially avoid June for trying their hand at promotion, as in June 2015, it was 32 out of 50 or 64%, and in June 2016, it was 23 out of 27 or 85%!

All these figures just leave me astonished that nothing has been done about it. I asked someone recently with knowledge of both recruitment and mathematical probability, and their view was that properly conducted merit selections in these circumstances would never select more than 10% of internal applicants and would probably be lower. Applying for a promotion inside the Department of Education, takes a lot of heart, soul and effort on the part of an applicant. They are entitled to assume that a system that advertises itself as merit-based, accountable and fair is just that!

The Department of Education goes to some length in its public statements, to assert a very different and noble picture to what is actually occurring on the ground, in its schools, in what ought to be a now a discredited promotion system. Hopefully unwittingly, the Department specialises in 'fake news' as it loftily claims that amongst its core values are 'integrity' and 'fairness'.

In its document on 'values' the Department says:

> *"Public schools ... have always stood for equality of opportunity and fair play ... New South Wales public education models the values that represent ... its concern for equity and excellence."*

On its claimed value of 'integrity and excellence' the Department of Education has this to say about its staff:

> *"You are part of a system which promotes integrity and excellence...values based public education and training system respects every one of its staff...When you work in the public education system you can enjoy the satisfaction of promoting a fair, democratic and tolerant Australian society, while reaping the personal benefits of a fair and nurturing work environment."*

This all does remind me of my school days studying George Orwell's '1984' with his hilarious account of opposites: 'The Ministry of Truth' and 'The Ministry of Peace' immediately come to mind. I am sure neither the current Minister for Education nor the current Secretary of the Department of Education would be familiar with the Department's own damning monthly reports on promotion. They should be asking why and calling the system to account. Alternatively, just formalise the system and let principals appoint who they want. Or bring back the old seniority system where talent at least got eventually promoted and new personnel were regularly brought into schools. But, I am very confident that nothing will happen. Perhaps I should check progress again in 2027.

2. Focussing on student and teacher learning

New South Wales Department of Education schools have much to be proud of. They accept all children, achieve wonderful results and have many hard working and dedicated teachers. Both my wife and I and both our children attended state schools. However, so much more could be achieved to prepare our school students for the future, if school leaders were properly trained, equipped and selected, to lead centres of learning rather than just operating a school building environment. Unfortunately, this is no less a problem in 2017 as it was in 2005 when I intended to do something about it.

One very positive initiative of the Greiner Government's Education Minister, Terry Metherill, was the introduction of a new position into high schools called the 'Leading Teacher'. This was at Deputy Principal (DP) level and was fully focussed on improving teaching practices in the classroom and the learning outcomes of both teachers and students. Sadly, the position in time lost its designated title and morphed into just another deputy administration role. Unfortunately, this meant that the critically important role of a DP equivalent in the school, leading the improvement of teaching and learning in the classroom, disappeared as the position became overrun with the traditional standard all-consuming DP focus on a daily diet of 'dunnies, drains and delinquents'. As is so often the case for senior management in our schools, 'operations' get precedence over how to increase the quality and performance of our classrooms. No wonder there are concerns about the slipping of student achievement against other OECD countries.

I intended to recreate the position of Leading Teacher, and insist that schools including their principals, were given the training, resources, time and staff, to do what they were supposed to do; fully focus on teaching practices in the classroom and the learning outcomes of their students.

School senior executives always claim that they are doing this, but in reality, few actually do, or even know how it should be effectively done. There are many notable exceptions, but unfortunately, far too many of our schools are run by quasi building managers rather than leaders of classroom excellence. If the latter were the single overwhelming priority of school leadership, as it should be, then the Department of Education, would have to substantially overhaul the development and selection of the kinds of teaching personnel traditionally selected for senior school positions. I sincerely doubt if either the government or its Departmental leaders will do so.

I have no reason to assume that the constant challenge of school management and operations, rather than educational leadership, in replacing potential school leadership time and effort, is any different in our private and independent schools.

Chapter 13: The premiership denied

If only parents, community and Government knew just how much school leadership time was wasted on 'administrivia' and how little was genuinely spent in creating first class learning organisations! They would not be impressed.

In 2014, one of the academic experts in this field, John Hattie, lamented that probably only about 5% to 10% of New South Wales school leaders are instructional leaders, focussing on their actual impact on improving classroom teaching practices and learning outcomes. Regrettably, far too many of the rest run their organisations less as learning centres, and much more as a Landlord and Tenant building arrangement: spaces fit for occupants, toilets working, food facilities available, rent and bills paid, power and heating on, newsletters, notice boards and special events organised, staff attending, student customers herded in, recalcitrant stakeholders appropriately secured and so on.

All those tasks, though important, take so much time and effort, that some senior school executives must wonder if they have 'left the Education building' and taken up a new career managing a shopping centre or a popular holiday resort. Whilst all those tasks need to be done, they could be handled more efficiently by appointing a non-educator Chief Operating Officer to each school rather than wasting the valuable time and expertise of our educators. Principals and deputies could then focus on what Government and community think they already focus on: improving the learning outcomes of their school and inspiring their teachers to do great things in the classroom. This is what will lift numeracy and literacy standards across the board – not filling senior school executive time with administrative tasks!

3. Appointing the best principals

With that in mind, I had intended to create a specialist panel to find and appoint a small number of inspiring educators as school principals. They would have been put on contract for a fixed term, paid a lot more money and with further financial rewards based on growth in student learning and teacher quality. It would have been an experiment worth undertaking, but no doubt the reactionaries in the Teacher's Federation would have resisted with great vigour. I think it is still worth considering as ought a requirement, that only those who have completed a Master Degree in Educational Leadership be eligible for promotion to Principal.

4. Mandating the New South Wales Quality Teaching Framework

One area which troubled me greatly in 2005, and still troubles me now in 2017, is the failure of the Department of Education, and non-government schools, to insist that all teachers implement the research and evidence-based 'NSW Quality Teaching Framework' (QTF) into their classroom teaching practice, rather than it just being a departmental tool and a voluntary guide. It still astonishes me that 'Quality Teaching' is not mandatory for teachers and schools. To properly ensure that our teachers are using the very best classroom teaching practice will require extensive training, mentoring, monitoring and evaluation. This is what school leaders should be filling their days with. A good starting point for them, would be to assess the extent to which teachers are implementing the QTF in their classrooms.

These are just a sample of the things I intended to implement if appointed Premier. I just omitted the main requirement of implementation: Having the numbers in the ALP Caucus!

Chapter 13: The premiership denied

Obeid and Iemma plan for the succession

In January 2005, Egan announced his retirement from politics. For nearly 10 years, he had been Carr's right hand man and effectively Chief Operating Officer of the Government. It was inconceivable to many of us that Carr would want to serve for long without him and we interpreted this as Carr's first step towards a carefully planned retirement. What then convinced us that this was the case, was when Carr made no opposition to the suggestion that Joe Tripodi fill Egan's vacant position in the ministry. Carr had never been known as a big fan of Tripodi.

In late January 2005, I had lunch with Mark Arbib, the then ALP General Secretary and had an engaging discussion about the post Carr future. He posed the difficult question: "What do you say to the argument that you have been damaged by rail and that you would, as a result, be in a difficult position to win an election." I put my case then, as I did a few months later, that rail was long gone as an issue, that by the election I would have been out of the portfolio for four years, that if it re-emerged as an issue, it would be tough on whoever was at the helm and I believed, I was the most capable of the post Carr choices. I must not have made a convincing impact or more likely, he never intended to listen to the case that rail was doing well.

In early 2005, I was more than a little concerned with Iemma's intentions of wanting to become premier, despite Obeid's assurances to the contrary. I met with Iemma in Parliament House and he surprised me with his expressed wish to move into federal politics. Knight had suggested that I try and get closer to Iemma, so I invited him to a BBQ at my home a few weeks hence. And then I went too far. I offered him the Treasury portfolio if I were to become Premier. Iemma was always a cool, non-emotional sort of person, but I was surprised when he made no sound and no response to what I had just offered. I had been expecting something quite different. The lack of interest and non-response to being offered a huge role in my administration, not only perplexed me, but caused me to query with Obeid if Iemma was really interested himself in running for the premiership. I suspected this potential as early as February 2005.

I was even more alarmed on the 22nd of February 2005 when Iemma sided with a whole phalanx of non-Terrigals to vote for Paul McLeay for a minor position in the right caucus. The two sub-factions of the NSW ALP parliamentary right known as the Trogs and the Terrigals, had all agreed that the position would go to Tony Stewart who won the position 26 votes to 20; 21 Terrigals out of 26 voted for Stewart and only 7 Terrigals out of 20 had voted for McLeay. All the senior leadership of the Terrigals had supported Stewart except for Iemma. I was very concerned that Iemma would do that and even more so, that Obeid would be dismissive when I raised concerns about it. I began to smell a rat.

I met with Obeid who fobbed off my concerns about Iemma in classic Obeid style: "Carl, I have heard that some are mentioning Iemma, but I can't see him being interested. He's got four young kids and his wife won't let it happen. I wouldn't worry about it." Obeid never enlightened me as to who the 'some' were, but as events soon unfolded, the 'some' emerged clearly: Eddie Obeid, Joe Tripodi, Ian McDonald and no doubt, Morris Iemma himself.

At the end of February 2005, I got a call from Iemma: "I'm sorry mate, but I can't make the BBQ at your place this weekend. Something has come up." I replied: "Morris, it's the same date next month, March not February." I predicted correctly to my wife Ann, that Iemma did not wish to socialise with me and would again find that 'something had come up'. It was around this time that even

Chapter 13: The premiership denied

Ann sought an assurance about Iemma from Obeid who gave a convincing response: "Morris is not interested; he's got four kids."

If I needed any further evidence that Iemma was not for reaching, it was when I happened to learn one day in idle discussion with him that he had not read "To Kill a Mockingbird" which I told him had had a profound impact on me as a young man, as it also had for millions of people around the world. I sent him a copy of the book with a covering note and a few days later at a caucus meeting he said: "Carl, I got a book in the post the other day, with a note from someone who had obviously forged your signature." I stopped trying after that.

My concerns were again fuelled when I was told that Obeid had been a sole visitor to Iemma's home on Easter Saturday 2005. I was never able to ascertain what had been discussed or the purpose of the visit. I assumed that it was probably not one in my best interests.

In May 2005, I met with Obeid and Tripodi at Club Marconi located in Bossley Park, just up the road from where I lived and in the heart of my former electorate of Smithfield.

We discussed at length the likelihood of Carr soon retiring and their strong support for my candidacy for the premiership. As I stood up and said: "Sorry guys, but I have to get to the electorate office for some appointments with constituents", I felt confident and comfortable. But as I walked some distance through the club and before I would be out of sight, I turned to give a wave goodbye and the two of them were staring at me in silence and suddenly looked quite uncomfortable. It crossed my mind that their body language suggested that they had just had quite a different conversation about me than the one we had just had together. I was the one then feeling uncomfortable, but quickly remembered all of Obeid's assurances and dismissed uneasy thoughts out of my mind. I believed what they had said.

Obeid had often said to me that I needed to look the part if I wished to lead the State and a short time later, in June 2005, Obeid joined me at Stewarts Gentleman Outfitters in George Street and waited with me as I tried on some suits. He sat in a lounge chair chatting to the proprietor and only seemed vaguely interested, which I found strange given his keenness to attend. Obeid then took me around to a shoe shop and after being fitted, I bought a pair of impressive shoes to go with the suit. After that, it was lunch nearby with Obeid and the Stewarts proprietor. Obeid's phone rang: "I'm with Carl. You should join us for lunch" and he then said; "That was Roozendaal. He is keen for a ministry and you should spend some time with him".

This whole episode was a ruse, which was the first of many others to come. If there was an Oscar category for acting in the political environment, then Obeid would have got an Academy Award.

Twice a year the Premier's Chief of Staff and the General Secretary of the ALP would conduct an audit of the portfolio with my Chief of Staff and my Head of Media. This was done for all portfolios. It was a thorough audit of the challenges and opportunities in the portfolio over the coming weeks and months. We treated the process seriously and prepared accordingly.

On Monday, 25th of July 2005, my Chief of Staff, Brent Thomas and my Head of Media, Jim Hanna, attended a scheduled audit meeting with Carr's Chief of Staff, Graeme Wedderburn and Mark Arbib. When Brent returned to the office, I was anxious to learn how they had gone and he said; "It was really strange. It was the easiest one of these I have done. There were no issues of concern

Chapter 13: The premiership denied

to them and they seemed happy with what is going on in the portfolio. Pretty easy really". A long time after the leadership challenge had come and gone, I bluffed Wedderburn with; "You gave it away you know with the easy audit you and Arbib did on my portfolio only two days before Carr's announcement. It was obvious that something was happening" and he responded; "We had to go through the motions". I was expecting a defence not an admission!

On Wednesday, 27th of July 2005, as scheduled in my diary, I had arrived at 9.00 am at the large Parramatta Police Centre to witness first hand a large-scale police event training scenario involving an act of terrorism and the police response. It was impressive, interesting stuff and one of the many occasions with the police high command which had made the portfolio a whole lot more enjoyable than the transport one had ever been.

I had only been watching this unfold for about 15 minutes when I received a phone call from my Chief of Staff, Brent Thomas, advising that Carr had just announced his retirement effective 3rd of August and that he would be calling a caucus meeting on the following Tuesday for the election of his replacement. I immediately felt an enormous surge of electricity through my body. I had campaigned for this day for just over 10 years and now my time had come. I felt overwhelmed with emotion and excitement. I was ready. I was going to be Premier. I had the programme. I had the plans and the speeches and the right people. It was exhilarating stuff. For about 20 minutes on that day, I actually thought I was going to be the Premier. However, I was about to be violently disabused of that notion.

Iemma put out a story which the press dutifully reported, that he had been in the car on the way to the airport to travel to Alice Springs to attend a Health Minister's Ministerial Council when he was shocked to learn of Carr's resignation. It was presented as if he was taken completely off-guard and just there and then decided "oops I think I will run for the premiership". I never thought of Iemma as an actor, but this one is foremost as one of the most effective acting jobs I had seen in politics.

On the second day of the leadership contest, a good contact in ALP HQ advised that he had seen Iemma visit the HQ office no fewer than six times in the week leading up to Carr's announcement. Surprised indeed.

I hopped in the car and rang my wife Ann who at that time was a consultant within the Department of Education and at that point was in the middle of a training workshop. I tracked her down and asked her to join me at the press conference I proposed to hold. I then rang the Deputy Premier, Andrew Refshauge, who confirmed what had occurred, that he and the soft left would be fully behind me and then wished me well on the campaign that was about to unfold.

And then I called Eddie Obeid: "Hi mate, Carr has finally announced he is going" and Obeid was jubilant. I said to him: "Ann is meeting me in the city and I will be doing a press conference with her at Parliament House to announce I am running" and then he floored me in a way no other remark has ever floored me in a phone conversation before or since: "That's a team decision" he said, to which I responded: "What do you mean, it's a team decision." The best Obeid could come up with then was: "We are all in a team and the team has to be involved in making a decision like this. I would hold off on doing a press conference until you have had a chat with Joe and me."

I was devastated and emotionally shattered by the conversation. I had long suspected that Obeid had been quietly

Chapter 13: The premiership denied

setting Iemma up for the succession with Iemma's full knowledge and acquiescence, but I had accepted Obeid's assurances that this was not the case, that Iemma was not interested, that he had too many young children, that his wife would not allow it and that I was the man. I cannot describe the devastating sense of betrayal that the phone call with Obeid had on me and still has on me now. I rang my Chief of Staff, Brent Thomas, who was blunt in his response about Obeid and his 'team decision' mantra and said: "Fuck'em, let's do it without them; do the press conference and then we'll go see those bastards."

I called Iemma and for the first time in the 20 years I had known him, he neither took my call nor returned it. That was confirmation enough that something was up, and only confirmed when one of our confidants informed me that Iemma was definitely in his ministerial office and "as we speak is in a huddle with his advisor, Peter Barron". I was not sure that day, just how many daggers I was going to have plunged into me in one day, but this was the third in a matter of less than an hour: Obeid first, then Iemma and now Barron. There would be more, a lot more, before the contest was over, but this was an awful lot to suddenly take in. Eddie Obeid had been a friend and loyal supporter for 15 years. Morris Iemma had been a friend, mate and confidant, and factional and Party fellow traveller for 20 years.

Peter Barron's behaviour was particularly disappointing at the time. I had long admired Barron as an extraordinary political strategist to both Hawke and Wran and early on in my ministerial career, I drew on his obvious expertise to help guide me towards being an effective and successful minister. We would meet at least once or twice a year regularly throughout my first 10 years of ministerial life. This included the period of 1995 to 1999, when

Iemma was still languishing on the backbench during the eight years it took him as an MP to get into the ministry.

As the years unfolded, I had assumed that it was obvious to both Barron and I, that the purpose of his guidance was towards the goal of replacing Carr. When Barron was later challenged about it, the best he could come up with was: "I never committed to him. If I had, he would have had my exclusive commitment."

Over the years, I was fortunate to have benefitted from the sage advice of former Wran Government Senior Media Advisor, Brian Dale and his wife Sandra. Brian was rightly credited by Wran as a major factor in the unexpected ALP win at the May 1976 New South Wales State Election. Brian and Sandra stuck with me through the whole contest and beyond, remaining loyal and supportive.

Ann and I did the press conference which went very well in front of a full complement of the gallery except for my unintended introduction of my new nickname: "Sparkles".

I had believed Obeid's assurances about Iemma not running, as Iemma seemed to me to be the antithesis of the sort of personality the leadership job required. He had always been seen by all as a backroom numbers man. He was quiet, reserved and introverted whereas I was outspoken, confident and extroverted. He seemed to dislike being in the spotlight whereas I loved it. He always came across as a little shy with an unknown crowd whereas I thrived in such an environment. I had thought deeply about the policy direction we needed to take and I was very confident that Iemma would not have given this anywhere near the attention to detail I had given it.

Chapter 13: The premiership denied

I had always known that the critical role of Premier was to be master and arbitrator of all the great party and governmental policy challenges and debates which must occur within a regime trying to do as much good as possible for the people of New South Wales. I am not sure that Iemma would have seen it like that.

Anyone who was honest about our respective qualities at the time also came up with similar comments. I knew the contrast, I am sure Iemma knew the contrast and I am sure Obeid and Arbib did too, but they all soldiered on as if it did not matter. Advancing the best interests of New South Wales was never discussed nor presented.

At the news conference to announce my candidacy, I wanted to use words that would clearly identify the contrast in personality between Iemma and me, without actually denigrating him. I said: "I will bring sparkle and verve to the job…" Everybody knew that Iemma would bring neither sparkle nor verve to anything let alone the job of being Premier of New South Wales.

Brent Thomas and I then went up to Obeid's office for an 'audience' with Obeid and Tripodi. And that is probably the best description of the unpleasant encounter it was, which just a day earlier, would have been called a 'meeting' with trusted colleagues. I had known Tripodi by then for 20 years. As a 17-year-old local high school student, he had joined my Fairfield West branch of the ALP and I had taken him under my wing and tried to advise and mentor him for many years. I had been a visitor to his parental family home in Fairfield West, had attended his wedding, and when he mired himself in a sex scandal, I telephoned his mother to make sure she was ok. The 17-year-old Tripodi I had met all those years before and loyally befriended, was now the 37-year-old assassin of my political dreams. A 20-year friendship was about to end abruptly.

Interestingly, Obeid did little of the talking in our brief meeting and left it to Tripodi to deliver the 'message'. It was acrimonious and pointless to say the least. It went as follows:

Tripodi: "Why did you do a press conference before speaking to us?"

Me: "Are you kidding? You and Eddie have already made a decision to support Morris and from what I can see, you made that decision a long time ago."

Tripodi: "Mark has briefed us on the polling, which shows that Morris is the best candidate to take us to the next election." Eddie mumbled agreement and said almost nothing memorable except that he supported what Tripodi had said. I think he must have been a little embarrassed by it all.

Me: "I don't care what you two think. I'm going to test this and see what the caucus thinks."

They did not look happy. Brent Thomas then piped in with the most sensible comment of this short unpleasant occasion: "Let's go. We've wasted enough time here already."

As expected, Mark Arbib then asked to meet me in my ministerial office. Arbib had long been well liked by all who had dealings with him including the left. He had been a welcome contrast to his predecessor, Eric Roozendaal, who was a more difficult personality to work with. Arbib usually worked his natural charm and hail-fellow well met bonhomie to the last detail in all his interactions with people. This brought him friends, influence and control. Folks liked him and liked working with him including myself.

Chapter 13: The premiership denied

But in this meeting, a very different Arbib emerged. He was taciturn, abrupt, irritated and arrogant. He did not even bother with the bonhomie pleasantries which by then he had truly mastered. He expected me to kneel and concede before the weight of his mighty opinion that Iemma was the one and only person to lead us to a 2007 election win. At this point in time, for reasons still unbeknownst to me, Arbib was regarded as a political guru, to be respected and followed. In time that would change, particularly after a stint in federal politics. But, in late July 2005, he had great sway and respect amongst many in the Party, including MPs whenever he spoke.

Arbib explained that he had done some polling which showed folks really turned-off when asked about poor rail performance during my time as Minister for Transport. He was not interested one bit in even discussing a counter view. I put to him as I had put to him over lunch the previous January, that trains were no longer an issue and that the Liberals would only be able to run on it if it did become one and if it did, it would be a problem for whoever was Premier. I sensed from his body language that he knew what I had said was right, but he was not to be swayed from his predetermined path no matter how good the argument.

I had assumed that Arbib had procured some thorough statistically valid polling from a large cohort of the electorate. I was astonished to learn from him, well afterwards, that he had relied, not on polling as we all understood that term to mean, but on small focus groups who had been asked their opinions. This is notoriously unreliable as a means of determining what the whole electorate is thinking. I would learn much later that this was Arbib's preferred way of gauging public opinion. There is nothing wrong with getting what is known as qualitative data from small groups of people to drill down on some issues, but it should never be used for quantitative purposes to argue that 4,000,000 voters think a certain way. This is just what Arbib did to determine who should be Premier. The absurdity of such a process should have been dismissed by all as a laughable way to select the Premier of the State. But no one challenged it. Mark had spoken and that was it.

Arbib would have known that had he done statistically valid polling, he would have found that I was a whole lot more electable than he wanted the caucus to believe. It was why, I am sure, he never relied upon or referred to such polling. Even when the Sydney Morning Herald published the results of such an independent statistically valid poll which showed me as being electorally competitive against Iemma and others, Arbib brushed it aside as no more than an irritation to delivering his selected candidate for the job of Premier. But, I would still be slandered by Arbib, Obeid and others as unelectable based on what a few folks had allegedly said in a focus group. Allegedly, because so far as I am aware, no one in the parliamentary caucus actually saw the focus group results. That ten people off the street in an evening chat about who should lead the Labor Party, was the means by which Arbib justified Iemma as his personal choice for Premier, was beyond ridiculous. That no-one was even shown the results and how they were arrived at, just emphasises the tawdry nature of the whole Iemma sales pitch. It was enough for the large majority of ALP right MPs to be simply told what was in it.

On Thursday, 28th July 2005, the Sydney Morning Herald published the results of a Newspoll survey of a random sample of 664 people conducted between the 3rd and the 9th of June 2005.

Chapter 13: The premiership denied

It made for interesting reading:

- 47.8% rated Iemma's performance as Health Minister as very good, good or fair, but 37.3% rated it poor or very poor, and

- my own performance as Police Minister was rated by 61.6% as very good, good or fair and just 19.9% as poor or very poor.

When these same folks were asked "Who should accept most responsibility for problems with the rail system?":

- a whopping 51.5% blamed Bob Carr
- 20.7% "didn't know"
- 18.0% blamed Michael Costa and
- a low 8.2% blamed Carl Scully.

On the question of "Who was the best candidate to lead the New South Wales Labor Party?", the scores were:

- Morris Iemma: 2.2%
- John Watkins: 7.9%
- Craig Knowles: 9.2%
- Frank Sartor: 11.0%
- Carl Scully: 11.6%.

None of these figures fitted in with the Arbib narrative that because of my record in rail, I was as a result, unelectable. He, Obeid and Tripodi, with the full support of Ian McDonald and most of the hard left, soldiered on as if nothing had happened. No wonder Bob Carr would say to me years later; "contrary to what Arbib had been telling the Caucus, polling at the time showed you were electable".

Despite Arbib obviously already having made up his mind on the issue, I still did try to reason with him. I pointed out to Arbib what I thought was the single most important thing a new Premier should have, and that was to have an exciting innovative programme to hit the ground running with. I said to him: "I have spent over a year developing plans for the next five years through and beyond the 2007 election and to position us to win the election after that." Arbib was contemptuous, dismissive and disinterested: "I know, you're going to abolish the vendor's tax. Anyone can do that." That was the extent of the interest the General Secretary of the Party had in a vision and programme for New South Wales. It would not be the first or only time, I had cause to view this man as a light weight operator.

Neither Arbib nor Iemma ever asked me for the details of the policy agenda I had prepared, and as far as I am aware, nor were any of my staff. No one ever asked for Iemma's agenda or plan for New South Wales, as Shorten and Albanese were for Australia, in their own quests for leadership in the ALP, after the Federal Election of 2013. That the new Iemma Government in New South Wales eventually ran out of steam was no surprise to me. All the focus, thought and energy was on just winning the premiership and then on winning the 2007 election, not on what to do with that win, why we should be elected and what we needed to do to put in place a long-term agenda to keep the community with us. It was just: "Let's win the next election" and nothing else. Very limited, ordinary, and disappointing stuff for the people of New South Wales. Arbib and Iemma were only interested in managing the shop and had no interest in the kind of transformational leadership required to make a real difference to how society worked and operated. I had long before the July 2005 leadership battle, privately articulated in writing with my senior staff, why I wanted to be premier, what I intended to do with the position, and my plan

Chapter 13: The premiership denied

to inspire both the community and the government with passion, ideas and change. I am very confident that Iemma would never have reduced to writing why he wanted to be premier and no doubt, would have bristled at the intrusion, if he had been asked to do so, before the Obeid, McDonald, Tripodi and Arbib quartet lined up in his corner.

I brought the discussion with Arbib to an abrupt halt with: "You and Obeid can get fucked. I am running and I don't give a shit what you and he think about it. The two of you with Iemma have obviously cooked this up some time ago, but I want to see what caucus thinks about it."

I then hit the phones with colleagues and embarked on what turned out to be a three-day soul-destroying exercise. I had spent 10 long hard years performing as well as I could in many difficult portfolios, often in the face of quite onerous odds, undermining from within and almost constant attack from the media and talkback radio. Despite all that had been thrown at me, I had delivered motorways, rail lines, housing estates and port facilities and was making a good fist of the police portfolio. I believed that a Premier needed to have had this sort of long political combat training in delivering, arguing the case for change and coming through successfully. It was obvious to me that whilst Iemma had spent two years in the tough Health portfolio, he had experienced a relatively peaceful six year of ministerial life, and I thought that would count against him. I believed he was simply not combat ready for the task of Head of Government. In the end, sadly, after his disappointing period of premiership, I was proved right but at the time, very few were interested in hearing it.

And none more so than Arbib and the Obeid/Tripodi attack duo. Having brushed aside any relevance to limitations on Iemma's personality and his suitability for leadership, Arbib now argued that a lack of solid exposure to the cut and thrust of daily ministerial life was not a liability for leadership, but actually an asset that the Party intended to draw on. This was extraordinary nonsense then and remains nonsense now, and just another example that Arbib, Iemma, Obeid and Tripodi were all intent on their choice and no matter what argument was put for a contrary candidate, they would craft a case against it.

Arbib started to peddle his stuff with the Caucus: "Carl has got too many barnacles from all his grief in Rail. Morris is a clean slate on which we can write what we like." Imagine a large corporation having that sort of rubbish put to them about why a candidate ought to be the new CEO. But it was dished up to MP after MP and they swallowed it hook line and sinker. If any still needed convincing, then Arbib would just refer to his mysterious polling which nobody had seen, and which nobody would see.

I am still astonished how MPs just fell into line. I was certainly accustomed to faction and party discipline, but I was also very used to having to bring every MP with you no matter how large or small the issue was. I had seen first-hand just how independent minded many MPs could be from time to time.

Arbib, Obeid, Tripodi and Iemma all hit the phones in a concerted four-pronged attack, which I had no chance of overcoming. When ambitious MPs could see that Iemma had been pre-selected by the General Secretary of the Labor Party, anointed by the factional godfather Obeid and supported by the faction spear carrier Tripodi, they all fell into line very quickly without so much as a murmur of discontent. It never occurred to them that perhaps being so ambitious to get into the ministry, now or in the near future, may in fact not be in their or the Party's best long term interest, if it meant electing a Premier who was not best equipped

Chapter 13: The premiership denied

to do the job well. Trying to have a conversation like that with MPs in mid-2005 was like talking to a brick wall.

Arbib did the 'science' and presented the reasoned approach that from a rational and quantitative assessment I could not win the 2007 election, but Iemma could and therefore, was the only candidate to support. Obeid herded the cats by repeating this view, calling for all Terrigals to support the General Secretary and appealing to them to be team players and protect their path to promotion.

Tripodi was the nastiest of all. He would cajole MPs with the line: "Scully is not fit for leadership. He does not even believe in immunisation. How can we have a guy like that leading us?" Tripodi who had been a friend and confidant for such a long time, really did upset me when this was brought to my attention. He had been a regular visitor to my home and knew my wife and children very well. When one MP rang to tell me that Tripodi had adversely reflected on an aspect of how we had brought up our children, I decided there and then that he was no longer a friend of mine and that from then on, I would have as little to do with him as was practically possible. I did tell Tripodi later that I understood MPs making professional decisions and that was fine, but that he had gone way beyond that and that was the reason why we would never again be friends.

It was not all sad and bad news. Rather surprisingly, Richard Amery and the Trog sub-faction of the NSW ALP parliamentary right, expressed full and strong support for me. It is one of the most ironic experiences I had throughout my career. I had campaigned with Obeid and Iemma and later Tripodi against the Trogs for more years than I could remember. But then, as the Terrigals deserted me in droves, the Trogs stuck firm. Astonishing! Richard Amery even said to me at the time: "I don't know why your mates are backing Morris. It is rather lost on me and if I were you, I would keep a new suit pressed and ready as I'm not sure this bloke is going to work out." He did not need a crystal ball to know that this was going to be the case. In just three short years, Iemma would self-immolate in a ball of flames with Michael Costa over their clumsy attempt to privatise a large part of the New South Wales electricity system.

Andrew Refshauge, the long-term Deputy Premier, continued to be a very strong supporter of mine, as did most if not all the members of the soft left sub-faction he led. Refshauge and I had been working closely together over the previous two years, to get his sub faction left colleagues comfortable with the idea of me succeeding Carr. It had worked well. We had agreed that he would continue as Deputy Premier, would have a major role in Cabinet and would be an important part of the way forward. We would have been a great team. It was obvious that neither he nor Iemma wanted to work with each other and after the ballot, sadly, he left politics.

The soft left led by Refshauge, and the hard left led by Ian McDonald, had roughly the same numbers in Caucus, but the Trogs were swamped by the rusted on Terrigals. I had to try and reach more than a few in both the hard left and the Terrigals if I was to have any chance of success. I knew that the hard left was a tall order. Iemma was close to Leo McLeay, the then Federal MP and former Assistant Secretary of the ALP and right hand man of Graham Richardson. McLeay had over the years, developed a close friendship and solid political relationship with Anthony Albanese who was a dominant player in the New South Wales hard left. Iemma was close to McLeay and I assumed he would, as a result, be more likely to be able to lock in the hard left for his candidacy. Ian McDonald then led the New South Wales

Chapter 13: The premiership denied

parliamentary hard left, and by mid-2005 was well known for spending a lot of time with Obeid. I assumed correctly, that due to the closeness of the relationship between Obeid and McDonald, they would likely be both pushing the MPs subject to their influence to support Iemma.

I had rarely spoken to McDonald in 15 years as an MP and I was not about to change that now. But, I did decide to test his influence by reaching out to two hard left ministers who I believed, had a reasonable professional regard for me.

I called Carmel Tebbutt, wife of Albanese, a fellow minister and very much a member of the hard left. I had always found her a pleasant and engaging person who seemed to be the most likely hard left member at least to have a conversation with, on who best to serve as our new leader. I was soon disabused of that too.

I gave my introductory spiel to Carmel over the phone and got a very surprising response: "I am in a team and I support the decision of that team to vote for Morris." I then said: "Carmel, can you honestly say to me that you think that Morris Iemma is clearly the better candidate for Premier" and I again got back: "I am in a team and I am supporting the team decision." I tried again: "Yes, but can you look me in the eye and tell me honestly that you think Morris Iemma is the better candidate" only to again get: "I am in a team and I support the team decision". I wondered for a moment if I was listening to a recording or if this was her backhanded way of saying that she knew I was the better candidate, but could not break ranks with the Ian McDonald controlled hard left.

I had long pushed this discussion to the back of my mind, until I saw an article in the Sydney Morning Herald in late November 2013, announcing that Carmel Tebbutt was calling for the direct election of the New South Wales Parliamentary Leader by the ALP membership. I certainly would have relished a Shorten/Albanese style broad ALP membership contest with Iemma back in 2005, but I have a strong feeling Iemma would have shunned the scrutiny and declined to be a candidate. Perhaps a Scully/Watkins battle in the branches would have been the more likely and more interesting contest. At least Watkins had a little more charisma and interest in policy.

I also tried rusted on hard leftie, Bob Debus but to no avail. Despite being a regular visitor to his marginal electorate of Blue Mountains, pouring millions of dollars of road funds into his electorate, and even hosting a fundraiser which raised thousands for his campaign, he did not even return my phone call. A few days later, as we both walked down to Government House for the swearing in, I asked Debus if he had injured his dialling fingers. At least he looked a little sheepish.

With the most approachable hard lefties either batting me away or not talking to me at all, I was left in no doubt then, that if I did not get any traction with members of the Terrigal group it would soon be all over. These were MPs with whom I had worked closely for years, socially, professionally and politically. In many cases, I had helped secure their first wins in Parliament or their subsequent re-election as MPs. Some would say that that was my job as a Minister, but compared to Iemma, the attention, the hard work, the care and detail I had given to each of these MPs, did not of itself deserve a vote for me, but it did in my view, create a reasonable expectation that I would, at least, have a good conversation about the pros and cons of each candidate. What followed gave me the impression, that it would have been whole lot better for me, if I had spent the previous 10 years attending to MPs demands and expectations as Iemma had done over the previous six years. I would have had a whole lot more time at home with my wife, and spent a lot more quality time watching my children grow up.

Terrigal, after Terrigal battered away all and any overture I made to put my case for the premiership. My experience was best summed up by a frank Graham West after the ballot was well over when he fessed up: "After our 45-minute phone call, I immediately rang Kristina Keneally and told her to expect a long phone call from you and the only way to avoid it, was tell you up front she was supporting Morris." I had called Kristina and recalled vividly the tart conversation we had had, if it can be called that as my "hello Kristina" was immediately met with: "Carl, I'm voting for Morris. I have already made up my mind." That was the extent of the intelligent discussion I had with our future Premier about who ought to be the future leader of our Party and why. West was also a disappointment, as he had succeeded Michael Knight in Campbelltown who, on his departure from politics, had said to me: "My gift to you is Graham West." Some gift. But this was still relatively tame stuff.

Then things became really nasty. A rusted-on supporter in the Upper House rang me to say that despite promising me the day before to vote my way, he had been reminded by the Party office that it was they and not me who had put him in Parliament and that they expected him to vote the way the Party had told him to vote, and that was for Morris Iemma. He was in tears as he withdrew his support.

This was then followed by another call, also from a rusted on Upper House MP who had been told that if he voted for me, he would not be on the ALP ticket for the Legislative Council when his time came up for re-election. He had, only a few days before Carr announced his retirement, introduced me to a former colleague as "the next Premier of New South Wales". He was also in tears as he advised me that he wanted another term in Parliament and now was not able to support me.

And then came the same if not worse, from a close Terrigal colleague in the Lower House who had long expressed a wish to see me as Premier and for him to serve one day in my Cabinet. He rang to say that the Party office had pressured him considerably and had plainly told him that if he voted for me, then there would be no place for him in the Ministry after the election. He too was in tears as he told me that the Scully dream was over.

However, one player who stuck by me through thick and thin was David Campbell, then a Minister and the former Lord Mayor of Wollongong. He told me that regardless of what Iemma, Obeid, Arbib, Tripodi or anyone else told him to do, he was voting for me as he thought I was the best candidate for the job. They certainly made him pay for that in the following few years, for what Tripodi referred to as his disloyalty.

Knight called in during the middle of all this and asked a confronting question: "Who is doing all the calling around for you? Which MPs are doing the hard slog for you as Obeid and Tripodi are doing for Iemma?" I knew that Knight was also close to Iemma and given the circumstances, avoided answering the question. However, it left me feeling very lonely and isolated. When we see the footage of Bill Shorten in 2010, in an office with colleagues on the phone, and clearly in the middle of pushing for the demise of Kevin Rudd in favour of Julia Gillard, it is obvious, that an MP cannot win a leadership battle on the phone on his own. Knight's question rammed this home to me, long before the Rudd/Gillard/Rudd Federal phone canvassing debacles of the recent past.

Chapter 13: The premiership denied

I knew by then that my 30-year dream to become Premier was not going to happen, although I had always understood that it would be a tough thing to achieve. I would not have minded so much if we had selected an MP who had a natural ability for political leadership such as: Egan, Knight, Knowles, Refshauge, Whelan or even Watkins. That the baton was about to be passed to someone who had no plan for New South Wales, was not exactly charismatic or able to demonstrate obvious leadership potential, made it that much harder to accept. There had been no real and fair assessment or weighing up of the candidates by the Party. Just an opinion expressed by the General Secretary, and then supported, enforced and imposed by faction leaders, Obeid, Tripodi and McDonald, and that was it! Within one of the two great party organisations which compete for votes at our democratic elections, there had been no real democratic process to select the head of government. There had been next to no discussion of which was the best candidate and why. It was obvious that the very few had predetermined the outcome for the many, and had done so well before Carr made his retirement announcement in July 2005.

I rang Iemma mid-afternoon on Friday, 29th July 2005, and announced I was pulling out of the ballot and that he would have my full support as Premier. It was one of the hardest things I have had to do in my life. It is still tough now, all these years later, to recall it. I called Arbib who surprised me yet again: "But we want a ballot. We want the caucus to endorse the new Leader." I had been tipped off that as Iemma's victory was looking more and more assured, that more and more MPs were coming over to his cause and that the impending ballot for me would not be pretty. I have always referred to this as the 'winner's surplus'. In a leadership ballot, there are always more than a few MPs who sit back and only commit to a particular candidate once he or she has

50% of the vote assured. This is why some ballots can look a little lop-sided. Everyone wants to be seen by the new Leader as a supporter.

Unlike any other General Secretary, Arbib, talked too much and let slip in the ALP Headquarters during the contest, that he and Iemma were looking for a crushing win which would be a great start to marketing the new Premier. This was quietly passed onto me, enabling me to deny them that indignity.

After I announced my withdrawal from the ballot, it quickly became all about who would get what portfolio. In Carr's day, the Premier would never have allowed the General Secretary of the Party to make calls to ministers to inform them about what portfolio they were getting in a new Administration. But in a taste of things to come, this is exactly what occurred. As soon as Iemma had been appointed as the new Leader, Arbib called me and said: "We have decided to leave you with Police, but due to the way you have conducted yourself, you are going to get Utilities as well, which puts you in charge of both Sydney Water and Power." I was left feeling like an errant schoolboy who had been rewarded due to unexpected good behaviour.

I understand that at about the same time, Iemma told Tripodi; "You can have any portfolio you want" and Tripodi quick as a flash responded; "I want Roads". And the rest, as they say, is history. It is very unusual for someone to be given this sort of offer, unless he or she was a Deputy Leader or someone very close to the Leader. Clearly, Tripodi was being rewarded for effort but unfortunately, given a job in which he would struggle.

Iemma in his three short years as Premier would make two disastrous ministerial appointments. The first, Tripodi in Roads, would lead to the post opening Cross City Tunnel debacle and as

Chapter 13: The premiership denied

a result, marked the end of Labor's motorway building programme. The second, was appointing Costa to Treasury which directly lead to the destruction of the Labor Government after an appallingly mishandled attempt to again sell a large part of the State Electricity assets. Iemma was unable to see the limitations of these two individuals when most others could.

Just a few days after Iemma had been appointed Leader, I met with him in his new office prior to his formal swearing in as Premier. It was a very emotional time for us both, but I was floored when he said to me: "Stick around. I'm not going to break any records in this job, so I wouldn't be going anywhere if I were you." Unbelievable. I could not believe what I had just heard. I had always thought that if I succeeded Carr, that I would either be carried out in a box, defeated at the polls or removed by an ungrateful Caucus, but the thought of doing a short stint and bolting had never entered my head. I was amazed, confused and angry all at once. Why had he taken the job, and denied me the opportunity, if he only saw it as a transitional thing before he went on to do something of more interest to him. If MPs had bothered to grill him about his long-term commitment to the job and had he given an honest answer to the question, I doubt he would have been elected Premier!

About a month into the new Government, Iemma and I did a joint news event at a Sydney Water site and he again, unsolicited, returned to the same theme: "Don't go anywhere. I won't be in this long term." I said: "Morris, you must have known that the job was going to be tough. Why did you take it on?" and his plaintive reply of "good question" left me feeling sad, because our new Premier was stuck in a place he did not want to be in. I would have given my right arm for the job and stayed in the position forever, but here was a guy who had been handed the head of government position on a silver platter and hated it! He wasn't what sometimes amusingly and inaccurately gets directed at Carr as the 'reluctant leader' but now appeared as the 'resentful leader'. I just found the attitude extraordinary and not one I would expect to hear from a head of government anywhere, anytime. Even many years after he had left politics when my sister Marie introduced herself to him at his local shopping centre, he lamented: "I never wanted the job you know."

On the day I withdrew from the leadership ballot, I went home feeling a little numb and shell-shocked, but I thought that would pass. But in the middle of the night, I woke up dry-wrenching with pain and grief. The pain was physical and not mental. I felt physically sick as if I had just been killed from the inside out. I doubt many people will ever experience that kind of pain. I had dreamed and pursued the great mantle of being Labor Leader and Head of Government from the age of 17 to now 48. It had been almost in my grasp and then rapidly disappeared, not because a better and more capable man presented himself for office, but because particularly close friends and colleagues who I had known for what by then felt like half a life time, had turned on me in such an unexpected and toxic way, that they could never be friends or colleagues again.

It was a traumatising experience to not only have been denied this long sought-after position, but to have been denied it by people I thought were my friends, including Morris Iemma himself – that was heart wrenching. It was harder still when Iemma made it clear that he didn't really want to be Premier!

The following Monday, I was back at work. I was emotionally wrung out. I had to go through the pretence that all was well and Morris and I were all part of one big happy family. I threw myself into the Utilities and Police portfolios and in time, gradually accepted the situation.

In quick succession, I had to deal with Tripodi and his handling of the Cross City Tunnel and then of course, the Cronulla Riot.

In April 2006, I had a private meeting with Iemma and sought his assurance about my still being on the front bench after the 2007 election. I said to him: "If you are of the view that you want generational change, then I would like to know and I will prepare accordingly and quietly leave at the next election". He expressed complete surprise at me raising this matter and gave me the assurance I had been looking for. Somewhat ironic in that just six months later he did the exact opposite.

CHAPTER 14

The dream ends – Iemma strikes again

It was a huge contrast working for the new Premier when compared to Carr – it was palpable.

Carr was a master communicator, whereas Iemma was the master mumbler. Carr listened to the advice of his staff and his ministers to get the facts and would then workshop in his own mind how he would deliver the message. Iemma would do a briefing prior to a press conference but if he needed reinforcing, then he would call Peter Barron for the lines to use, which he would write down and then repeat in the press conference. Carr was the master of the one-liner, whereas Iemma could never manage one. Carr was decisive and Iemma was dithering. The decisions Carr made may not have always been to the liking of a minister, but at least he made them. Iemma just could not make a decision even if his life depended on it. Carr was tough, but never needed to make a decision to look the part. Iemma struggled to look tough and often felt the need to appear to be so.

An example of his dithering occurred after my debrief on the Water portfolio from Frank Sartor, which was probably the best and most comprehensive of any handover I would get in my long period as a Minister. Sartor advised me that I needed to urgently put to Iemma the need to bring together all the myriad of people

Chapter 14: The dream ends

and agencies that had a role in Water policy. There was Sydney Water, The Department, the Sydney Catchment Authority, The Water Unit in the Cabinet Office and the Premier's own water advisor, Mark Aarons, who seemed to be a law unto himself. Iemma had not yet issued the administrative arrangements for his Government, so I took the opportunity of putting to him that he needed to bring this all under one minister who would have full responsibility and accountability for Water. At the end of my submission, he just said: "Let's keep a watching brief on it". I went back to the office and advised my staff that "I did not get a 'yes' and I did not get a 'no'. All I got was a nothing". That was classic Iemma!

A huge contrast to how Police Commissioner, Ken Moroney, would handle the investigation into the Cronulla riots, was the case of Macquarie Fields riot, in which Moroney kept the investigation in-house and under close scrutiny. The investigation and report was conducted by Deputy Commissioner Dave Madden, and its final contents were agreed after several drafts were examined and workshopped with the Commissioner and his senior staff and officers as well as mine, along with input from Les Tree as head of the Ministry of Police.

On one occasion during one of these workshops, when we got to a draft section which was critical of the role played by Commander John Sweeney, Moroney stepped in and said: "I am not having this all sheeted home to Sweeney. The system let him down. He didn't let us down." The offending part was removed. I assumed that Moroney would follow a similar process for Commander Mark Goodwin who commanded the police response to the Cronulla riots.

Several changes to policing were introduced as a result of assessing the police response to the Macquarie Fields Riot. The main one being the establishment of a dedicated Public Order and Riot Squad with its own personnel, equipment and commander.

Shortly after becoming Premier, Iemma went close to sacking Frank Sartor, who in a radio interview had spoken about discussions that he was trying to have with an Aboriginal activist in relation to the much-needed upgrade of the Redfern Waterloo Aboriginal Housing Precinct. Sartor had used some colourful language which he then promptly retracted during the same interview. When I asked Iemma about it, he said: "I was about to sack him, but because he had immediately apologised I decided not to." I was surprised at how the Premier had almost flippantly weighed up in an instant, the pros and cons of sacking a minister, for what seemed to me an unfortunate turn of phrase but not a dismissible offence.

After the leadership battle, I needed to get out of the country and Iemma approved me going on a two-week trip to the USA to study policing and counter terrorism. I had some great meetings with the Los Angeles Police Department (LAPD), the New York Police Department (NYPD) and the Federal Bureau of Investigation (FBI) in Washington. It was just the tonic I needed.

However, while I was away, Arbib decided that Iemma needed to look decisive and convinced him to announce that we were going to build a new desalination plant to secure Sydney's water future. It was all the more astonishing when Arbib explained that he, rather than the Premier, had come to this conclusion, after some small focus group he had run, was strongly in favour of it. Carr had settled a reasoned and well considered position on a desalination plant which was that we would be ready to start building one when the Warragamba Dam went below 30% capacity. I thought we were still committed to that position.

Chapter 14: The dream ends

There is no way Carr would have ever allowed a $1B piece of infrastructure to be announced because of what 10 people off the street may have said in an Arbib focus group discussion. But this is what happened in August 2005. No discussion with the Minister, no consideration by the Budget Committee and no advice from Sydney Water, which would have to run the tender and oversee the construction of the desalination plant. Just a press release issued to the Sydney Morning Herald the next day. Incredible stuff announced without any reference to me or my office. So, focus groups having underpinned the selection of Iemma as Premier, were now being used to determine infrastructure priorities. Amateur hour had arrived at both Macquarie Street and Sussex Street!

Incredibly, both Iemma and Arbib denied the focus group reality when questioned about it by the Sydney Morning Herald which reported on the 17th of June 2017 as follows:

> *"Mr Iemma told Fairfax media the claims were 'not correct'...how the desalination plant project was handled was 'entirely consistent with all procurement guidelines...I don't know what he's referring to'...Mr Arbib said: 'it's a ridiculous claim'".*

This is an extraordinary denial by both senior political players who ignored the proper processes of cabinet to publicly announce a political commitment to a huge new piece of infrastructure. Sydney Water, the responsible agency for running a tender process was blindsided by the announcement, treasury had not assessed its merits and the budget committee of cabinet had not considered it. To then justify this amateur approach by pointing to a subsequent tender process is disingenuous.

But don't just take my word for it.

Mark Aarons was the water policy advisor in Iemma's private office and this is what he had to say on the matter in an article in The Australian newspaper on the 10th of August 2010 with the rather apt title: 'Focus groups and factions tear heart out of Labor':

> *"Iemma's greatest failing was to let the machine into his government's policy making processes...Under Carr, there was an iron clad separation when it came to running the government. Iemma opened the door...Arbib...had developed focus group polling into an art form. The trouble was that a tool meant to guide political strategy was substituted for political judgement...the Arbib...theory is that these people...should...predominate in policy setting."*

Aarons then set out a devastating indictment of the application by Iemma and Arbib of focus group decision making to the $1B desalination plant:

> *"As soon as Arbib had engineered Iemma into the leadership, he persuaded him to immediately tender to build a desalination plant. When I joined Iemma's staff four weeks later, this decision was already unravelling. From early 2006, polling demonstrated that the focus groups had led the government up a blind alley...Suddenly, Arbib was at my door pleading for me to find a way for Iemma to do a backflip with triple twist and spin".*

Clearly the denials of Iemma and Arbib are contrary to fact, contrary to my recollection and contrary to what Iemma's own staffer outlined just a few years after the event. But the denials are understandable. No political figure or leader wants to be outed for running an amateur hour administration.

Chapter 14: The dream ends

After experiencing at close quarter the bizarre way in which Arbib, as ALP General Secretary, came to a definitive conclusion on important policy matters, I would have welcomed the opportunity for a discussion with Kevin Rudd as Prime Minister in early 2010. I would have enlightened the PM that Arbib had picked a Labor leader and the need to build a desalination plant, not on any conventionally reliable way to weigh up such momentous decisions, but on what a few battlers off the street may have said in a group think political chat around the table one evening. Perhaps then the PM may have been a little reticent to accept Arbib's advice, as a then relatively new Federal Senator, to dump the 'great moral challenge of our time' commitment to deal with climate change. This extraordinarily important 'decision' was rightly treated with disdain by the community, directly causing a catastrophic collapse in the polls, the demise of Rudd himself and almost the Labor Government itself at the July 2010 election. When I asked for the detail on how the PM and his government, had arrived at such a momentous reversal of our commitment to help protect the planet, all I got was what looked pretty much like the kind of analysis Arbib had applied on the desalination plant and on who should be the next premier.

Tripodi's mishandling of the community, and media reaction to challenges in the post opening period of the new Cross City Tunnel Motorway just poured fuel on the flames, destroyed our reputation as serious infrastructure builders and heralded in a stupor where fear of building was the order of the day for over six years. Tripodi's sacking of Paul Forward, CEO of the RTA, sapped energy out of an already reeling RTA. It never recovered. Arbib, for some reason, thought it was a great way to differentiate Iemma from Carr. It failed.

Much has been written about the Cronulla riot itself and the revenge attacks which followed in late 2005.

The protest at Cronulla beach about foreigners visiting their beach was an ugly display of Australia at its worst. Inebriated white trash turned up in hundreds to protest and oppose all foreign looking people from daring to tread upon what they regarded as their Caucasian turf. The protest very quickly progressed from being offensive to being criminal. Police were attacked and marauding crowds of drunken youths went in search of anyone who did not look the same as they did. The most uplifting and yet most offensive scene was outside Cronulla Railway Station when a lone police sergeant was filmed sweeping his baton at many ratbags trying to assault a young Indian couple who had just alighted from the train on their way to the beach. This police officer saved this couple from significant injury and in my view, was the hero of the day.

About 150 police officers eventually brought some semblance of order to the place, but not before some very worrying and scary moments. None of us could believe what had happened in what we thought was our modern, tolerant multicultural country.

The reaction of the thugs from Western Sydney Middle Eastern gangs was swift. By the following night, a car load of them jumped out to knife a Cronulla local in the back for no other reason than he did not look like they did. The victim had just happened to be putting out the rubbish bin. Next and caught on film, was the harrowing beating a Caucasian received whilst just walking along his local street. And then the Bra Boys, a surfing gang from Maroubra did a really silly thing. One of their leaders said that the Lebanese gangs would not dare take on the Bra Boys. Just as I expected, three car loads of them turned up and using a crate full

Chapter 14: The dream ends

of baseball bats, smashed up a street full of cars whilst yelling for the Bra Boys to come out and face their tormentors.

Sporadic attacks were appearing across Sydney. This was not a typical riot which is fixed in a place for a period of time, but was mobile across Sydney. To deal with this, new tactics had to be developed rapidly. We had established a new Public Order and Riot Squad after the Macquarie Fields Riot earlier in the year, but this was a new threat. To deal with it, the Highway Patrol became the means and navigation for a riot squad on the move. When about 20 Lebanese youths were harassing shoppers and families at the entrance of Castle Hill Shopping Centre one Thursday night, we dispatched several Highway Patrol vehicles each containing four members of the riot squad. I am told that the thugs ran like the wind as soon as they saw the batons and shields of a small platoon of riot police running towards them. I wish I had seen it.

There were so many outbreaks of lawlessness across so much of Sydney and beyond, that I sought and received Cabinet approval to expand the powers of police to designate areas under their specific control to manage and resolve a potential riotous situation. It flew through the Parliament and prior to the following weekend, the police had designated large swathes of the City, Wollongong and Newcastle as restricted or 'no go' zones.

I was not satisfied with the Commissioner allocating only 600 police to do the job, on what I worried was going to be an even worse repeat of what had occurred the previous weekend. The Commissioner got the message when I threatened to bring in the army to restore order to our streets. Under the command of Assistant Commissioner, Mark Goodwin, 2,000 additional police were brought to bear on resolving once and for all the riotous behaviour which had been breaking out all over the place. Literally hundreds of kilometres of our coastline were put in lockdown, police resources, including planes, helicopters and even inflatables off a few beaches all joined in with what looked like on the ground police infantry. Order was restored, folks began to return to peaceful lives, the police returned to barracks and the shock jocks stopped fomenting discontent.

The Premier and I sighed with relief that a situation, which could have easily ended up in a burning city out of control, had been avoided and resolved. The two of us had been in constant contact during the crisis as I was with the senior Police command, the head of the Riot Squad and a number of local commanders.

I was still shattered from my experience in losing the leadership and as soon as the Cronulla situation had calmed down, I left for four weeks to Europe, Russia and the Middle East to liaise with Police and counter terrorism experts. In London, The Metropolitan Police were able to show me the CCTV footage of the 2005 London bombers travelling all the way from Leeds before unleashing their venom on an unsuspecting city. It confirmed in my mind the right approach was to use cameras to deter and detect crime in a major city.

In Paris, I was able to get briefed on progress on the prosecution of Willy Brigitte and similar tactics employed by French police in dealing with mobile riots in their suburbs.

In Moscow, it was an hilarious meeting straight out of a blend of Hogan's Heroes and James Bond with a serious 'we know nothing' response to even the most basic questions on the Beslan hostage crisis of 2004 and the follow-up of the Chernobyl nuclear explosion in 1986. It would be my only official visit to Russia, but confirmed what many had been saying: "Under Putin, the old Soviet Union has returned." When I then followed up with a meeting with our Australian Ambassador and he asked how the

Chapter 14: The dream ends

meetings went with the Russian security agencies and I told him: "they were hilarious", he responded: "that's not good".

However, the trip soon ended abruptly with a call from the Premier saying: "We need you home. These clowns running the cops have run amok since you have left". Arbib called soon after, wanting me on the first plane home.

Even before peace had returned to the streets, the Commissioner had established a task force of skilled detectives to start sifting through all the CCTV footage, witness statements and evidence to start the massive process of tracking down and prosecuting all the culprits who had engaged in such disgraceful criminal behaviour.

The easiest starting point was all the footage of the initial 'whites only' protest gathering on Cronulla beach which initiated Sydney going into meltdown, as well as CCTV footage around Cronulla railway station. The police were quickly rounding up hooligans, rioters and individuals responsible for assaults and worse. The community supported by the shock jocks started to complain and ask what were the cops doing about catching the Middle Eastern criminals who they argued, had done worse than anything their local thugs had done.

Commissioner Moroney then went freestyle in my absence and claimed that the detectives did not have any camera footage of Middle Eastern attacks, but had plenty of film of the criminal behaviour of a number of Sutherland's finest. This sounded plausible until it was demonstrated to be untrue. The Commissioner and the Government got roundly attacked and I was then called home.

Then Moroney took a step which should have only been a stone in the pond of turmoil that this whole affair had produced, but for me, it would be the start of what would ultimately end my political career. To make himself look responsive to all the heated criticism, Moroney announced a sweeping inquiry of all aspects of the management of the riot and the subsequent investigations to identify and prosecute individuals.

I was briefed by Moroney on my return and he advised that he had asked retired Assistant Commissioner Norm Hazzard to do the investigation. I initially saw nothing wrong with that or even noticed that the investigation of this riot would be external to a degree compared to the one conducted following Macquarie Fields, which had been done internally under the close and watchful eye of the Commissioner.

Norm Hazzard had been the Head of the New South Wales Police Counter Terrorism Unit, a highly-regarded police officer and I had spoken at his retirement night. I did not see any issues in that regard.

However, I became a little concerned a short time later when Deputy Commissioner, Andrew Scipioni, gave me a call and advised that the Cronulla Riot Police Commander, Assistant Commissioner, Mark Goodwin, was very upset with the selection of Norm Hazzard. Scipioni could not have been blunter: "Mark has complained to me that he and Hazzard never got along and that he believes Hazzard is there to do a job on him". I think Scipioni was trying to do me a favour. I should have listened. I made some discreet enquiries and was informally told that both Goodwin and Hazzard were not exactly close and that Moroney may have decided to give Goodwin a hard time.

Chapter 14: The dream ends

I was not alarmed enough to overrule the Commissioner and direct him to do what he had done after Macquarie Fields, which was to have one of the Deputy Commissioners carry it out. I thought highly of Hazzard and assumed that he would do a professional job in carrying out the investigation.

What concerned me most was that inquiries always have a tendency of finding things out and uncover matters that usually leave people in an unfair light compared to what should be the case if all the circumstances of what they faced were properly aired. As far as I was concerned, Mark Goodwin had been given perhaps the toughest single police assignment in living memory and had come through with flying colours. He had marshalled 2,000 police officers, used every single type of equipment, technology and vehicle at his disposal, and all and every policing technique to restore order to the streets. In my view, he deserved a medal not condemnation from an inquiry. And that is exactly what I had intended to say publicly if I had survived long enough to do so.

I then pretty much left Hazzard to do his investigation and get on with it. But, after many months had passed, I began to ask about progress on the report which I thought should have been already all over by early 2006. At my request, Moroney brought Hazzard to my Parliament House office to give me my first briefing on where the investigation was at.

When I asked the opening question, Hazzard left me gobsmacked: "The investigation has been concluded and the report is now at the printers". I immediately smelled a rat. That Moroney would allow a hand-picked investigator, unannounced and without consultation or feedback to just unilaterally complete his report and send it to the printer defied belief. I went straight to the Commissioner: "Ken, you have got to be kidding me. You have sat back and allowed Norm to take months and months to prepare a report and then without reading it, you let it go to the printers?"

I must have called Moroney's bluff to possibly present me with a fait accompli, as he rather unexpectedly responded with: "Norm, are you sure it has gone to the printer? Could you find out if we can put that on hold so we can have further discussions on it?" Hazzard then made a call on his mobile to someone and asked that the printing of the report be put on hold.

I made it quite clear that as far as I was concerned, all we had was a working draft that needed to be subject to discussion with several people including me and the Commissioner. I asked Hazzard if Mark Goodwin had been consulted on the contents of the report and his reply was less than convincing: "He has had every opportunity to put his case and has done so" to which I replied: "Yes, but has he been shown your draft report and been given the opportunity to respond?" and he responded "No". I assumed that there may have been a possibility that Moroney had not actually read the report, so I asked that a copy of the draft be made available to my office and to the Commissioner immediately.

I decided to read the draft report only after the Commissioner, my Chief of Staff and the Director of the Police Ministry had reviewed the document and Goodwin had been given the opportunity to respond. Whilst I would be briefed on the general findings by Moroney prior to the issue blowing up publicly, I had not yet read the full draft report. As with Macquarie Fields, I had intended to wait until all the major players had given their input, giving time for Hazzard to absorb that input so we could then work on what would then be an advanced draft.

I was aware then that the document, as with the one on Macquarie Fields, was likely to go through several iterations before it was completed, and I wanted to see it and read it when it was much closer to a finished document, which the Commissioner and I could then conclude. This had been an effective and productive process on the Macquarie Fields riot, so I saw no reason to assume that it would not also be so be with the Cronulla riot. How wrong I was!

I was anxious. Moroney was going on a three-week study trip to the USA, Parliament was due back soon, an Opposition MP had already effectively outed the advanced state of the working draft, and time was not a premium. I was always anxious in my time as a Minister of the ever-present possibility of the Upper House passing a resolution calling for the production of all papers on any matter of interest to them. I worried that if this occurred on the Cronulla Riot investigation, that we would have an incomplete document and in no position to control or direct the story on how we intended to respond. The first thing we were always going to be asked was: "What are you going to do about the recommendations?" My only weakness was trying to ensure that Goodwin was given a fair go at being properly recognised for a job well done and for the Government to be on the front foot. Had the draft document been called and produced, no harm would have been done to me either politically or personally.

The real cause of my demise was that I was trying to protect the Government and Commander Goodwin. Contrary to popular misconception, the draft report did not have any concerns for me personally or politically. I had not even read it. If it had been leaked or even printed and concluded just after my meeting with Hazzard, there would have been a short-term period of great interest in the cops and not much from me except to say, "I will be considering the recommendations and come back to you soon".

Bob Carr would have known that and weathered the storm, but Morris Iemma with his finger on the sack trigger was no Bob Carr!

The week before Parliament was due to return in October 2006 took me up to far north Queensland and to the Torres Strait at the suggestion of my Queensland counterpart, Judy Spence. It was a fascinating part of Australia and I learned a lot about how they police in those remote communities. However, one very big drawback of this trip and one which I believe later had a huge impact on my normally astute manner in dealing with tough situations, was that a long pre-existing back injury returned with a vengeance.

Ironically, on the Monday of the following week, Cabinet met in the electorate of the MP for Miranda, Barry Collier, whose electorate was next door to the Cronulla electorate. My back was so bad that I had to stand throughout the Cabinet meeting and at the end, when I was about to leave to get some much-needed acupuncture treatment, I was asked to join Iemma in the usual community Cabinet meeting press conference.

A local journalist from the St George and Sutherland Leader asked me about the status of the Cronulla riot report. I was surprised, as he had not raised an issue about it with my office which, based on past dealings with him, I would have normally expected him to do. I correctly said that the Commissioner was working through some documents and that I expected the process to be completed soon. What surprised me further, was that rather unexpectedly, Channel 9 News ran big on the question with a close-up of my face giving what they reported as a guarded answer. It looked to me like they had used the local journalist as a muse for their story.

Chapter 14: The dream ends

In caucus the next day, I had to stand for most of the two-hour meeting as my back was excruciatingly painful. My wife had urged me to take the day off that morning and in hindsight, I should have listened to her! For over 11 years as a Minister, I always used to have pre-Question Time briefings with my senior staff in which we would try to second guess what questions the Opposition might ask and then workshop the answers. We should have all known that they would ask about the Cronulla Riot Report. However, we had become complacent! I did not know it at the time and nor did the Opposition, but as I walked in to Question Time that day, I had only eight days left in my ministerial career.

The quick and fast journey to a painful and public end to my ministerial career all really began with the words I used to respond to a question from Peter Debnam on behalf of the Opposition.

On the 17th of October, 2006, Debnam asked:

> "It has been six months since the Cronulla riots and revenge attacks, and the public have a right to know why they suffered one of the worst breakdowns of law and order in New South Wales. Given that the police report was completed at least six weeks ago, will the Minister explain why he is trying desperately to delay and bury the report?"

I responded:

> "Perhaps Opposition members can give me a copy of that report and I will consider its contents. They know that the report process has not yet been completed so they have invented a story where none exists. It sounds good ...Watergate, Nixon, cover-ups, and conspiracies. It all makes for good copy ... it was a conflagration ... Quite reasonably, when an incident

> such as that occurs, the Police review the causes and contributing factors and, most importantly, consider how they might improve their operations."

If that is all I had said, I would have been in a whole lot better place than I ended up, but I continued:

> "...these myths about a report. I contacted the Commissioner of Police. I rang him a short while ago and asked him about the status of the report. His advice was that the report had not yet been completed...that Norm Hazzard had still to interview some operational police before he could finalise it. When I receive the report, I will consider it."

At this stage, I had spoken to Moroney and he advised that he had made several pencilled notations in the document that Hazzard had prepared. It was clear to me and the Commissioner that some work still needed to be done before what was at most a draft but more accurately a working document, could be classified as a completed report.

None of what I had said here could be classified as misleading the House. None of what I said was incorrect or untrue. The report process was incomplete and the report itself was some way off from moving from a working draft to a completed publishable report.

I continued:

> "The report processes have not been completed. When they are finished obviously, I will be presented with the report by the Commissioner of Police."

So far so good. Had I just said: "It is the Commissioner's report and I will consider it when I receive it" then I would have been a

Chapter 14: The dream ends

Minister of the Crown for a whole lot longer. Still there is nothing in this answer on that day which is anywhere near misleading.

That is where it could and should have stayed as an issue if I had not ventured to do an interview with Channel 9 Reporter, Adam Walters, to clarify the status of the report. My media advisor cautioned against it and I should have listened, as what I thought would be an easy stand up to explain why the report was not finished and what was outstanding, turned into a slippery road to political ruin.

I was so focussed on explaining the process that required to be followed, that it had not occurred to me that I needed to manage the author, Norm Hazzard. My failure to do so was disastrous. I was aware that the report was critical of Commander Goodwin as I had expected it might be. Moroney had yet to provide his detailed comments and Goodwin had certainly not yet been allowed the opportunity to comment on what Hazzard had proposed to say about him. I still expected that the process would allow for the final report to include Goodwin's response to what was said about him.

On camera, I said to Channel 9 TV News:

> "... there had been an oversight in the preparation of the report. It's not appropriate to finalise a report when the senior command involved in the Cronulla riot operations hadn't been properly interviewed or consulted. There was a bit of a deficiency in the report process that is now being rectified...obviously if it came to conclusions, he must give those officers the opportunity of putting their views before he finalises his opinions and recommendations."

In hindsight, I should have simply said: 'The report is nearing completion and is now subject to further consultation before being finalised'.

There is nothing unusual in what I had said on camera. In fact, that night, Moroney issued a statement confirming he had been given a draft copy before going overseas and said:

> "I've asked Mr Hazzard to conduct further consultation with senior commanders. I will be meeting with him next week...**until that interview process is completed, the report is not finalised.**"

Even better, if I had merely had Moroney issue this clarifying statement and said nothing to camera I probably would have survived. But, Hazzard was for some reason deeply offended by what I had said. Without any reference to me, he spoke to Andrew Clennell, a journalist of the Sydney Morning Herald and expressed some quite ill-tempered views about what he seemed to have interpreted as a personal slight to him. It just never occurred to me that Hazzard, a former Assistant Commissioner of Police, would go public and attack the Minister for Police. But that is what he did. It effectively cost me my political career.

The headline banner on Thursday, 19th October 2006, screamed across the front page: "Riot's Report Author's Fury over Scully" and it went downhill from there:

> "The furore over the unreleased report on police handling of the Cronulla riots deepened last night as its author contradicted the Police Minister's version of events. The recently retired assistant police commissioner, Norm Hazzard, 41-year veteran of the force hit back at claims by the minister, Carl Scully, that the report on the Cronulla riots was 'deficient'".

So, now an incomplete draft was elevated by the press to a completed report, because its author disagreed with my description of his work, and not because of the status of the report itself.

Even the character-attacking front page of one of Sydney's leading newspapers could not say then or later that I had misled Parliament. Its only point of attack was that the author of what everyone then knew was still a working draft was now attacking me because I had called the work to date as 'deficient'. And that is exactly what a minister's job entails when work done in his or her portfolio is found wanting in the opinion of the minister. That an employed consultant would react so publicly and so aggressively, to what he regarded as a reflection on his integrity, was at the time, simply unfathomable.

My career now hung on a thread because of something as superficial as this. If only I could have brought Carr back for a few days. Once I saw the Sydney Morning Herald front page early that day, I was sure my time would soon be up. Iemma would want to try and look tough and decisive by wasting a senior minister on what to Carr would have been an indulgent whim.

It was this story in the Sydney Morning Herald which first caused the trigger happy Premier, Morris Iemma, to start to think about what he might have to do about me. Would I or should I have to go. Iemma and the panic merchants in his office, almost never looked beyond the headlines, as Carr would have done, and seen a first-class media beat up. A bad headline to Iemma and his crew meant looming disaster and the need for a head to roll.

The SMH story went on:

> "Mr Scully, who has insisted all week that a report by Mr Hazzard into the riots and their aftermath was not complete, was forced to admit last night that it had been given to Commissioner Moroney's office a month ago. Mr Scully justified his statements to Parliament by saying Mr Hazzard had not interviewed or consulted enough officers in his report, so it was incomplete."

At this point, so far so good. Hazzard knew Moroney had some issues with the draft and he understood I expected Goodwin to be properly consulted on the draft before finalisation. But **Hazzard then threw all caution to the wind.**

> "I totally refute what the Minister for Police has said in relation to his comments depicted on television tonight. I am appalled he would make such a statement without verifying his information. There is nothing in the report that verifies or justifies his comment."

Those comments effectively ended my career in politics!

I cannot describe how devastating this emotive language was. It was unmeasured, totally out of proportion to whatever I had said that might have offended the man, and almost seemed designed to harm. I had thought I had enjoyed a good rapport with Hazzard. At the time, I did wonder if Hazzard had 'help' in contacting the SMH, and then in his choice of such incendiary and politically forensic language. I still wonder the same to this day.

Up until Hazzard overreacted and dropped a bucket on me, the story was bumbling along as one which was a little difficult

Chapter 14: The dream ends

and needing care and attention, but everything I had said and done to that point was completely consistent with the reality – the report had not reached its finality as "the report processes had not yet been completed." This was true then and it remains true now when I reflect on it all these years later.

What Hazzard did, either wittingly or unwittingly, was to comprehensively undermine that position. The entire wolf pack of the parliamentary press gallery, the shock jocks and the Opposition, came to the irrational view that Hazzard had now confirmed that the report had actually been finalised, I had sat on it and now I was attacking the messenger. The inflammatory Hazzard response was only concerned with his view that I was unfairly 'attacking the messenger'. That Hazzard made no other claim, did not stop several print journalists from embellishing it, joining the dots, and then misleading their own readers with colourful exhortations about the report being finished, that I had sat on it, and worst of all, I had misled parliament about these 'facts'.

The fact that Moroney in the same SMH story referred to the document as a "draft" and that "until that interview process is completed, the report cannot be finalised" was entirely ignored. An esteemed copper had spoken and that was the end of it.

I was again grilled about it in Question Time that same day and stuck to the line that "it can never be a final report until those officers have been given the opportunity to respond."

When a minister is getting a pasting in the media, there is one and always only one person who matters, and that is the Premier. My Chief of Staff at the time, Gary Sargent, came back to my office just after Question Time on the 19th October with a worrying report: "Mate, I was just up in the Premier's office and something just occurred which worries me greatly. I saw Barron, Arbib and Kaiser (Chief of Staff) walk into Iemma's office and as Arbib closed the door he gave me a look which told a thousand words. I am convinced they are up there now discussing what to do with you. Remember this is the bloke who sacked Paul Forward for nothing and I am sure that Barron and Arbib are not up there arguing your case."

With Carr, you always knew he would stick by you as long as it took to get through a difficult media period. But not Iemma!

The pressure was now enormous to release the document in whatever form it was currently, which the Commissioner duly did.

On the 20th of October 2006, the Illawarra Mercury best summed it all up:

> *"Political pressure yesterday forced the release of a sensitive, half-finished report showing NSW police misjudged racial tension in the lead-up to Sydney's Cronulla riot. NSW Police Commissioner Ken Moroney in Los Angeles, ordered that an edited version of the draft report be made public in a bid to end speculation of a cover-up that he said was damaging the force."*

How could I have 'mislead the House' when saying there was no report if the so-called report was "half-finished" and still in a "draft" form?

The Daily Telegraph was predictably hysterical. But even it said:

> *"Moroney was forced yesterday to hold a late-night press conference on the other side of the world,*

Chapter 14: The dream ends

admitting he was releasing a half-finished report because of public pressure."

The Commissioner of Police, on the record, clearly stating, that it was a "half-finished report" would in nearly all circumstances, have satisfied the press and the shock jocks, that maybe the minister was telling the truth that the report was not yet finished. But not on this occasion.

The press then had a field day alleging I had mislead or even lied to Parliament. Some started even suggesting it was time for me to go. I was worried about my position. I even rang my 'friend' Eamonn Fitzpatrick, who was then Senior Media Advisor to the Premier, and asked if my job was on the line and when he claimed he had heard nothing to suggest that, I knew something was up. He would never have made it in Hollywood on that performance.

I called David Tierney who was both a close friend of Iemma and a trusted confidante of Graham Richardson. Tierney claimed my job was safe but then made a strange remark: "He stuck by you over the Cross City Tunnel. Even though he got strong advice to sack you over it, he stuck by you". I was astonished at this remark and asked: "Sack me for what? I delivered a Motorway with the approval and support of the Cabinet, the Budget Committee and the Treasury, as well as the Premier and Treasurer. What on earth was I to be sacked for?" Tierney was unable to articulate any sackable offence I may have committed. It just cemented in my mind that with Iemma, if a minister received any bad media, then the option of a political firing squad was at least on the table, and if it continued, then Iemma at the very least, would have his finger on the trigger. I am sure Tierney did not mean to confirm my suspicions I was on thin ice, but his attempt at reassurance certainly did the opposite.

It is hard to describe the sheer frenzy that the press wolves and sharks had whipped themselves into. Every journalist and shock jock in Sydney had decided that in the Court of Public Opinion (that is, in their opinion) I had lied about the existence of the report, covered it up for base political motives and had shock horror, even mislead Parliament, for which I should now be politically executed.

Iemma was clueless that real leadership often required an ability to calmly take the heat, stay the course and ensure a long-term outcome is achieved when calmer waters are finally found. That is not to suggest that Carr and his staff were saints in the way they handled ministers and the media, as many a former minister can now attest, but it was quite clear that when your back was to the wall, Carr was in there defending you. Iemma would not!

But I did not have Carr in my corner, I had no one, especially not the Premier. I was again in tough times with a panic merchant at the helm who had none of Carr's ability to manage difficult media nor loyalty to his ministers and department heads who worked hard for him.

I started to get calls from two close friends who were former work colleagues and who were respectively close to Barron and to Arbib. They told me that on advice, Iemma had come to the view that it was time to tell me to announce that at the March 2007 State election I would be retiring from politics. I was shattered.

At a time when I needed to draw on all the emotional strength I could muster, here were two close friends draining it out of me. I had never before nor since felt as lonely or isolated as I did at that point. This was the one time I needed emotional bolstering and not the opposite.

Chapter 14: The dream ends

My wife Ann has long believed that both friends were at the time more focussed on ingratiating themselves with Barron, Iemma and Arbib for personal and political gain, rather than concerning themselves with my future, which is what friends would normally do. Ann still believes that one of them was solely motivated by career advancement and replaced friendship with our family with political expediency.

I still like to hope, that both were motivated by a desire to make sure I was fully aware of the danger I was in. But at the very least, they should have been aware that I did not need them to remind me of that. I was already fully aware that I was walking on thin ice. These two long standing friends allowed themselves at best unwittingly, to be used as direct conduits from Barron (and probably Iemma) and Arbib straight into my head. No wonder I found it hard to think straight. My political career was falling apart.

The former work colleague closely linked with Barron and Iemma even went through an absurd process of getting a copy of a list of all the Government authorities I could be appointed to if I left cooperatively, as if the ALP had learnt nothing from the attempt by Greiner to appoint Terry Metherill to the Environment Protection Authority. That had led to Greiner being forced to resign as Premier. In the days that followed, I actually had several of these ridiculous conversations. I well knew that if Iemma was about to force me out, I would be cast adrift and on my own. There would be no Government job for me. I was right on that score, as I knew I would be.

The only guy who mattered in all of this was the Premier and here were two messengers who were close friends, delivering damning messages from the Party Secretary, the Premier and his personal Strategist, telling me that my time was up and I had to move on. It was well-nigh impossible to stay mentally focussed on survival, when all this was swirling around me.

I knew that I had experienced some tough press in the past, but to be forced out just for tough media treatment, left me confused and devastated. I felt like my world was ending and I had nowhere and no one to turn to for help.

If Carr's approach had been to remove Ministers when they were attacked and denigrated by the media, then he would have had to get rid of quite a few ministers including Knight during the 'Olympic ticket fiasco', Whelan during the 'Jones police attacks', Knowles during the 'Camden/Campbelltown Hospital saga' or the 'Cryptosporidium/Giardia Sydney Water crisis', Egan following the disastrous 'privatisation of electricity' or even me following the 'Waterfall train disaster' or 'poor rail performance' in the lead up to the Olympic Games. These were all his most senior and capable ministers managing really tough portfolios and from time to time, a tough portfolio blew up into a media conflagration. Carr knew this and never panicked. Iemma was simply not in the same leadership league!

On Saturday, the 21st of October 2006, one of my media advisors, Peta Fitzgerald, organised a press conference at my home for me to clear the air on the way I had conducted myself and the things I had said regarding the report. Peta is the daughter of former MP Kevin Greene and is now managing government relations and communication at the University of Wollongong.

That evening, I attended a police function with the Premier who said; "I need to talk to you about the future. Let's chat after Monday's Cabinet meeting." I called one of the two friends I had been speaking with who confirmed that Iemma would tell me it was time to go. This was shattering news. I was not ready to go.

Chapter 14: The dream ends

On Sunday the 22nd of October, the Sunday Telegraph reported that:

> "Carl Scully yesterday expressed regret over his handling of a police report into the Cronulla riots, but refused to resign. Mr Scully is under pressure after telling State Parliament last week the report was unavailable, without making it clear that a draft version had been given to Police Commissioner Ken Moroney. He admitted yesterday he had confused Parliament, but said he believed he had not mislead MPs. 'I regret the fact I was not clearer with what I meant by a final report' Mr Scully told reporters. 'If I could have my time again, I would have said that the commissioner has a working document-he had a draft-and it was going to take some time to complete. There were, in fact, working drafts, working documents that the commissioner had.' Opposition Leader Peter Debnam said it was clear that Mr Scully should be sacked."

This was the best that a major newspaper could come up with.

Because I had said in Parliament:

> "... the report process has not yet completed...these myths about a report ... (the) Commissioner of Police ... advice was the report had not yet been completed"

instead of simply saying:

> 'A draft report has been presented to the Commissioner of Police'

meant for many excitable journalists, that I had misled the Parliament and for some journalists at the time, even lied to it. In the normal course of parliamentary exchange, what I had said and done would have simply gone down as the usual cut and thrust of the 'bear pit'. In fact, when compared to some of the answers given by Ministers at both state and federal level, my contribution seems innocuous.

Two examples make for an interesting comparison:

1. Minister Prue Goward

Minister Goward made a claim in the New South Wales Parliament in February 2013 regarding the number of Department of Community case workers. The claim was shown to be wrong when a report surfaced from accounting firm Ernst and Young. No steps were taken to correct the record even when it later emerged that she had been at a meeting when the report was tabled, that her office had been sent a copy but she had 'not read the report'. Some months later, on the 13th of August 2013, the minister claimed that 'there is no moratorium and there has never been a moratorium on caseworker recruitment'. The claim was false and instead of simply correcting the record, her staff tried to have Hansard add the words 'by me' at the end of the sentence to substantially change the meaning of what had actually been said by her in the house.

This 'incident' if it could be called that, quickly disappeared from view and is now substantially forgotten even by media scribes and MPs of the day.

2. Treasurer Peter Costello

Perhaps an even starker example is that of former Howard government Federal Teasurer, Peter Costello. In response to a question from the opposition on the 7th of November 2005, Costello denied that he had received Treasury advice on possible adverse impacts of proposed legislative changes to workplace relations. Following a Freedom of Information application, the Australian Newspaper was able to claim that a 'Treasury executive minute' on the very same subject had been sent to Costello on 6th of October, a full month before he asserted in Parliament that 'this report had not even been written'. Costello batted away the claim of misleading the house by saying he was referring to a report not a minute.

These two examples emphasise my point about the ethereal and ill-defined nature of what constitutes 'misleading the house' and the consequences, if any, which ought to follow. Neither Prime Minister John Howard nor Premier Barry O'Farrell were the least bit interested in either the story or giving up a ministerial scalp because of 'air swirling around the minister'. These heads of government exercised a choice which incredulously, Iemma would later claim he lacked.

During what would be my last Cabinet meeting on Monday, 23rd of October 2006, Iemma and I made eye contact a couple of times and he genuinely looked uncomfortable. He and I then had a private meeting in his office. He made a valid point: "This should have been a triumph for you, but instead you have managed to achieve the exact opposite." There was no mention or discussion of my future except a cryptic: "Let's just get through this week."

I called one of the two friends who had informed me of my impending position to discuss the conversation I had with Iemma, and he said to me that "Iemma could not bring himself to tell you the bad news, but don't kid yourself that he has not come to the view he thinks you should go." I then realised that this friend was not talking to Barron, but had a direct line personally to Iemma and was allowing himself to be used as his messenger. That was hardly the kind of emotional battering I needed, as I braced myself for what would be a pretty unpleasant week in Parliament. Both, as my friends, should have refused to be messengers of such awful news and done what they could do to lift my spirits and advise me on how best to survive the week ahead. But as former New South Wales Premier, Jack Lang, once famously said, in drawing a horse racing analogy with political intrigue: "In the race of life, always back self-interest; at least you know it's trying". And staying supportive to a man on the slippery slope was not backing 'self-interest'. Friendship in politics is a temporary and relative thing as I had found in the leadership battle and again now as my political career hung on the edge of oblivion.

But what was most disconcerting and left me feeling about as professionally isolated as it can get, is that on Tuesday, 24th of October, Iemma at a press conference had been asked three times if I would be a minister still by the time of the March election and each time he failed to answer. The Australian Financial Review summed it up the following day by stating that there was "increased speculation that Mr Iemma may dump Mr Scully from his front bench-if not before the election, then certainly after."

During Question Time on the 24th of October 2006, I was asked by Debnam if I would now resign. I used the expected question to explain what the status of the report had been and that I could have been clearer in the language I had used. I would remain a Minister for just one more day!

I said in the House:

> *"Last week when asked a question about the Cronulla report, I should have answered the question by informing the House that the report had not been concluded, it was not complete, and it had not been finished. I should have made it plain to the House that*

Chapter 14: The dream ends

> *a working draft had been made available to the Commissioner of Police for his perusal and was subject to further interview with the author and to a submission by affected officers, and that the process had some way to run. I regret not making it clearer to the House. I should have used more precise language."*

The record shows I had been clear enough, that I had already said these things, but the media needed to hear that I respected their view, that I had not been clear enough in my explanations about the status of the report. They were not in the mood for being satiated.

The next day, the 25th of October 2006, the Sydney Morning Herald quoted almost verbatim what I had said in the House and in a reference to Iemma's studied refusal to back me and ran with a banner:

> *"Scully skates on thin ice with no help from Iemma."*

But, the Australian Financial Review claimed in its story on the same day that in Question Time *"a contrite Police Minister admitted he had mislead Parliament."*

Senior journalists and reputable newspapers were so convinced I had mislead Parliament that they were now misleading their readers by saying that I had admitted I had mislead Parliament. And all done with conventional journalistic impunity.

At no stage in my answer the previous day had I said any such thing. Saying "I regret not making it clearer to the House. I should have used more precise language" is so far from an admission of 'misleading Parliament' as to make me wonder if it did not matter what I had said in the House, as the media would have still interpreted it as a full acknowledgement of my 'guilt'.

Simon Benson, a senior journalist with The Daily Telegraph, then took it to a whole new level:

> *"He has brought his government into the trough with him. Misleading Parliament is a very serious matter. While Scully is an honest man, he does get a bit cute with the truth…***His bending of the truth over the report into Cronulla has unnecessarily tarred the government with 'liar, liar' brush***. So yesterday, under orders from the Premier, Scully was forced to apologise to Parliament for misleading it over whether he had seen the controversial report."*

This is just extraordinary stuff and a great example of a journalist himself in full 'spin' mode. I did not "apologise"; I was not "forced to apologise"; I did not lie; and I did not mislead the house. It also provides an excellent example of an established and respected journalist, endeavouring to hold an MP to account, but ironically, not subjecting himself to the same standards of scrutiny or accountability. This is certainly one 'story' I regret not commencing proceedings for defamation against both the journalist and his newspaper.

Misleading the house is a quaint and ancient notion that allegedly requires a ministerial resignation whenever it occurs. However, there is no parliamentary or statutory definition of what is meant by the term, so it is left vague and open to varied interpretations. There is not even a fair and accountable process where an MPs guilt or innocence can be questioned and independently determined. If what I had said and done actually constituted misleading the House and warranted a resignation, then many a ministerial career would have been brought to abrupt halt, both before and since my time in office.

As one MP said to me recently: "If what you had done warranted removal, then half the cabinet would have been removed before the end of our first term of office".

So, despite the facts, by the morning of the 26th of October 2006, I was universally regarded by the press, as having 'mislead the House'. I knew from back channels that as far as Iemma was concerned, 'my time was up' and I had no confidence at all that I would be allowed to weather the media storm and move on.

The Leader of the National Party asked me that day in Question Time:

> "Given that on last Monday week the Minister **phoned the ABC television newsroom** claiming that that night's Channel 9 News Report was untrue, has he now apologised to the ABC and other media for lying about the report and his knowledge of it?"

This was such an easy question to have batted away. I still find it unfathomable that I answered in a way that allowed Iemma to swoop and execute. I should have just said: "Enough has been said on this issue" and sat down.

The almost trivial exchange which ended my political career then went as follows:

Me: "Perhaps I could answer that question if Channel 9 can tell me who in my office rang and at what point I rang and what I said. Then perhaps I could answer the question."

As more than one front bench colleague was later to remark: "You had clearly not properly heard the question and got held to account in a way you should never have been."

Stoner: "You rang the ABC."

Me: "Now you are lying."

And then I sat down and thought nothing more of it. A short time later the parliamentary press gallery was in a rage of excitement that I had apparently again 'mislead the house' with the four words: "Now you are lying".

The press gallery then asked the ABC for a response to what I had said in the House. Amazingly, the ABC then itself became part of the story rather than a reporter of events.

The ABC's editor of news and current affairs, Paul McIntyre, issued a statement that afternoon saying that I had spoken to the executive producer of **radio news**, Trevor Thompson, sometime between 7.00 and 7.30 pm on the relevant day, and that I had inquired as to whether ABC news (i.e., ABC radio news not ABC television news) would be responding to a Channel 9 news story about a report on Cronulla riots of last year."

The ABC statement went on:

> "In the course of a brief conversation, the ABC's executive producer asked Mr Scully if there was a report to comment on. **Mr Scully replied that the report had only got to drafting stage, so there was not a report to comment on.**"

I should have been off the hook. The ABC had stated clearly that I had called ABC "radio news" and not the "ABC television

Chapter 14: The dream ends

newsroom" as asserted by Stoner. When interjecting with "you rang the ABC" he was clearly referring to the assertion in his question that I had called the television newsroom not just the ABC.

It is only all these years later, on cold reflection, that I now see how easy it could have been to escape the Iemma noose, at least on that day. I don't know how I missed it, or how my staff missed it. All I had to do that day, was walk into the chamber and advise the House that the statement of the ABC meant that Andrew Stoner himself had mislead the House by asserting incorrectly that I had called ABC Television News. Maybe Iemma would have still drummed me out on some other pretext, but he would not have been able to do so on that day for what the press then claimed was a second act of misleading the House.

In Carr's day, his senior staff would have been in a huddle with my team poring over the exact words in Hansard and assessing how best to get through the drama. But not in Iemma's day! If anything, Iemma's senior staff were more inclined to encourage their boss with a good political shooting, than in undertaking the much harder task of working with a minister in resolving the difficult media issues of the moment.

I rang Mike Kaiser, Iemma's Chief of Staff and said that whilst I did not recall the conversation with the ABC, I felt that I should correct the record in the House by saying that as there was a memo, I now accept that a conversation with the ABC must have taken place.

When I used the words: "now you are lying", it was for me, more about some cut and thrust of what the 'bear pit' is renowned for, rather than a technical response to some kind of court room style cross examination. And now I can see, with the benefit of hind sight, that even on that standard, I should have come through unscathed. For this short exchange to have become the pretext for sacking a senior minister now looks rather unjustified based on the evidence.

If Graeme Wedderburn as Carr's Chief of Staff, had been at the end of the phone, he would have said straight of the bat: "We've checked this out and you're in the clear. Don't worry about whether you had a conversation with ABC, or what you might have said, what matters is that Stoner asked you about ABC TV news but you clearly spoke to ABC radio news. This is more than enough for you to defend your position and to attack Stoner for misleading the house".

But, I had Mike Kaiser on the other end of the line, not Graeme Wedderburn.

Kaiser supported my going back into the House, but I should have picked up the signs that he was sending me into a 'political killing zone'. I mentioned to him that it had been a tough few days and that I had been in almost constant and excruciating back pain from an old skiing injury to which he said: "Why don't you say you are on medication?" and I responded, "but I am not, that would be untrue". Clearly, as far as Kaiser was concerned, he and Iemma had already removed me from the Cabinet.

I then walked into the House and spoke for the last time:

> "I wish to provide a supplementary answer to a question I was asked during Question Time today .... I answered that it was untrue because then, and now, I do not recall that specific conversation. Over the past 10 days I have had scores and scores of conversations with many journalists and many,

> many newsrooms. In the face of the ABC newsroom insisting I made the call, and with no means of proving otherwise, I must accept that I did actually make the call ..."

I could have added 'so what', as the ABC memorandum detailed a conversation which was completely consistent with the same message I had given to any journalist who would listen: the report was at draft stage only, but that was all Iemma claimed he needed to be able to say: "I want your resignation."

After I had 'corrected the record', Sargent and my Media Advisor, Martin Wallace, then went to sell this to the press gallery, but they came back with advice that it was now the story of the day that I had 'mislead' Parliament again. What particularly concerned them, however, was that as they were about to walk into another section of the 6th floor media offices, Iemma's entire media team, led by Eamonn Fitzpatrick and Josh Murray, and supported by two junior media advisors, emerged from the lifts and splayed out in all directions as if on a mission. Sargent said: "I don't know what they were up to, but I don't think they were about to do you any favours." How right he was!

At that point, Sargent got a call from Iemma's Chief of Staff, Mike Kaiser, advising that the Premier wanted to see me immediately. My heart almost stopped. I knew it could not be good given all that had just happened. I walked into the Premier's office and without any discussion or interest in what I might say on anything, Iemma said: **"I want your resignation"**. He didn't even make eye contact when he said these fateful and awful words. I asked to talk to him privately and Kaiser and Sargent then left the room. The Premier was blunt and disinterested. When I asked to be allowed to weather this one out and then announce at the end of the session that I was retiring he responded: "It's too late for that. I said to you on Monday 'let's just get through this week', well we did not get through this week".

In a daze, I went back to my office and rang my wife and a small coterie of friends. It was hard to hold back the tears. I signed a resignation letter which was duly delivered to the Premier's office. Gary Sargent and Martin Wallace were asked to come up to the Premier's office on the 8th floor and assist with the settling of the wording of a press release announcing my departure, but when they arrived, the draft was already on the screen and ready to go. Clearly, the Iemma media team had been asked to draft the press release well before either I, or my team, knew I was about to be sacked.

David Campbell happened to be there and witnessed a very happy Ian McDonald parading his signature Cheshire cat grin outside the Premier's office. It is still unclear to us all, why McDonald was so happy that evening! As a convicted felon now rotting in one of Her Majesty's prisons, McDonald is unlikely to be grinning anymore!

I then held a very emotional press conference and left the building. No man had done more to wreck my dreams, aspirations or career than Morris Iemma. I received an absurd phone call on the way home from Arbib, offering me an appointment as a judge after the election or if I wanted it, the pre-selection for the Federal seat of Fowler, based at Liverpool. I wondered what planet he lived on, or if he had been smoking something. When I asked him, who was going to run the Government after Iemma left mid-term, he made it clear that he was only concentrating on winning the next election. And when I followed up with: "He must have told you he is leaving mid next term as he has told me the same thing. So, I ask you again. With me gone, who is going to run the show

Chapter 14: The dream ends

when Iemma leaves" and all I got again was: "We are just focussing on the next election."

Iemma put the boot in for good measure: "It was simply a case of one mistake too many" and that the Government could not allow "the air swirling around the Minister to continue." So, this was the real reason for dismissing a minister. What was that supposed to mean? Whatever were the mistakes was never made clear to me by Iemma and nor was the level of turbulent 'air swirling' required to justify sacking a senior minister.

Looking back on this affair, it is clear to me, that I was sacked, not because of what had actually transpired that day in the House or previous days, but because Iemma was sick of the media attention on the Cronulla Riot Report, and as he had done so often in the past, came to the view, that a sacking was what was needed to close off the whole issue. In other words, there was never at any stage, any identifiable action, offence or misdeed on my part, which would have warranted my dismissal. Calling the work done by Hazzard, as a 'draft' or 'work in progress' or 'subject to further consultation', were all correct and supported by the facts and media coverage. All these years later, I remain convinced, that Iemma had no grounds upon which to justify my removal, and only did so, because he panicked in the face of robust media criticism of my handling of the Cronulla Riot Report issue. Exercising not choice but a leader's whim.

Iemma could never draw on the poise, resolve and patience which came naturally to Bob Carr in dealing with difficult media issues, just inexperience, apprehension and impetuosity. Carr would have made a choice to weather the short-term storm but Iemma convinced himself he had no choice!

Iemma never once said to me that he believed I had mislead the House or that I was being sacked for it. And nor could he have. He would have well known that what I had said fell well short of that. One of my good union leader mates agreed that if there had been similar Unfair Dismissal provisions for MPs which workers across Australia now take for granted, that I would have been reinstated. And this from a Labor Party in Government committed to fair process in all industrial relations settings!

It was also a very tough time for my wife and two teenage children. Our son, James, was in the middle of his HSC exams trying to study as scores of journalistic vultures hung around at the front of our house waiting for a camera shot, bouncing balls on the road to amuse themselves, and even using our bins to dispose of their takeaway food containers. Our daughter, Sarah, was being teased at school and all in all, it was probably the least pleasant week my family would suffer in my 17 years as an MP.

A few days after my forced removal, Sargent told me he had had a very troubling conversation with a rather frank journalist from one of the newspapers who said: "You should know that while you were putting the case for Scully, Iemma's office were assuring us that he was gone and that Iemma was about to ask him to resign."

Eamonn Fitzpatrick and Josh Murray and their two sidekicks, had indeed been busy and certainly not doing me any favours. What emerged from this exchange between a senior gallery journalist and my Chief of Staff, was that the press had been informed of my departure prior to Iemma letting me know that such was his intention.

I have always assumed that there was no good reason for such a story to have been fabricated by this senior journalist, but I would

Chapter 14: The dream ends

still welcome an opportunity to hear from this gang of four, as to whether they actually did, as suggested. Until that occurs, I will continue to assume the veracity of the claim. Unsurprisingly, none of those involved has ever apologised for doing this. I do not know who directed Eamonn Fitzpatrick and Josh Murray to descend to the sixth floor as they did that day, but it is inconceivable that they would have done so without the knowledge and approval of both Iemma and his Chief of Staff, Mike Kaiser.

I am still incredulous that a Premier and his senior staff would behave this way. It was neither warranted nor necessary, especially given that when asked, I submitted my resignation. Furthermore, we did all belong to the same Party and the same Government which I had loyally served for a very long time. I am still perplexed why Iemma, who I had known for over 20 years, would not even bother to have a conversation with me before deciding to pass judgement. John Della Bosca, hardly a friend of mine in either the Cabinet or the Caucus, let it be known that Iemma had interrupted a Budget Committee meeting that he and John Watkins were attending, to announce his intentions. Della Bosca claimed he put the case that my removal was not called for but that Iemma remained unmoved.

Iemma some months later asserted to one of my staff "I had no choice", almost as if he was apologising for a hand he was forced to play, and virtually having no discretionary role in the matter. A convenient absolution of responsibility which I am sure Bob Carr would have regarded as an absurd and unconvincing thing to say about a matter on which he clearly had a choice. Iemma could have said during the turbulent media treatment I had received: "I have confidence in the Minister. He has not misled the House and if we win the election, he will be a member of my Cabinet." That is how Carr handled those sorts of situations. In fact, Carr told me some time after I had left politics that during one period when the daily press was demanding my scalp for alleged 'rail offences', he rang the editors of the two Sydney daily newspapers and said: "You can call for Scully's scalp as long as you like. You are not getting it. You can get fucked." There was no way Iemma would ever have had the nerve to provide that kind of confident leadership!

Iemma had had a soft ride in Sport and Public Works for four years before landing the tough Health portfolio for two years prior to becoming Premier. He had to deal with the fallout of Knowles' Camden and Campbelltown Hospital issues, but never once had an issue where the media were baying for his blood. Plenty of his ministerial colleagues had experienced this during their many years at the Cabinet table, but not Iemma. In fact, this lack of combat experience, far from being an obvious leadership negative, was a positive Arbib selling point: "He has a clean slate upon which we can write what we want." That was a thirty something's approach to selecting the CEO for the largest state administration in the country!

So, when it came to either handling a very tough media issue or managing a minister through one, Iemma was a novice. Carr would never let the media dictate when a Minister was to go and if anything, it would just make him dig his heels in more. But not Iemma! By not confronting the attacks front on, leaving his minister out in the cold, and not answering direct questions about my future, he exacerbated the noise and demands for my removal, and then used the very exacerbation he had himself fuelled, to convince himself, that he had no choice. Only he could have lowered the din, but instead chose to allow the noise to rise unabated to a point where he convinced himself that: "enough was enough".

Chapter 14: The dream ends

I fronted again at the last caucus meeting for the year the following week. At the end of the meeting, Iemma asked me to come up for a chat. I think he must have been feeling a little remorseful as he was friendly and engaging: "Mate, I was going to hand it all over to you. I told you I was not in this for the long haul."

But he added a very frank acknowledgement of why in his view I had to go: "It was five months before an election. If it had been five months after an election, I probably would not have worried about it." At least I finally received the real reason for my forced removal – the imminent election and nothing else!

After that, the encounters were increasingly unpleasant as I think his advisors were telling him that the best thing for him and the ALP was if I withdrew as a candidate at the next election.

I was inundated with supportive phone calls from well-wishers. On the second day after the sacking, I got a call from no less than two former Prime Ministers and one former Premier: Bob Hawke, Paul Keating and Bob Carr, and even from former Treasurer, Michael Egan.

Carr was astonished that I had been sacked for what he regarded as being the subject of too much media attention: "You should never have been dismissed for that. The most I might have done was counselled you to be more careful with your words, but probably not even that."

Egan was equally surprised: "This was just in the 'oops' category and soon enough the media would have moved on to another target."

Others in the caucus and in private industry lamented that I was a threat to Iemma and his cronies and that was the real reason for my removal.

I now had to decide if I was going to disappear into political obscurity or re-contest my seat of Smithfield. I was the endorsed candidate and had I chosen to run again, I would have been allowed to do so.

I had had enough. My wife had had enough and we both knew it was time to go. Having media crews and TV cameras camped outside our house for days on end, just to catch a photo glimpse of any of us, did little to make political life any more attractive. Few have to put up with this level of unpleasant scrutiny. I still wonder how the journalists and cameramen involved would handle it if the tables were ever turned upon them. Whenever that does occur they tend to have very thin skins about it.

Ann was convinced that the same characters who had denied me the premiership were now mostly the same characters who had encouraged Iemma to have me thrown out of the Cabinet room. She strongly believed that they were never going to let me back into the ministry. I had toyed with the idea of working hard on the backbench, doing my penance, and then returning in due course to the Cabinet room.

Whilst I am confident that Obeid, Tripodi and McDonald would not have wanted me in the top job, I have often wondered whether I may have still got there. Thinking and knowing are two very different things.

In late 2006/early 2007 I was in no fit emotional state to decide this sort of critical decision. I do wish I had had at the time, one or two close political friends, who were able to caution me about making such a rash decision to leave politics for good. But in that regard, I was on my own. No one came forward to proffer that kind of sage advice. I should have let the March 2007 election come and go, remained as an MP and when emotionally fit, made a final decision on my political future.

It was in this climate that Chris Bowen, Joe Tripodi and Anwar Khoshaba, jointly anointed Anwar's son, Ninos, as the new ALP candidate for Smithfield, in the likely event I was not going to run at the next election. I acquiesced in this, as I thought it was a fitting way to acknowledge all that Anwar had done for me. However, the haste with which it was done, before even the political corpse was cold, left me feeling discarded by the Party both locally and in Macquarie Street. It was a very lonely and isolating time for me. Not one of them made any attempt to persuade me to stay and just assumed I had already left politics from the night of my sacking. Ninos went onto become the MP for Smithfield at the 2007 election but lost the seat to the Liberals four years later at the 2011 election.

Iemma and I met in his Parliament House office in January 2007 just weeks before the next election. He was distant, disinterested, aloof and at his mumbling best. I said that in weighing up whether to run again or leave, I needed to know what my prospects would be and I got the only animated response in an otherwise particularly unfriendly encounter: "I'm making no commitments". It sounded like it had come straight out of Barron's mouth and left me feeling that he had been coached to be as unsympathetic as possible to my plight as a way to encourage me to leave. I said: "In that case then why would I stay" and he replied: "Well if I was you, I wouldn't."

And that was it. My future in politics was over. Not long after the election, I rang the new opposition leader, Barry O'Farrell and he made an interesting point: "We all thought that you would do your penance and then come back into the ministry after the election. We were all surprised when you announced your retirement." He was even more surprised when I recounted the January conversation with the Premier.

I assumed Iemma and I would never speak again. However, over 9 years later, in October 2016, we did run into each other on George Street, outside the entrance to Wynyard Railway station, as I waited to meet up with my daughter Sarah. Iemma and I had an awkward but civil conversation for about 10 minutes. Any lingering anger from me had long passed but the two of us knew without articulating it, that we would never be friends again.

Chapter 14: The dream ends

CHAPTER 15

Privatising electricity – The destruction of a Labor Government

It is ironic that Iemma would not even last 18 months after the March 2007 election, before the failed and deeply flawed attempt to sell the New South Wales electricity industry engulfed both him as Premier and Michael Costa as Treasurer. It was a high price to pay for a commitment which had not been mentioned in the lead up to the election, and was not needed to save the finances of the State nor essential for any possible future capital investment in the electricity industry. It is still a mystery why Iemma unexpectedly pursued the issue with such gusto straight out of the election blocks and put Costa in charge of it.

What a contrast to Mike Baird as New South Wales Premier, in the lead up to the March 2015 election, where the major plank of his campaign was to finance new public infrastructure from a partial sale of poles and wires. Iemma made no mention of his intentions at any stage in the long lead up to his election of 2007. It is highly likely that work would have been done quietly on such a proposal by Treasury in preparation for an election win. If that was the case, then clearly it was not shared with the Cabinet, the caucus, the party or the wider community.

Such material prepared by Treasury at the behest of Iemma and Costa, might now be labelled as just 'working drafts' or 'half-finished' documents and were not yet completed reports, ready for full Cabinet and community consideration. They would provide interesting background to the almost surreal political world into which Iemma and Costa descended the Labor Government, relatively quickly after the March 2007 election.

Iemma justified his considerable focus and strenuous commitment to the sale of the electricity generators on two major, but intertwined flawed claims. The first, that a significant increase in power generating capacity was required for New South Wales and the second, that this could only come from private sector investment. The first claim, in my view, would not have withstood the test of close scrutiny making the second redundant. That is, if the claim that more power was needed was wrong, then how it was going to be financed would be irrelevant. I had been the minister responsible for the power industry up to early 2006, and all the forward projections for demand showed New South Wales did not need more new base load power stations until at least 2017 and probably beyond.

An amusing anecdote which confirms this is worth recounting:

I was appointed by Iemma in August 2005 as Minister for Police and Minister for Utilities. The latter gave me responsibility for the water and power sectors all of which consisted of publicly-owned assets authorities which managed and operated them. I had enjoyed enormously the many years of building major infrastructure in roads, ports, housing and public transport and I initially wondered if I might be able to bring the same kind of drive to the power industry and ignite the halcyon days of New South Wales generator building of the 1970s and 1980s.

Shortly after being sworn in, I met with the Head of the Department of Energy and told him bluntly: "The only thing I want you focussed on is to ensure I build a huge new base load coal-fired power station". I had been warned he was a bit of a 'greenie' and I did want to tease him a little. He certainly started to turn a little green with my opening salvo before responding: "But we do not need any more power generation capacity. We have an oversupply as it is and we will not need any new capacity for at least a decade." I said: "I know".

I would have been the first in the ministerial queue to build a new $2B public asset, but we simply had no need for one. This was not guess work but a sound view of the government's Department of Energy based on detailed forecasts of the electricity needs of New South Wales for the next 10 years. The Cabinet Office concurred with the figures and the policy approach that no new generating capacity needed to be built for a very long time. It is inconceivable that Treasury would not have been aware of this work.

Treasury never once put the view to me that we needed to urgently prepare for new power generating capacity. So, on the 17th of February 2006, when I left the power portfolio to concentrate solely on police, there was a clear and unchallenged consensus within the New South Wales Government as well as the Treasury, that no new generating capacity was required for at least 10 years.

Just 9 months later, on the 22nd of November 2006, Premier Iemma during Question Time in the Legislative Assembly, would refer favourably to advice about the capability of the state to meet demand for electricity:

Chapter 15: Privatising electricity

> *"According to the National Electricity Market Management Company (NEMCO), New South Wales is the best placed of all the states to meet electricity demand and offer reliability...that relates to peaking capacity and baseload."*

This statement by Iemma was consistent with the advice I had received as Minister from the Department of Energy and with reality.

The next day, on the 23rd of November 2006, Treasurer Michael Costa, during Question Time in the Legislative Council, would even more emphatically confirm this:

> *"There is no energy crisis in New South Wales...In fact, New South Wales has surplus energy...we do not have an energy shortage."*

This advice on being able to reliably meet the demand for electricity well into the future, and the confidence of both the premier and the treasurer in publicly articulating it, reflected the over capacity for power generation built by the Wran Labor government from the mid-1970s to the early 1980s following several blackouts across Sydney. These were the years of huge power station construction and will never return. That was known in 2006 and it is still known now over 10 years later!

However, in April 2007, just 5 months after their joint statements in Parliament of New South Wales having sufficient power generating capacity, both Iemma and Costa would claim the exact opposite. Their new found and sudden need for future additional electricity formed the almost entire basis for justifying the sale of the publicly owned generators. This was allegedly because New South Wales could not afford to pay for the huge capital cost which they claimed was now needed to build new generating capacity, and which they claimed could only come from the private sector.

The case for sale was convoluted, disingenuous and unsustainable. It was that flawed and inept approach, I believe, that killed a State Labor Government.

Iemma, Costa and the Secretary of Treasury, John Pierce were all determined to sell the electricity generators, but to justify their decision they had Treasury commission a report from Professor Anthony Owen, which unsurprisingly, supported the proposal to privatise a large part of the publicly owned electricity industry.

Despite the trio grabbing Professor Owen's report as sufficient justification for their pre-determined position of needing to sell the generators, because a new power station would be needed by 2013-14, the report was somewhat more equivocal than their words and behaviour might have warranted.

On just page 3 of his long report, Professor Owen was clearly less than adamant about the issue:

> *"New South Wales continues to experience a declining rate of growth of electricity consumption…*
>
> *…Some submissions to the Inquiry have argued that the need for new baseload supply will occur later than 2013-14. They have asserted that enhanced levels of energy efficiency, higher levels of supply from existing generators, renewable technologies, and additional sources of distributed power suggest that this date can be extended significantly into the future."*

They were right!

Chapter 15: Privatising electricity

The equivocation which should have alarmed Iemma and Costa was again on page 3:

> "**On balance**, *I have decided to recommend a risk-averse approach and focus on the 2013-14 timeline.*"

So, nothing emphatic. No clear cut and unambiguous view one way or the other. The future of a Labor Government was then underpinned by no more than an 'on balance' weighing up of the evidence and nothing more certain. Too much was at stake to have put so much faith in something so vague.

Despite this, Iemma went full steam ahead and on the 21st of June 2007, Iemma provided the Parliament with an update on his intentions:

> *"We are now pressing ahead on the most important economic decision that we will make in this term of government- a decision on how we secure our energy future to provide families, businesses and industries with the electricity they need…*
>
> *…We need to take steps now to secure future base-load electricity capacity in this state to ensure a reliable energy supply to homes and businesses in the coming decades."*

Just 2 years later, Transgrid, responsible for assessing future power needs for the State, would demonstrate the unsustainability of Iemma's claim in its 2009 Annual Planning Report. The Owen Report confirmed that the State had a total generation capacity of 85,000 Gwh (Gigawatt hours). Transgrid as usual, gave three scenarios for future power need. The highest demand level would reach that figure in 2017, but the other two possibilities would be well beyond that date. So just two years on from Iemma's 'we'll all be ruined' claim if a new power station was not built by 2014, the forecasting authority was throwing iced water on the notion.

The Owen Report also made it clear that it was not exactly at arm's length from the government which had commissioned it:

> *"The Secretariat for the Inquiry was drawn from a number of NSW Government Departments, and the material in the Report was largely contributed by people from the same Departments."*

It is inconceivable that senior Treasury officials, with a vested interest in a pro-sale outcome, would have not been involved closely in what the report 'found' and recommended. It is not known to what extent, if any, that John Pierce or other Treasury officials discussed with Professor Owen on what side of the coin his 'on balance' view should fall on, as to when in his view, a new power station was needed. It would be interesting to know.

Iemma had determined on his course of action prior to the March 2007 election, but unfortunately chose not to reveal his intentions to the electorate. Some years later, I was told by a Iemma Cabinet minister of a conversation he had with Iemma just a few days before the election as the two departed from a campaign event at Darling Harbour. The then minister was trying to get a commitment on a policy issue relevant to his portfolio. It is alleged by the former minister that Iemma said:

> *"Don't worry about that issue. We are going to do something much bigger after the election, but we can't talk about it now."*

When pressed somewhat on what it was, the former minister alleges that Iemma then said:

> *"We're going to sell the power industry but we can't talk about it until after the election."*

The former minister then gave Iemma a small sample of what was to follow and which cumulatively was to drive both Iemma and Costa out of Parliament and eventually, drive the government out of office:

> *"You won't be doing that with my help."*

The Carr and Egan failed attempt to privatise power in 1997, as with the disastrous 2007/08 attempt by Iemma and Costa, both had a party and union movement deal on the table, to sell one generator for a few billion dollars and sell no more. The deal was twice rejected and the plan to privatise as a result, twice failed.

When I asked a minister at the time why Cabinet had not insisted on committing to sell just one generator at a time, he said that the Treasury Secretary, John Pierce, had briefed the Cabinet and convinced all of the ministers that the market needed the certainty that all of the generators were to be sold. It is almost unbelievable how much 'fake news' was fed to the Cabinet, the caucus, the party and the community on the whole sale issue. Even a commitment to sell all generators and the retail business would require a piecemeal sale of it in tranches. It simply could not be sold all at once so a commitment to do so made no commercial or political sense. Each generator is a huge sale item and as each was put on the market, potential investors would have factored in the risk that the Government may get cold feet and not proceed with further sales.

The Kennett Government in Victoria had sold its entire publicly-owned electricity industry in this way more than 10 years before Iemma and Costa embarked on their own journey. The Baird Government in New South Wales embarked on the same journey. It is incredible that ministers just accepted Treasury's claim and then effectively followed their leader and Treasurer as they all jumped off a political cliff.

So many of the claims and arguments presented during this time just do not stand up to close scrutiny. That lots more power was needed was incorrect. That only the private sector could or would finance it defied belief. That the whole generating industry had to be sold and not part of it, was not only plainly wrong, but clearly unachievable.

If Government really believed that extra generating capacity had to be installed for businesses and households as a certainty, then only it could guarantee it. The market does not invest to guarantee supply of anything. It invests to underpin share price and to maximise dividends to shareholders. And this would have been clearly demonstrated, if after sale, demand for power exceeded available supply. The price of electricity would rise, providing better returns and wealth to shareholders. To assert that a new privately-owned electricity market would defy 300 years of market capitalism and invest, not for selfish shareholder reasons, but for community benefit, as if it were to be funded from a magic pudding, was just plain disingenuous.

If Government wanted to guarantee rather than just hope for new power capacity, then it would have had to deliver it itself. If in turn, it did not have the funds, then it would have needed to simply sell one generator for about $2B and invest the funds in new capacity. Party officials and union leaders had already put the sale of one generator on the table, but that was shunned by Costa and Iemma. If the issue was solely about alleged need for new generating capacity, then this would have been the only way it could have been guaranteed and achieved. Sell a generator, bank the funds, build a new power station and then move on. Despite the ambitious rhetoric about the generosity of the private sector doing public good even Iemma had his doubts:

> "...*if no such investment occurs when there is a clear market need for it the government will be able to pursue a baseload power station development in New South Wales to ensure our security of supply*".
> (Hansard June 4th, 2008)

So, by June 2008, just 8 weeks before the issue would end in flames for Iemma, Costa and the long-term survival of the Government, the generators had to be sold so as to finance unneeded extra capacity by a new publicly spirited capital market. But, just in case that market was unexpectedly only focussed on profit and wealth then the Government would build it anyway.

The Department of Energy was, I am told, mostly a bystander in the 2007/2008 period. Treasury took charge of the drive to sell as well as the development of policy positions and material to justify and underpin it. The Department's personnel and opinions were not required.

It would now make for an interesting analysis, to consider in detail the briefing notes and research on future long-term power needs prepared by the Cabinet Office and the Department of Energy prior to March 2007 and then contrast these documents with what was produced by Treasury before and after the 2007 election. It is now 2017 and it would be no surprise to anyone that the Department of Energy advice to me as late as February 2006, that no new major base-load generating capacity was needed for at least 10 years, was correct!

A paper published by the New South Wales Parliamentary Library in 2014 found that:

> "...electricity consumption in New South Wales remains virtually unchanged in 2012-13 as it was in 2002-03...electricity demand has been declining across the National Electricity Market since 2007-08...growth in electricity demand...is forecast to be subdued over the next few years."

Data from the Australian Energy Market Operator (AEMO) makes for sobering reading. It shows a steady year on year decline in annual electricity generation from 2008 through to 2011 and then a precipitous decline each year from 2012 through to 2014.

This is set out below:

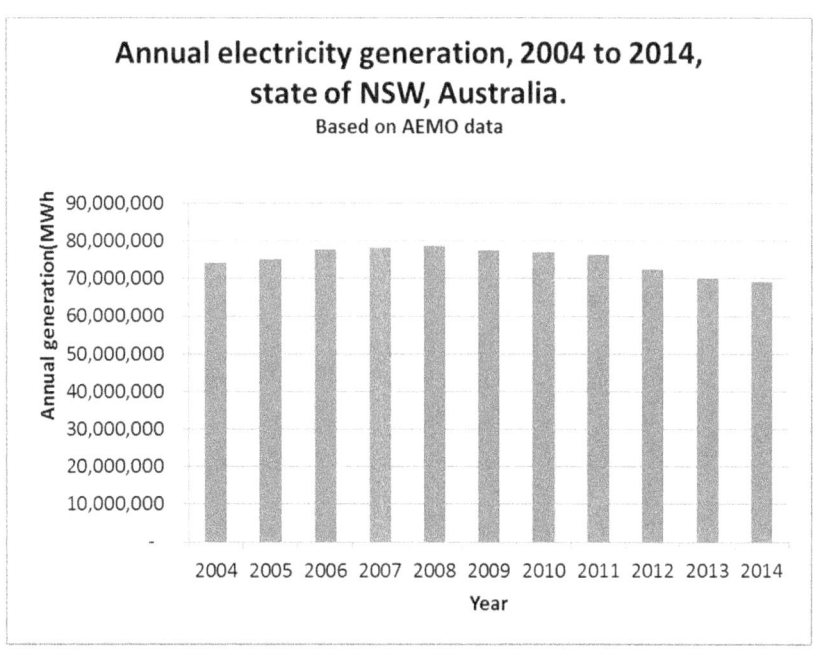

Source: http://carbonpolicy.org/australian-electricity-demand-and-consumption-2004-to-2014-nsw-and-vic/

Chapter 15: Privatising electricity

The reason for the constant decline in power generation was because the demand for electricity from New South Wales households and businesses also declined.

This is graphically shown below:

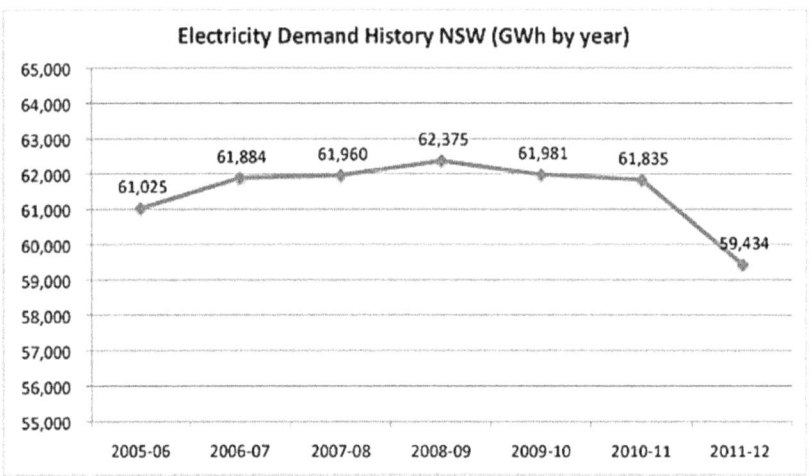

Source: https://reductionrevolutiopn.com.au/blogs/news-reviews/6285442-nsw-electricity-demand-drops-by-4

Despite the advice from and knowledge within the Department of Energy, and the reality at the time, Iemma would claim in Parliament:

> "...the critical need to be prepared for additional baseload capacity from 2013-14."
> (Hansard June 4th, 2008)

> "We have reached the point in the state's development where the next investment in baseload must occur."
> (Hansard August 29th, 2008)

It remains a mystery as to how and why Iemma, Costa and Treasury were all able to arrive at a position, where they all felt comfortable in arguing against reality on an issue, which in the end set fire to the Labor Government from which it and the Labor Party never recovered. Despite that reality, confirmed by what actually occurred into the future, Iemma would go on to claim in Parliament, in the party room, to the media and at the ALP conference, the very opposite as the reason for embarking upon a venture which not even Carr and Egan could achieve. He seemed to put the rest of the Government on hold as he focussed on this issue to the detriment of all else.

Having embarked on such a massive policy initiative with dubious foundation, Iemma then handed the carriage of it to the one person least able to build consensus in Government, reach out empathetically to stakeholders and come to a deliverable conclusion – Michael Costa. Had Iemma been able to see this as everyone else could, he would have never given the carriage of such a dangerous battle to someone so unsuited to compromise, consensus and settlement. If a cross factional duo like John Watkins and John Della Bosca had been given joint carriage of the issue, then a substantial and deliverable settlement would have been quickly found. The union movement and the party officials had on the table, an agreed position of supporting the Government in selling the retail arm of the electricity industry and one generator. This would have been grabbed by anyone else including maybe even Carr and Egan in their day, and would have delivered $5B to the Treasury.

Even at this late point, Iemma should have taken charge, accepted the deal and moved on, but incredulously, he left Costa to reject the deal and then went to war with his own party, his own caucus and the union movement. No wonder it all ended in tears! Perhaps this was a way to escape a job he never wanted in the first place. If so, it was a dramatic way to leave!

Chapter 15: Privatising electricity

Carr and Egan had tried their hand on this identical issue in 1997 and both backed away when it was rejected by a solid margin at the annual conference of the ALP. At least they had some negotiating skills and still could not get it over the line. The ALP and the trade union movement forces that had arrayed against Carr and Egan in 1997, were the same forces that again arrayed against Iemma and Costa in 2008. It was as if no regard had been given to the enormous risk of political failure in taking on something which had demonstrably failed just a few years before. On a much grander scale, it reminded me of the French failed invasion of Russia in 1812 being ignored by Germany as it commenced its own doomed invasion of the same country in 1941. The Carr administration survived, but the Iemma one did not. Political history lessons had not been learnt. In my view, the cause of the fall of Iemma, also directly contributed to the demise of the whole Labor Government at the 2011 election. As far as the electorate was concerned: 'enough was enough'.

The questionable methods of approach of Iemma and Costa on electricity privatisation, which bordered on the absurd and at times almost comical, can be best summed as Plans A through to C, which each became increasingly more difficult to achieve until disaster struck.

Plan A: 'Back to the future'

Sell all the generators and the retail businesses, and assume the caucus, the party conference and all affiliated unions will follow suit, and not oppose it as they had in vigorous fashion in 1997. It was just a rerun of a bad dream doomed to failure.

The naiveté of the plan was breathtaking.

In 1997, the State Secretary of the Electrical Trades Union (ETU) was removed from office for supporting Carr and Egan on privatisation. His replacement was Bernie Riordan. In 2008, Bernie was still State Secretary of the ETU but by then, he was also the ALP State President and Convenor of the ALP right union secretaries. He had been an implacable opponent in 1997, and was always going to be in 2008, except the second time round he was in an even stronger position to win the day. And he did!

Plan B: 'Communication breakdown'

When the ALP Annual Conference rejected the Iemma/Costa plan, the duo should have done what Carr and Egan had done 11 years before, and accepted the decision on the chin and moved on. Instead, Iemma decided to draw on 'support' from the new Prime Minister, Kevin Rudd. Apparently, Rudd before the December 2007 federal election, had promised to support the privatisation plan, provided Iemma stayed quiet on his intentions until after the election.

So Iemma delayed informing the electorate for a second time and both times within the same year. First, to the people of New South Wales at the March 2007 state election and then second, to the Australian people at the December 2007 federal election.

After the debacle of the ALP conference in 2008, Iemma called in what he thought was Rudd's commitment, and then bizarrely, interpreted that commitment as justifying an expectation on his part, that Rudd would draw down considerable political capital, and rail road the ALP National Executive to overturn the overwhelmingly carried NSW Party conference decision. It was an absurd and almost fanciful expectation. Rudd delivered on his own expectation of what was meant by support, by providing a letter expressing it. That was it. If ever there was a better example of a complete communication failure between two significant political CEOs then I am yet to hear of it. The naivete of Iemma at this point was simply breathtaking, as was his decision to find yet another plan to sell a large part of the publicly owned electricity industry.

Plan C: 'A parallel universe'

Despite rejection by the New South Wales ALP Conference and the road to the National ALP Executive blocked, Iemma decided to bat on. Labor MPs always faced expulsion from the party if they voted against an ALP caucus decision. However, in this case, there was already in place a caucus decision of Labor MPs which supported the sale, but that decision was now at odds with a subsequent yet massive majority ruling of the ALP Annual Conference, to oppose the privatisation of electricity.

We had all grown up in a Labor party which treasured and guarded the sanctity of policy decisions set by the ALP Annual Conference, as it also did, the inviolability of policy implementation decisions set by decisions of Labor MPs. It was always assumed, if not taken for granted, that one would follow the other, or at least, Conference and caucus would never ever, be in a state of irreconcilable conflict.

However, Iemma had now taken the party and its MPs to a position of such conflict, that only a conflagration could bring the matter to a close. Everyone except the two key protagonists, Iemma and Costa, could see this unnecessarily unfolding as each new, yet ever more difficult implementation plan was rolled out.

Unsurprisingly, some Labor MPs were threatening to support the party and its conference decision and therefore, oppose the Government and the supporting caucus decision it had secured.

Complicating matters further, the State ALP President chimed in with a guarantee that no MP would lose party membership or preselection, if they voted in Parliament against any legislation put forward to support the sale of electricity.

In other words, if Labor MPs voted against a Labor government and a decision of the Labor caucus, the Labor Party itself would protect and ensure affected Labor MPs with their continued membership of the party, and as Labor candidates at the next election. Carr and Egan had left the scene on their attempt long before this sort of politically suicidal scenario started to emerge. But not the Iemma/Costa duo.

Iemma and Costa then came up with their most bizarre scheme of all, which left many of us wondering if the two of them had left the building, and entered a parallel political universe. They had amazingly assumed, that the party of business, the Liberal Party, and its often-unbridled support for the privatisation of any publicly owned asset, was so overwhelming, that political enmity against the worker's party, the ALP, would be cast aside, and its Liberal MPs could then be drawn upon as a political resource, to ensure victory for a Labor government over its own party and a few of its troublesome Labor MPs. Just incredible stuff to say the least.

The Labor premier and his treasurer believed that any Labor MPs voting in the Legislative Assembly against legislation supported by the ALP caucus decision, would be more than made up for by the support of pro-electricity privatisation Liberal Party opposition MPs. This would have been a new kind of political Utopia, where sworn party political opponents could be imagined as defending their political enemies against their own party renegades. You could almost hear the Labor giants of the past refraining: 'What were they thinking?'. I am sure that the great Jack

Chapter 15: Privatising electricity

Lang, Labor premier of New South Wales in the late 1920s to the early 1930s, at a time of enormous political and party upheaval, would have been unflattering in his denunciation of the Iemma cross-party survival strategy.

One of the declared Labor defectors during the Iemma/Costa parallel universe strategy, had a chance encounter with a senior Opposition Liberal MP (who would later become in government, and as expected, a major proponent of privatising electricity) and said to him:

> *"Are you guys going to support this package on privatisation?"*

The reply was prophetic:

> *"No way. We are going to divide you on this issue."*

Of course they were. Anyone but Iemma and Costa would have seen that coming.

A few days after that conversation, the Leader of the Opposition, Barry O'Farrell, announced that they would be opposing the legislation. With that, Plans A, B and now finally C, had all failed. Iemma and Costa resigned leaving the party and the Government they had led in an unrecoverable mess.

The drive to sell had caused a major convulsion in the party, the union movement, the caucus and the community. A 'House divided' for very long will soon drain public support and sympathy and that is exactly what occurred to the New South Wales ALP because of this issue.

By mid-August 2008, the winning two-party preferred position the Labor Party had secured in its election win of March

2007 had evaporated to below 50% from which it never recovered, in every poll conducted all the way to the catastrophic election loss in March 2011, with Premier Keneally at the helm. Many explanations have been proffered to explain the disaster. None is more convincing than the permanent erosion of public support caused by Iemma and Costa, not for wanting to sell part of the electricity industry, but for the inept way they went about it. Much could have been calmly achieved by selling one generator and the retail business with $5B in the bank, a union and party convulsion avoided and public goodwill maintained. The alternative and unnecessary sliding door which Iemma and Costa entered on the issue, destroyed the Government.

Iemma and Costa both paid with their jobs well before then, but the party paid a higher price. The public was unforgiving at the March 2011 election, and rightfully so.

Much nonsense has been written about Iemma being the victim of betrayal by his parliamentary colleagues and by Labor Party and Union officials who allegedly had no business doing so.

However, a leader must always work and negotiate major changes in party policy through party and stakeholder forums. In doing so, the process compels compromise and 'give and take' to ensure a productive outcome. Wran did this in the late 1970s on privatising lotto, Keating on introducing foreign banks in the mid-1980s and what Iemma should have done on privatising electricity in 2007/08. In addition, a leader remains leader whilst he or she continues to have the confidence of the MPs he or she leads. It was Iemma himself who chose the path he did in an uncompromising 'winner takes all' approach that led to a party convulsion, a collapse in polling numbers, loss of confidence from MPs, and finally, the permanent evaporation of public support for the party and the government which it spawned.

There was no betrayal, but simply an unnecessary political mess requiring Iemma and Costa to depart the field of battle that they themselves unnecessarily chose to create.

Given what had happened to me at Iemma's hand, could it be actually Iemma himself who twice misled the public? Perhaps first, to the general public in not divulging before the election of March 2007, that he intended to embark on the biggest privatisation programme the State had ever seen. And second, when he claimed that the State would soon have a huge unmet demand for power.

Did Iemma mislead the Parliament in November 2006 when he claimed that New South Wales had plenty of power generating capacity? Alternatively, did he mislead the house on many occasions in 2007 and 2008 when he claimed the exact opposite, that the State did not have enough future power generating capacity? The proximity in time of these two-polar opposite public positions of Iemma as premier, makes a compelling case, that Iemma did in fact 'mislead the house' in either 2006, or if not, then during 2007/2008.

Drawing on Iemma's own words, was the latter then, 'simply a case of one mistake too many' and that after the awful way in which Iemma and Costa had handled the electricity privatisation affair, the Party 'could not allow the air swirling around the [Premier] to continue.'

But Iemma and Costa leaving did not stem the decline in the party's fortunes, which were effectively doomed once Iemma determined on a course of a 'winner takes all' policy position, and then decided to put Costa in charge of it. As much as Rees and Keneally tried to turn the tide, the public had by August 2008, effectively given up on the New South Wales ALP and the March 2011 election was merely the moment it was formalised.

It all remains as inexplicable now, as it did back in 2008. A typical calm and considered, but reforming Labor Government in the McKell or Wran tradition, would have quietly negotiated its way to selling $5B worth of retail and generating assets, leaving plenty left over if new capacity was really needed. Going not just beyond this, but way beyond it, deserves an explanation from the two men who took the Government to such a perilous position. None so far has been satisfactorily provided by either. They both owe an explanation to the political party which delivered them so much.

By then, I had known Iemma for over 20 years and during this time, his only unstinting passion was his almost inexhaustible pursuit of ALP Machiavellian factional and Party manoeuvring. He did have a long-expressed interest in public housing, but in my view, this was only to ensure that as many ALP voting housing tenants as possible were transferred into marginal seats.

Iemma's 'crash through or crash' approach on electricity privatisation and his determined effort in rewriting not only how the industry looked and worked, but also how the ALP went about its business, was as unexpected as it was ill-advised. Where did his decisions come from? And having seen what damage had been done, why did he cling to the same plan? As the great Prussian Field Marshal, Helmuth von Moltke once famously said: "No battle plan survives contact with the enemy." It would seem that neither Iemma nor Costa had read enough about leadership and strategy to understand the art of compromise and risk management to have avoided the catastrophe that befell both of them and the party. And sadly, it was all avoidable. Iemma did not need to elevate the issue as the defining issue of his premiership. But having done so, and much like British Prime Minister David Cameron on the issue of remaining in the European Union, when the issue failed, he too failed. Perhaps like Cameron, Iemma was rather inclined not to complete a full term anyway?

I am told that in the middle of the debacle, Iemma's former boss and mentor, Graham Richardson, advised him: "You can't take on the party machine and win." As a former Party Secretary, he was certainly in a position to know.

Iemma had made it clear that he never intended to be a long-term Premier and would not go beyond mid-term after the 2007 election. Maybe he wanted to go out with a major legacy in place, and perhaps cared little about the fallout and consequences, as he intended to leave anyway. I think, given the long-term damage it all caused, an explanation is warranted. I don't think we will get one anytime soon.

Costa is probably easier to understand. The last person to project compromise-building empathy, it is little wonder when resistance built, he just got louder and angrier, and the winning post just drifted further and further away. Iemma it would seem, was the only person who could not see this, as it all unfolded in full public view.

Perhaps the Costa approach can be best summed-up by a corporate lunch attended by Chris Bowen, with Costa as the ministerial guest of honour. Apparently, an architect attending the same lunch took great exception to some disparaging remarks made by Costa about architects and when the architect told all how offended he was, Costa responded: "Excellent. Excellent. You have made my day." What more need be said, except perhaps a query to Iemma, as to why he promoted Costa to Treasurer in the first place.

I have often wondered if one price Obeid extracted from Iemma in return for the premiership was an undertaking to appoint Costa as Treasurer. About a year prior to the mid 2005 retirement of Premier Bob Carr, Obeid was still at least going through the motions of supporting me for the top job, and made what I thought was both an extraordinary and ludicrous suggestion about Michael Costa:

> "You should appoint Costa as Treasurer. He could be your Egan."

Carr had effectively appointed Michael Egan as the Government's Chief Operating Officer, leaving Egan to do most of the hands-on work required for fitting politics and policy into the prevailing financial position of the day. Carr was certainly hands-on when a difficult media issue blew up, but otherwise he seemed sometimes almost like a non-executive Chairman.

I had no intention of empowering anyone like Carr had empowered Egan, and especially someone so unsuited to such a senior role as Michael Costa. I knew Obeid and Costa were close and very comfortable in each other's company, and I had noticed very clearly how Obeid did not take any role in stopping Costa from his yearlong public attacks on my record as Minister for Transport following the March 2003 election.

I think now, that at the time, in Obeid's mind I probably lessened my case for the premiership when I responded to Obeid:

> "Eddie, you have got to be kidding. There is no way I would ever appoint Costa to such an important position. He does not have the temperament for such an important job and in any case, I would never reward someone who spent so much effort publicly

Chapter 15: Privatising electricity

> *denigrating me without justification. Eddie, that is just not going to happen."*

Obeid never raised the issue again. But I did with Iemma himself.

When Iemma became Premier in August 2005, he appointed himself as Treasurer with an indication that in a few months' time he would hand over the portfolio to someone not yet known. None of us thought much of it until early January 2006 when rumours within the Government began to emerge that Michael Costa was about to be appointed. That many of us were simply horrified at the idea, would be an understatement.

I even went up to put my case to Iemma's Chief of Staff, Mike Kaiser who simply responded:

> *"I have given up. He is in his office if you want to talk to him about it."*

I did talk to Iemma about it. But Iemma was insistent that the appointment would go ahead and that Costa 'had promised to behave himself'. I gave up, but left the Premier with a blunt message:

> *"You will rue the day you appointed Michael Costa as Treasurer".*

As it turned out, Iemma and I were both right. Costa did 'behave himself' through to the March 2007 election, but I like to think that just maybe, with what happened afterwards on electricity privatisation, that Iemma would indeed have rued the day he made that appointment.

The question to Iemma remains: Why on earth did he appoint Costa as Treasurer and did Obeid make the same request to Iemma as he did to me? I don't expect an answer anytime soon.

CHAPTER 16

The aftermath – transition, renewal and new beginnings

The period from my dismissal until the election in March 2007 was surreal. I was still an MP, but with little responsibility. I was just the Member for Smithfield again.

Despite having been removed by Iemma not for anything I had said or done, but because of huge, disproportionate media reaction, I was still left with a public image that I had mislead the House twice, which to me sounded like a dishonesty offence.

My parents were good, hardworking, honest folks who instilled in all of their five children the essential ingredients of a good life: hard work, education, a generous spirit and above all, honesty and integrity. I believe all five of us have lived by those standards in full.

It still grieved me very much that after having lived a private and public life of honesty and integrity, I had been publicly maligned for having conducted myself in a misleading way requiring my departure from the Ministry.

Had Iemma allowed me to weather the storm, the media maelstrom would have passed, and in time, would have been seen

Chapter 16: The aftermath

by me, my colleagues and probably even the journalists themselves, as a typical few days fun from the media in putting a senior politician in the box and then character assassinating him.

Carr would have had the nerve and poise to let it pass and would have stood by his minister, but Iemma having thrown me to the wolves, simply confirmed the indignant groupthink that the political journalists of the day had been writing. This wounded me very deeply and did not heal for a very long time. When I shared my views with former Deputy Premier, Andrew Stoner one day, he generously advised that no one on his side of the House, even for a moment, thought that I was dishonest. Even though it was many years after the event, it was still good to hear such an assessment not only from a former political opponent, but from the very one who asked me the question which precipitated my demise.

There is no counselling available or offered in the political arena. There was none available, nor offered, when I had to confront severed limbs, blood and bodies by the side of the railway tracks at Waterfall.

There was none available and none offered, when I was thrown out of the political building on a Premier's impetuous and panicky whim. Not in response to anything I had done, which could even vaguely warrant consideration, yet alone justification, for my dismissal in any workplace, but in response only, to the superficial, loud and distracting din, created by a wolfpack of journalists rather enjoying the baying for a public hanging, after what they regarded was my trial before their interpretation of the Court of Public Opinion. Iemma always saw media noise as substance, and the louder it got, the more substantive he and his short term focussed personal staff treated the populist tabloid witch hunts unfolding before them. This was not a team you wanted on your back when a frontal media assault was unleashed.

As politicians, we are supposed to be made of more 'sterner stuff' than the common folk, but even the thickest skin can absorb only so much.

I never could understand why people were ever so overwhelmed with sadness that they struggled to cope against dark thoughts. I now have a much greater respect for the hard journey they go through.

On the day of the March 2007 election, unbeknownst to me, Ann sent Iemma a text message: "Goodbye Morris, I hope your family never has inflicted on them, the unnecessary suffering you inflicted on mine. Ann" He had caused a lot of pain and grief to the four of us, and I didn't mind at all her telling him. As irony would have it, his own self-immolation on the sale of electricity would bring upon him his own share of suffering and grief. But at least, he had done it to himself and only 18 months later!

Despite thinking for a moment that Iemma had irrevocably wrecked my employability, quite quickly after my removal from Cabinet, I was approached to join a high calibre consulting firm in Sydney. In another irony, it would be the same firm that Paul Forward had gone to after Iemma had allowed his unfair and unjustified sacking, following the 'air swirling around him' over the Cross City Tunnel. It certainly was an adjustment to lose many privileges I had taken for granted for nearly 12 very busy years: my office, my personal staff and my status; but it was great to be able to throw myself into a new and unexpected career.

Chapter 16: The aftermath

I initially reported to Paul who was fantastic about it all and certainly helped my transition to this new role, as did our Managing Director, Rob Aldis who had brought me into the firm.

One of the sheer delights of having way too much time on my hands was that Ann and I rediscovered each other. We had always been good, but the burdens of parenting and the enormous demands of political office, meant that we had not always enjoyed the time together quietly that most couples take for granted. We started going on dates, long walks holding hands, romantic weekends and more. She even joked that we could now watch an entire movie without being interrupted by phone calls. We both felt like we had just met all over again. It was wonderful and a truly positive and life-changing aspect of having been thrown by Iemma into the abyss.

I joined the ALP at 18 and now at 60, I remain a loyal and faithful member, still convinced that it is the best vehicle to deliver lasting and better change for working families and for the general community. On occasion, I have had that faith tested, but it has endured.

When I joined the ALP in 1976, I had a burning desire to serve as an MP, lead the Party and do great things for the community. Most of what I set out to achieve as an 18-year-old, I had achieved by the time of my departure from politics in 2007 as a 49-year-old. I did not quite get to the top of the political tree which has been a lamentable disappointment I have had to learn to live with.

I have often wondered whether I should have contested the 2007 election, stayed a while on the backbench and made my way back into the Ministry. Iemma had made it abundantly clear that he would not complete a full term after the election and that meant there would be a chance, even slight, that I could make my way back to a possible tilt at the top job.

I am certain that the Obeid, Tripodi and McDonald troika, would have again thwarted my ambitions as they had in 2005, but I like to ponder that perhaps even they could not have put up a convincing case against me when there was so little experienced talent left in the ministerial ranks. By 2008, when Iemma blazed out of the place, I would have had 18 years' experience as an MP, including over a decade in senior Cabinet roles. At the same stage, the new premier, Nathan Rees, had had only 18 months as both a minister and an MP. No wonder one senior ALP MP at the time said of this extraordinary appointment: "It was like giving an 8-year-old kid a loaded .357 Magnum".

But in early 2007, I was so shattered by the experience of being thrown out by Iemma and the Party, I could not face another day in public life beyond the election date. I was in no fit mental shape to make such a momentous career decision and given what happened in the August 2008 to December 2009 period with no less than three separate Premiers at the helm, leaving when I did, has been my only, but lasting regret of my professional life. I should have stayed!

I do look back with pride on a long period of office during which much was done. It is a stark contrast to the little that was achieved under the Iemma/Rees/Kenneally revolving door administrations, especially the last four years of Labor Government.

I am sometimes asked to name the achievements I am most proud of.

Chapter 16: The aftermath

There are a few:

1. The M7 Motorway
2. The Bus-only Transitways across Western Sydney
3. Transport for the Sydney 2000 Olympics
4. The Eastern Distributor Motorway
5. Road Safety Initiatives
6. The Epping to Chatswood Rail Link
7. Building the Abbotsbury Parkland in my electorate
8. The campaign against John Lewthwaite
9. The M5 East Motorway
10. The Lane Cove Tunnel Motorway.

The list also makes a mockery of the unsustainable claim by some that a lack of public infrastructure through the sixteen years of Labor rule contributed to our electoral defeat in March 2011. However, whilst a great deal was delivered in the first 10 years, little new infrastructure was delivered in the last 6 years and I believe that did contribute to our decline and fall from public grace.

On average, MPs normally serve for a period of 8 years and a minister for a period of 4 years. I had served for 17 years as an MP and nearly 12 years as a Minister. Whilst I did not quite make it to Head of Government, I did have the privilege of being able to do some great things for the community. This has given me lasting pleasure.

Bob Carr gets criticised now and then by uninformed and lazy journalists for having presided over a period of little infrastructure building. The claim is false and demonstrably so. Whilst Carr was far more known for being a thespian Premier than an infrastructure Premier, his period in office was at a time of record public construction and he is entitled to claim credit for the achievements of his two main building ministers: Michael Knight and Carl Scully.

The Carr Government was serious, measured, capable and successful. We made a difference and left the place better for having been in it. The former Premier is well entitled to draw on the McKell Administration of the 1940s for both inspiration and comparison. But what a contrast with the Premier who followed him. Iemma was disinterested and disengaged, but at least for the period up to the March 2007 election, he had Peter Barron, Mark Arbib and Mike Kaiser to help him over the line. After getting a 'mandate', those three men for various reasons, exited the scene, leaving the Government to quickly morph into a shambolic mess, at war with itself and the Party which spawned it, over electricity privatisation. No wonder then, that the departure of Iemma and Costa, saw a quick descent into governmental farce with the Rees and then Keneally Administrations, and predictably in due course, loss of power.

Our last two ALP premiers both suffered from being elevated to high office long before they were ready to lead, and by a caucus denuded of talent. Neither our senior Party officials during a sustained period of time, nor their predecessors in office, had given more than passing interest to effective long-range succession planning. Any significant and properly run organisation will quietly pride itself in future-proofing the firm with a steady conveyor belt of talent. Politics is no different, with varying levels of talent required to provide not just future leaders, but ministers, parliamentary secretaries and value adding backbenchers. This talent pool was mostly empty by the March 2011 Election. Backbench Members of Parliament who should never have seen the inside of a Cabinet room were by then Ministers of the Crown. There was no one left to say 'no' and too few left to hold up the pillars of a solid modern reforming Labor Government. Sadly, well before the March 2011 election, the Government had simply stopped governing because as a collective entity, it no longer knew how.

Three examples are worth noting:

1. No new Motorways

First, when I asked a post Iemma senior minister why the Government had no plans for future motorway development, the reply was withering; "Because it will upset too many people." Government should constantly deliver, improve and reform for the community and in doing so, constantly arbitrate between competing interests. It is not for the faint-hearted and if done with diligence, there will always be loud and disappointed stakeholders. If not, then you are not governing. No motorways were planned or delivered during the whole six years of the Iemma/Rees/Keneally period. In an almost complete mockery of the excuse provided to me, the Liberal State Government is now building more motorways than even I could have ever imagined. And yes, unsurprisingly, some people are upset by it, but many tens of thousands will benefit every day of their motoring lives.

2. The non-Metro Rail project

The second, was the farcical Metro Rail proposal. After the 2007 election, Iemma pulled a $7B Metro Rail to North West Sydney project, literally out of his pocket. It had not been raised during the election campaign and no one knew where it had come from. Rees in late 2008, promptly cut the proposal in half, only to have Keneally in early 2010, cancel the project altogether at a wasted cost to the taxpayer of $500M. Amateur hour had arrived in Macquarie Street and on this example alone, the ALP was undeserving of re-election. The Liberal State Government is now building a huge mega billion-dollar rail project to the North-West suburbs of Sydney, which sadly, three separate Labor Governments were unable or uninterested in delivering.

3. Throwing $1.5B down the drain

The third example is the Rees/Keneally Governments allowing the M4 toll to expire in February 2010 a full year before the March 2011 election. This was a pointless attempt to salvage some support for the ALP from its Western Sydney heartland which was already waiting with baseball bats to whack 'their' government. It did not work. Retendering the expired toll contract would have generated at least $1.5B from the private sector which would have permitted the resuscitation of the much needed M4 widening and extension, and financed a large capital works fund for local Western Sydney council roads. Instead, we had a bunch of politically timorous amateurs unwilling to do anything which might vaguely pass muster as both innovative and delivering what the people of the region really needed. The baseball bats rightly hit their mark! The 'do nothing' decision to just let the clock tick over and the toll expire was so indefensible in terms of losing valuable infrastructure dollars, I did wonder if Prime Minister Rudd ought to reduce Commonwealth grants to New South Wales by the same amount. Needless to say, the current Liberal State Government is also building the M4 extension.

The period of March 2007 through to February 2010 was about as damaging and wasteful as any three-year period in the history of government in New South Wales. And amazingly, it spanned three Premiers! The Government came to a standstill as it went to war with itself and its own party over selling electricity, $500M was washed down the drain over the ludicrously mismanaged metro project and then a $1.5B cash payment for road building was ignored. I still find it hard to believe that a Labor Government literally threw away $2B in infrastructure funds. And those who oversaw all this simply retired with superannuation and pensions intact. Perhaps if that had been at risk some different decisions may have been made over several years and the public better off as a result. We will never know.

Thankfully, party officers recognised very belatedly, that one of their most important roles was to steer generational change and new talent into Macquarie Street. Both the 2011 and 2015 elections saw a large contingent of old guard make way for new and emerging talent. If the trend continues to the next election and beyond, then the ALP will soon enough have a large enough talent pool to underpin the next long-term Labor Government. But all this, just emphasises how bad it got by March 2011, and just how little was accomplished to achieve generational renewal while Labor was in office. As a major political party, Labor was organisationally asleep at the wheel!

Sadly, by March 2011 there was little fight left in those remaining and the keys to Government were just about left on the table for our political opponents. It did not help that almost no Ministers and too few Members of Parliament had ever experienced the hard grinding years of opposition and far too many had settled into the comfortable complacency of elected office. Government is very hard won and from the experience of 2011 and federally in 2013, it can easily be lost. The ALP State and Federal Oppositions are now, in my view, unnecessarily having to go through the back-breaking task of winning back community confidence towards a new era of Labor management. That confidence should have been kept and maintained whilst still in Government. To have spent most of my adult life in doing my bit to help Labor win state and federal elections, it is very distressing to have witnessed Labor in government, at both levels, perform so poorly in this period, that elections became virtually a 'no-contest' political bout.

It was during the Carr years of 1995 to 2005 that the vast Olympic venues were constructed as were five new Motorways, the Epping to Chatswood Rail Link and the extensive Bus-only Transitways across Western Sydney. By the time the Iemma premiership in 2005 rolled in, Michael Costa had already cancelled the M4 East Motorway and the Epping to Parramatta Rail Link, and then subsequently, Iemma and Tripodi attacked the Cross City Tunnel Motorway and in doing so, completely undermined the Labor Government's reputation and that of the ALP as the builder of public infrastructure.

From 2005 to 2011, the Labor Government's interest and energy in building big things for the community went into hibernation as it became overwhelmed with fear of itself, fear of its lack of capability in the Cabinet room to get any big projects underway and fear of electoral oblivion. The decline and fall of the New South Wales ALP as the pre-eminent builders of public infrastructure was a long and sad six-year process.

Perhaps my most lamentable reflection of my time in public life is to have witnessed as a bystander in private life the 'passing of the infrastructure baton' in 2011 to the new Liberal National Party State Government. It did not need to be so. Jack Lang had built the Sydney underground railway and the Sydney Harbour Bridge in the late 20s and early 30s. Joe Cahill had locked-in the Sydney Opera House in the late 50s and it was the Wran Government of the 80s which built Darling Harbour. It was fitting that Bob Carr would add to this enviable tradition with motorways, rail lines and the Olympics.

Chapter 16: The aftermath

The Iemma/Rees/Keneally Governments should have built the Northwest Rail Link as well as the M4 East and M1 to M2 Motorways, but instead they squandered the opportunity to do so. The current Liberal National Party State Government is now getting on and building major rail and road infrastructure across Sydney and fully exploiting the fact that the three post Carr Premiers were simply asleep at the infrastructure wheel. The baton passed. It will not be easily returned.

EPILOGUE

My third career as a consultant and advisor in the infrastructure sector began on the 7th of May 2007 with a small boutique firm known as Evans & Peck. I would spend nearly five years there as a Principal, building up and running their Sydney Business Advisory practice, as well as mentoring and advising CEOs, providing strategic advice on major projects and assisting clients on understanding how Government worked. It was very different to my life as a Minister and it did take a while to transition.

At the end of 2009, Evans & Peck was acquired by the Sydney headquartered global engineering and project delivery firm, WorleyParsons. I welcomed the great opportunities this might provide for new professional experiences and began to undertake international travel for the business. In January 2012, I transferred across to the parent company and took up a semi-global role as an International Business Development Director. It was a fascinating role which regularly took me to the Middle East, South America and to a large part of Africa. New South Wales politics soon began to look quite small in comparison.

Three people stand out in terms of providing me with a post political career: Rob Aldis, as Managing Director of Evans & Peck who was terrific in mentoring me into a new professional life, Roy Pearson, as WorleyParsons' Regional Managing Director for Europe and Africa who gave me opportunities to engage with the parent company in Africa, and finally, Gordon Cowe as the

WorleyParsons Global Lead for Infrastructure and Environment who moved me across from Evans & Peck and was always a strong supporter of my role in the company. I thank and acknowledge them all.

I retired from full-time employment in late 2015 and accepted an appointment from Minister Anthony Roberts, as Chairman of the New South Wales Mine Safety Advisory Council. It is a role I enjoy very much. In late February 2016, I commenced a part-time History degree at Sydney University, which I intend to mix with more golf and in due course, some travel.

I grew up in Chatswood and at age 26 moved with Ann to the south-western suburbs of Sydney to marry and have a family, and to start the long hard road towards a political career. We would spend the next 25 years in three separate homes in that area, but always within the boundaries of the Smithfield State Electorate. When I left politics, I had done so in a painful, humiliating and searing way which would take many years to heal. I needed a new life away from all that was so politically familiar. My roots and my childhood were grounded in Chatswood and the North Shore suburbs of Sydney.

In August 2008, Ann and I put Smithfield and a quarter century of our life in Western Sydney behind us as we moved into our new and beautiful home on the Upper North Shore of Sydney. Handing out 'How to Votes' for the ALP at a local high school in a blue ribbon Liberal electorate in the September 2013 Federal Election made me feel very much as a 56-year-old that I had gone back to the future as a 19-year-old, handing out election material for the ALP at Lane Cove Shopping Centre just before the 1976 state election. Déjà vu!

Our two children have grown and matured into wonderful young adults. James completed a Human Resources/Industrial Relations degree in November 2013 from Western Sydney University and has been working for nearly three years in that field. In July 2015, he started a Graduate Law degree at the University of Technology Sydney. Sarah having completed a degree in Social Sciences also from Western Sydney University, has now completed a Law degree at the University of Technology Sydney achieving First Class Honours and the University medal. In March 2017, she commenced her career as a lawyer. Ann and I are very proud of them – they both have great futures ahead of them. There were many challenging times for them growing up in the political spotlight and I am really proud of how they met these challenges and never once, in all those many years, complained or asked me to quit.

Ann retired from full-time work in April 2013 and set up her own education consultancy business. She completed her Master's degree in Educational Management and Leadership at the University of Sydney in November 2015 and her dissertation on the role of secondary Deputy Principals as educational leaders (rather than just managers and administrators) and their professional development needs, was ground-breaking. In early 2017, The Journal of Educational Administration published a scholarly article based on that research and in that same year, Ann commenced her PhD in the same area of study.

The passing of former ALP Premier Neville Wran and the unexpected early demise of Liberal Premier Barry O'Farrell, within days of one another in 2014, were timely reminders of both our mortality and the fragility of political life. This was even more emphatically confirmed in 2015 with the fall of Speaker Bronwyn Bishop, Treasurer Joe Hockey and Prime Minister Tony Abbott

Epilogue

over a matter of weeks. All of them must have been shattered by their unplanned and unexpected demise. It puts my own tough departure into better perspective. Even Kevin Rudd could laugh about his own and other political departures in a conversation with me after the Gough Whitlam funeral in Sydney: "You just get told to fuck off." Indeed. And that was almost a year before the Bishop, Hockey and Abbott troika, were given their marching orders.

As I enter my sixties, I look forward to not only proud reflection on an honest life well led, but also a period of happiness and fulfilment as Ann and I enjoy more and more time together, we watch our children prosper, and observe with a wry smile, the new young bucks of the great Australian Labor Party, making their way through the ranks towards a life of public service and commitment.

A nostalgic moment at home (November 2015) reflecting on all the years gone by; the highs, the lows, the great challenges and a life of public service and commitment.

It has been a long road well-travelled which I have enjoyed tremendously, and now I have set the record straight.

Photo by VincentLai Photography

A brief history of Carl Scully's political and business career

Solicitor	1983 – 1990
Member of Parliament	1990 – 2007
Minister	1995 – 2006
Minister for Roads	1996 – 2005
Minister for Transport	1997 – 2003
Minister for Housing	2003 – 2005
Minister for Police	2005 – 2006
Leader of the House	2003 – 2006
Principal, Evans and Peck Consultants	2007 – 2012
Director International Business, WorleyParsons	2012 – 2015
Chair, Mine Safety Advisory Council	2015 -

www.ingramcontent.com/pod-product-compliance
Lightning Source LLC
Chambersburg PA
CBHW071850290426
44110CB00013B/1095